YLDS

This book is published with the aid of the **Bookmarks Publishing Co-operative**. Many socialists have some savings put aside, probably in a bank or savings bank. While it is there, this money is being loaned out by the bank to some business or other to further the capitalist search for profit. We believe it is better loaned to a socialist venture to further the struggle for socialism. That's how the co-operative works: in return for a loan, repayable at a month's notice, members receive free copies of books published by Bookmarks. At the time this book was published, the co-operative had more than 250 members, from as far apart as London and Malaysia, Canada and Norway.

Like to know more?

Write to the **Bookmarks Publishing Co-operative**, 265 Seven Sisters Road, Finsbury Park, London N4 2DE, England.

South Africa
between Reform
and Revolution

Alex Callinicos

Bookmarks
London, Chicago and Melbourne

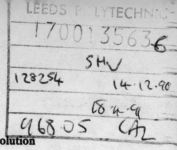

South Africa between Reform and Revolution
by Alex Callinicos
Published November 1988
Bookmarks, 265 Seven Sisters Road, London N4 2DE, England
Bookmarks, PO Box 16085, Chicago, IL 60616, USA
Bookmarks, GPO Box 1473N, Melbourne 3001, Australia
Copyright © Bookmarks and Alex Callinicos

ISBN 0 906224 46 2

Printed by Cox and Wyman, Reading, England
Typeset by East End Offset, London E2
Design by Roger Huddle, Artworkers, London EC1

Bookmarks is linked to an international grouping of socialist
organisations:

Australia: *International Socialists*, GPO Box 1473N, Melbourne 3001
Belgium: *Socialisme International*, 9 rue Marexhe, 4400 Herstal, Liege
Britain: *Socialist Workers Party*, PO Box 82, London E3
Canada: *International Socialists*, PO Box 339, Station E, Toronto,
     Ontario M6H 4E3
Denmark: *Internationale Socialister*, Morten Borupsgade 18, kld, 8000
     Arhus C
France: *Socialisme International*, BP 189, 75926 Paris Cedex 19
Ireland: *Socialist Workers Movement*, PO Box 1648, Dublin 8
Norway: *Internasjonale Sosialister*, Postboks 5370, Majorstua, 0304
     Oslo 3
United States: *International Socialist Organization*, PO Box 16085,
     Chicago, IL 60622
West Germany: *Sozialistische Arbeiter Gruppe*, Wolfgangstrasse 81,
     6000 Frankfurt 1

Contents

Preface and Acknowledgements

These essays represent a developing analysis of South Africa's crisis in the 1980s. As that crisis has evolved, so too has the analysis. At least some of any contradictions the reader may detect between the essays are likely to reflect the different dates at which the various parts of this book were composed: chapter five in particular, written especially for this volume, contains a rather more fully elaborated analysis of the contemporary relationship between apartheid and capitalism.

Various people have made valuable comments on part or all of this book in draft, among them Peter Alexander, Duncan Blackie, Chris Harman, Richard Kuper, Peter Marsden (who also prepared the book for publication), and John Rogers. I am grateful to all for their help, though naturally they cannot be held responsible for the result. I would like to dedicate this book, in comradeship, to all those in South Africa working not simply for national liberation, but for socialism.

Alex Callinicos
October 1988

★

Alex Callinicos is a member of the Socialist Workers Party in Britain. His previous books include **Southern Africa after Soweto** (with John Rogers, 1977), **Southern Africa after Zimbabwe** (1981), **The Revolutionary Ideas of Karl Marx** (1982), **The Great Strike** (with Mike Simons, 1985) and **The Changing Working Class** (with Chris Harman, 1987). He teaches politics at York University.

A note on population and terminology

The population of South Africa was estimated at 34,800,000 in June 1987. Under the apartheid regime's system of racial classification, the South African people are divided into four groups—25,980,000 Africans, 4,911,000 Whites, 3,069,000 Coloureds, and 913,000 Indians. Africans, in turn, are classified along tribal lines corresponding to the ten 'Homelands' or Bantustans (indeed, the total given above for Africans is too low, since it includes a 1985 estimate of 5,849,639 for the population of the four 'independent Homelands'—Transkei, Bophuthatswana, Venda and Ciskei—which are, according to apartheid law, no longer part of the Republic of South Africa).

The South African resistance tend to reject this entire classification as arbitrary, racist and divisive. They recognise, in addition to the fundamental antagonisms of class, only the divisions between white and black, where 'black' is used to refer to the entire non-white oppressed population. In this book, however, it will sometimes by necessary to use the words 'African', 'Coloured' and 'Indian', but these terms should not be taken to denote genetically or ethnically distinct groups, and should be regarded as having invisible quotation marks. On the basis of the above figures blacks make up 86 per cent of the South African population, and whites 14 per cent.

On 11 October 1988, one pound sterling was equivalent to 4.26 South African rand (R), and one US dollar to 2.49R.

Abbreviations used in the text

ANC	African National Congress
AWB	Afrikaner Resistance Movement
AZACTU	Azanian Confederation of Trade Unions (Black Consciousness)
AZAPO	Azanian Peoples Organisation (main Black Consciousness movement)
BAD	Department of Bantu Administration and Development
BOSS	Bureau of State Security
BPC	Black Peoples Convention
CAL	Cape Action League
CAYCO	Cape Youth Congress
CCAWUSA	Commercial, Catering and Allied Workers Union
COSAS	Confederation of South African Students (UDF-affiliated)
COSATU	Congress of South African Trade Unions
CUSA	Council of Unions of South Africa (Black Consciousness)
EPG	Commonwealth Eminent Persons Group
FAK	Federation of Afrikaans Cultural Societies (a front for the right-wing Broederbond)
FAWU	Food and Allied Workers Union
FCI	Federation Chambers of Commerce
FEDCRAW	Federation of Commercial, Retail and Allied Workers
FOSATU	Federation of South African Trade Unions
GAWU	General and Allied Workers Union
HNP	Far right-wing Reconstituted National Party
KP	South African Conservative Party
MACWUSA	Motor Assemblers and Component Workers Union
MAWU	Metal and Allied Workers Union
MK	Umkhonto weSizwe, military wing of the ANC
MWT	Marxist Workers Tendency
MWU	Mine Workers Union
NAAWU	National Automobile and Allied Workers Union
NACTU	National Council of Trade Unions
NEUM	Non-European Unity Movement
NRP	New Republic Party (liberal)

NUM	National Union of Mineworkers
NUMSA	National Union of Metalworkers
NUSAS	National Union of South African Students (predominantly white)
NUTW	National Union of Textile Workers
PAC	Pan Africanist Congress
PEBCO	Port Elizabeth Black Civic Organisation
PFP	Progressive Federal Party (liberal opposition)
POTWA	Postal and Telecommunications Workers Association
PWV	Pietermaritzburg, Witwatersrand and Vereeniging area
SAAWU	South African Allied Workers Union
SACCOLA	Employers' Consultative Committee on Labour Affairs
SACP	South African Communist Party
SADF	South African Defence Force
SAP	South African Police
SARWHU	Railways and Harbour Workers Union
SASO	South African Students Organisation
SATS	South African Transport Service
SSC	State Security Council
SWAPO	South West African Peoples Organisation (Namibia)
SWATF	South West African Territorial Force
TUCSA	South Africa's main white trade union federation
UDF	United Democratic Front
UMMAWSA	United Metal, Mining and Allied Workers
UWUSA	United Workers Union of South Africa (formed by Inkatha)
ZANU-PF	Victorious liberation movement in Zimbabwe

South Africa: The main cities and Bantustans

Pietersburg

TRANSVAAL

Witwatersrand

Pretoria

Johannesburg

NATAL

ORANGE
FREE STATE

LESOTHO

Durban

CAPE PROVINCE

Cradock

Port Elizabeth

Cape Town

Bantustans:
1 KwaZulu
2 Bophuthatswana
3 Transkei
4 Venda
5 Ciskei

Introduction

ON 9 JANUARY 1973 two thousand black workers at the Coronation Brick and Tile works on the outskirts of Durban went on strike for higher wages. They marched through the early morning traffic chanting *Filumuntu ufedsadikiza*—Man is dead, but his spirit lives.[1] Their action sparked off a wave of strikes in the Durban-Pinetown area, South Africa's second largest industrial conurbation.

The Coronation strike was the first stirring of what has become one of the gaints of international labour. Fifteen years later, the Congress of South African Trade Unions (COSATU) organised a million black workers: three million answered its call to join a three-day general strike in June 1988, defying the most repressive state of emergency in South Africa's history.

The Durban strikes of 1973 marked the end of the long night which followed the apartheid regime's success in crushing popular resistance to its policies in the early 1960s. A series of blows now struck South Africa's racist rulers in rapid succession. In April 1974 the Portuguese dictatorship was overthrown by a military coup in Lisbon. The subsequent collapse of Portugal's colonial empire in Africa meant that national liberation movements took power in Angola, Mozambique and Guine-Bissau. The attempt by the South African government in Pretoria to impose a black puppet regime on Angola ended in military humiliation. The liberation of Mozambique turned the flank of the white settler regime in Zimbabwe, guaranteeing the eventual victory of the nationalist guerrillas whose struggle finally ended ninety years of racist rule, with Robert Mugabe sweeping to victory in the independence elections of February 1980.

As the tide of black liberation lapped at the borders of South Africa itself, the apartheid regime faced growing defiance from its own subjects. On 16 June 1976 black school students took to the streets of Soweto, the vast complex of African townships outside Johannesburg. They were protesting against the imposition of Afrikaans, which they regarded as the language of their oppressors, as the compulsory medium of instruction in certain key subjects. The South African Police reacted by mowing the demonstrators down. The first to be killed was thirteen-year-old Hector Peterson—the first victim of the war between township youth and the security forces which has continued, with interruptions, ever since. Police brutality turned a protest into a rising which raged for over a year, only to break out again, this time chiefly in the townships around Cape Town, in 1980.

Popular insurgency developed against the backdrop of an increasingly serious economic crisis. 1973, the year of the Durban strikes, was also the year when the long world boom of the 1950s and 1960s definitively came to an end. South Africa, a major beneficiary of that boom in the 1960s, was profoundly affected by the great international recessions of the mid-1970s and early 1980s. The impact of global crisis was intensified by structural problems particular to South African capitalism, reflecting its failure to break out of the role of an exporter of primary commodities such as gold and to become, like South Korea or Brazil, a significant exporter of manufactured goods. The 1980s proved to be a decade of long-term economic stagnation, exacerbating the terrible poverty of black South Africans, especially in the horrifying rural slums of the tribal 'Homelands'.

The South African regime reacted to this multiple crisis by proclaiming its commitment to 'reform'. P W Botha, after becoming leader of the ruling National Party in September 1978, launched an ambitious programme to restructure South African capitalism. His most important single concession to the black majority was the legalisation of African trade unions in 1979. The aim of this and other measures—above all the 1983 Constitution granting parliamentary chambers to the Coloured and Asian minorities—was to create and to incorporate a privileged layer of black intermediaries, not to abolish white domination. The Commonwealth Eminent Persons Group declared in June 1986, after its attempt to achieve a negotiated settlement of the South African crisis had been scuttled by Botha and his ministers:

> Their actions up to this point do not justify any claim that apartheid is being dismantled. The argument that the considerable change which we have seen is directed to that end founders, irretrievably, on the rock of 'group rights' and white control.[2]

The various elements of the crisis—political reform, economic crisis, township rebellion and working-class militancy—came together in September 1984 to precipitate by far the greatest wave of mass resistance to white rule in South African history. For nearly two years the country was shaken by township risings far greater than anything seen in 1976 or 1980 and all the more threatening because they were accompanied by mass strikes mounted by the growing movement of independent unions, the most important of which united as COSATU at the end of 1985. As the guerrillas of the exiled African National Congress (ANC) stepped up their military efforts, the collapse of the regime, whether through negotiations or popular insurrection or a combination of the two, seemed only a matter of time.

It was not to be. The state of emergency imposed by Botha in June 1986 proved to be highly effective. Township organisation was smashed, its leaders driven underground, and even the much more resilient unions were forced onto the defensive. The regime continued, under pressure from both right and left, to implement its programme of authoritarian reform. Historical experience of the cycle of risings—1976-77, 1980, 1984-6—suggests that South Africa's rulers had only bought themselves time, that future and even greater explosions were inevitable. Nevertheless, the defeat suffered by the resistance in 1986 implied that future victory would require searching and critical analysis and reflection.

This book is a contribution to this process. Its origins lie in an earlier book, **Southern Africa after Soweto**, which John Rogers and I wrote at the time of the 1976 rising. There we argued that the development of industrial capitalism in South Africa had given rise to the system of racial domination, known since 1948 as apartheid. The conclusion we drew was that national liberation would require socialist revolution to tear out the roots of apartheid in capitalism, and that consequently the only effective agent of change was the black working class. Subsequent developments have vindicated this argument—especially the rise of the black workers' movement which was in 1976 still in fragile and embryonic form.

The essays gathered together in this volume further develop our analysis, tracing the origins and course of South Africa's crisis in the 1980s. They were written at different times and for different occasions. Chapters One and Two were written in 1980, and originally appeared as part of a book titled **Southern Africa after Zimbabwe**.

Chapter One outlines the structural contradictions of South African capitalism at the beginning of the 1980s—its continued dependence on primary exports, the growing capital intensity of production, the expanding economic role of the state, and the increasing strategic position in industry of semi-skilled African workers. All these factors are still very much present in South Africa today, despite, for example, the Botha government's attempts to implement monetarist policies and to privatise state-owned industries. Were I writing this chapter today I would, however, lay more emphasis on the dominance of the private sector by a handful of corporations, above all Anglo-American and Sanlam.[3] The chapter's concluding stress on the potential importance of the black working class has, of course, been well borne out by events.

Chapter Two analyses P W Botha's reform strategy as it took shape after his accession to the premiership in September 1978. It emphasises key features—Botha's links with the Afrikaner bourgeoisie of the Cape, his alliance with the military, the drive to centralise executive power—which have since become even more pronounced. White petty-bourgeois and working class resistance to Botha's concessions, whose importance the chapter stresses, received clear organisational expression after the formation of the breakaway Conservative Party in 1982 and the rise of the fascist Afrikaner Resistance Movement (*Afrikaner Weerstandsbeweging* or AWB).

The contradictions of the reform strategy are a major theme of Chapter Three, originally an article in **Socialist Worker Review** written in the summer of 1985, when the township risings were at their height. It also highlights the limitations of the popular resistance movement itself.

Chapter Four was written at the beginning of 1986 and first published in **International Socialism**. Like the preceding article, it too challenges the idea that the current wave of risings would bring down the regime, and anticipates the defeat which followed the proclamation of a state of emergency that June. But it goes beyond a critical analysis of the mainstream resistance organisations, such as the ANC, to explore in depth the politics of the left whose emergence had crystallised around the debate in the unions between supporters and opponents of a broad alliance with the ANC and its sympathisers.

The confrontation between the two sides to this argument, known respectively as 'populists' and 'workerists', brought into prominence the issue raised by John Rogers and myself at the time of the Soweto rising: was the immediate objective of the struggle merely, as the ANC claimed, black majority rule, or did the rise of the black workers' movement open up the prospect of socialist revolution? Chapter Four argues strongly for the second alternative, and insists that the struggle for socialism in South Africa requires neither simply the strong independent trade unions defended by the workerists, nor a broad party on the model of the British Labour Party or the Brazilian Workers' Party, but a revolutionary Marxist organisation fighting within the working-class movement for socialist ideas.

Chapter Five, written specially for this volume, brings the story up to 1988 and extends the analysis made in these earlier writings. It measures the extent and isolates the causes of the defeat inflicted on the resistance under the June 1986 emergency. It explores the crisis of the regime itself—its difficult relationship with private capital, the challenge from the far right, and the ambiguities and limits of the reform process itself. And it traces the history of the workers' movement since the foundation of COSATU, and the conflicts and setbacks caused by this leadership. The analysis set out here underlines the argument fully developed in Chapter Four, but running throughout the entire book, that the fate of the South African revolution depends on the emergence of a Marxist party in South Africa.

The debt of all these essays to the brilliant Marxist scholarship which has flourished among South Africans both inside and outside the country since the early 1970s ought to be evident. The book is, however, rooted in the broader classical Marxist tradition of Marx and Engels themselves, Lenin and the Bolsheviks, Trotsky and the Left Opposition, Luxemburg and Gramsci. Sometimes this approach draws the criticism that it is 'Eurocentric', applying an analysis particular to the Western capitalist world to very different

African conditions. I have always been puzzled by this argument. After all, the theory of permanent revolution which forms the unifying perspective of this book was first formulated by Trotsky to analyse the Russian Revolution of 1905, which took place in a country subject, like South Africa, to the process of uneven and combined development—the rapid growth of industrial capitalism in a backward, overwhelmingly peasant society. Russia indeed even at the time of the October 1917 Revolution was in relative terms far less industrial, proletarian, and urban than South Africa today. Trotsky generalised his analysis into a global theory of revolution in the backward countries during the debate in the Communist International over the Chinese Revolution of 1925-7, which took place in a society far less developed even than Russia.'

In any case, modern South Africa is a product, as an outstanding generation of historians have shown, of capitalist development, and is caught up in the rhythms of the capitalist mode of production as a global system. Indeed, the very patterns of struggle in contemporary South Africa are by no means unique. The most important development which these essays analyse is the growth of what Eddie Webster calls 'social movement unionism', where black workers do not simply organise industrially but assert their power politically, outside the workplaces. But this is by no means a phenomenon confined to South Africa, as Webster recognises, implicitly treating it as a common feature of what he calls the 'semi-peripheral countries', but which are perhaps better known as the Newly Industrialising Countries.'

One of the key developments of the past decade has been the emergence in a number of Newly Industrialising Countries of new and powerful workers' movements which mobilise for political as well as economic goals: Brazil and South Africa since the late 1970s, Iran in 1978-9, Poland in 1980-1, and South Korea in 1987-8. This politicised militancy reflects common features of these countries' development. All experienced in the 1960s, and some well into the 1970s, the highly concentrated development of industrial capitalism under highly repressive political conditions: authoritarian regimes enforced on workers the high rates of exploitation required for rapid capital accumulation. By the end of the 1970s, these states found themselves in growing economic difficulties as the world crisis unfolded, and were faced with working classes created by the previous boom but no longer willing to accept the conditions on which the growth had been founded. So, as the Western working class went into retreat before employers' offensives usually mounted under the banner of the free market, new workers' movements exploded onto the world stage in the semi-industrialised economies on what had once been the advanced countries' periphery.'

COSATU is thus an instance of a much broader phenomenon. The divisions within it between workerists and populists have parallels elsewhere. The new workers' movements were very conscious of their new-found industrial might, but typically lacked any deep-rooted proletarian political traditions of their own on which to draw. Yet they faced challenges which made any narrow focus on trade union issues disastrous. Forced to confront political issues, movements like COSATU or *Solidarnosc* in Poland came increasingly under the influence of variants of nationalism, in which solutions were sought in cross-class alliances, in 'popular' unity.

Once set against a broader background, the emergence of the black workers' movement in South Africa becomes more intelligible. But such comparisons lose much of their point unless practical lessons are drawn from them. In two cases, the co-existence of workplace-based militancy and populist politics led to catastrophe. The power of the workers' *Shoras* (factory committees) in Iran crumbled as the politics of Islamic fundamentalism exerted a growing influence on the urban masses. And Solidarnosc, the greatest of all these workers' movements, was crushed by a general whom its leaders believed could be persuaded to tolerate their 'self-limiting revolution'. In neither case was populism challenged by working-class politics which went beyond narrow syndicalism to defend a socialist strategy aimed at the conquest of state power by the proletariat. The experience of both these defeats has direct implications for South Africa, underlining as it does the need both to challenge populism and to go beyond workerism by developing the revolutionary socialist alternative.

These essays that follow are offered in the belief that classical Marxism, representing as it does the concentrated and theoretically clarified experience not simply of these recent movements but of 150 years of working-class struggle, is an absolutely indispensable instrument for revolution in South Africa. The analysis set out here is by no means definitive, but, like all contributions to the Marxist tradition, will no doubt require correction and elaboration in the light both of criticism and of subsequent experience. Its aim is to help stimulate the debate which socialists inside and outside South Africa urgently need if past defeats are not to be repeated in the years ahead.

Chapter one:
The Roots of the Crisis
(April 1981)*

SOUTH AFRICA TODAY is an extreme case of the law of uneven and combined development. Its three main characteristics may be described as follows.

First, it is a capitalist social formation, in which the mass of the population have been separated from the means of production and therefore, in order to live, must sell their labour power to the small minority which enjoys exclusive possession of these means of production and which is itself divided into a set of competing capitals geared to the accumulation of surplus-value extracted from the wage-labourers they employ.

Second, South Africa, despite the fact that the contribution of manufacturing to its gross domestic product is greater than that of mining and agriculture combined, remains a peripheral formation in the world economy, importing the bulk of its capital goods and dependent for foreign exchange on Western investment and the products of its primary industries, above all gold.

Third and uniquely, the overwhelming majority of the population, including most of the industrial working class, is denied both in law and in fact, on the ground of colour, the civil and political rights to which even the most backward dictatorship elsewhere pays lip service. In this chapter we shall try to indicate briefly how these features came into being and how they underlie the crisis which shook South Africa in the course of the 1970s.

---

*First published in A Callinicos, **Southern Africa After Zimbabwe** (London 1981).

Apartheid and Capitalism

Lenin wrote that the development of capitalism could proceed along one of two roads, which he called the Prussian and American:

> Bourgeois development may proceed by having big landlord economies at the head, which gradually become more and more bourgeois and gradually substitute bourgeois for feudal modes of exploitation. It may also proceed by having small peasant economies at the head, which in a revolutonary way, will remove the 'excrescence' of the feudal latifundia from the social organism and then freely develop without them along the path of capitalist economy.[1]

Capitalism in South Africa took the first, Prussian road, based upon the expropriation of the African peasantry by white settler landowners and the establishment of repressive forms of labour control in mining and agriculture. It is the continued dependence of South African capitalism on 'labour repression' that accounts for the apartheid system.

Racial oppression had been a feature of South African society since the Dutch East India Company established a settlement at the Cape to provide its ships with fresh food and water in 1652. The first two centuries of white colonisation were characterised by pre-capitalist forms of exploitation—slavery and indentured labour at the Cape and, further inland, feudal relations of production with settler farmers extracting rent in cash, kind or labour services from the African peasantry, who remained as 'squatters' on the land which had been taken from them by force.

The emergence of the modern form of racial discrimination was closely bound up with the development of capitalist relations of production, which came to predominate in South Africa only as a result of the discovery of diamonds in 1867 and gold in 1886 (although capitalist agriculture based on production for export had been established in parts of the Cape and Natal earlier in the nineteenth century). Conditions of production in the gold mines (a low average ore grade, fixed gold price and high development and overhead costs) required a plentiful supply of cheap labour. This was provided by the disintegration of African agriculture, whose extensive methods of cultivation presupposed ready access to fresh land.

The expropriation of much of the African people's land by

British colonists and Afrikaner settlers in the course of the nineteenth century undermined the communal mode of production that prevailed among these people. African peasants, no longer able to support themselves and their dependents out of their own production, and forced by the imposition of hut and poll taxes to earn more cash, went to work in the mines. They were recruited as short-term contract labourers and paid low wages, which reflected the fact that production in the Reserves set aside for Africans took part of the burden of reproducing labour power. The Native Land Act of 1913 eventually allocated less than 13 per cent of the land to the Reserves, too little to reproduce the population, thereby sustaining the pressure on Africans to work in the farms and mines; it also prohibited them from owning land outside the Reserves, eliminating a potential source of competition with white farmers. The migrants were controlled while in the 'white' urban areas by the pass laws, which placed restrictions on their movements, and housed in all-male compounds attached to the mines.

The expansion of capitalism in agriculture led to the establishment of similarly repressive forms of labour control by white farmers, with labour tenancy providing in large parts of the country a bridge between the old feudal arangements and fully fledged wage labour.

The development of capitalism in both mining and agriculture therefore rested on 'labour repression'. Indeed, it was upon a 'marriage of maize and gold', an alliance of mining and agricultural capital, that the Union of South Africa was founded in 1910 after the defeat of the Afrikaner republics of the Transvaal and Orange Free State by Britain in the 1899-1902 war. The Union was a compromise, reflecting the common interests that underlay the conflicts between the great mining houses integrated into British capitalism and the predominantly Afrikaner white farmers. Blacks were denied the vote, save to a limited extent in the Cape, while the parliamentary form of the state provided a framework within which differences between sections of the white ruling class could be articulated and reconciled. This accomodation has proved remarkably durable: with the modifications necessitated by the development of manufacturing industry, it survives to this day.

Before 1948 the South African state underwent two major crises, both of which arose from within the settler camp. The first was posed by the white working class, formed initially from predominantly British skilled men imported to perform tasks, especially in the mining industry, for which Africans did not have the training. It was then swollen by the influx of 'poor whites' into towns, many of them *bywoners*, Afrikaner tenant farmers pushed off the land by the rationalisation of agriculture. An attempt by the Chamber of Mines to cut labour costs by ending the white monopoly of skilled jobs and replacing expensive white with cheaper black labour led in 1922 to an uprising by the white miners of the Witwatersrand which was ruthlessly suppressed by the government of Jan Smuts. In the aftermath of the Rand revolt, the Pact government was formed in 1924, a coalition of the Afrikaner Nationalists and the white Labour Party, which legally entrenched the colour bar, reserving skilled jobs for whites, and encouraged the employment of 'civilised [white, predominantly Afrikaner] labour' in the state sector. These measures did not blunt the employers' offensive in the mines, where white wages were held below the levels prevailing before 1922.

The complementary interests of mining and agricultural capital were reflected in the second major crisis of the inter-war period which led to the formation of the Fusion government in 1932 when the world depression forced South Africa off the gold standard. This decision was followed in 1934 by the fusion of J B M Hertzog's ruling National Party with Smuts' South Africa Party, the latter backed by English-speaking interests; it favoured both mining and agriculture and stimulated a boom which continued until after the end of the Second World War.

This boom was marked by the very rapid expansion of secondary industry, stimulated, first, by a wave of import substitution caused by the introduction of tariffs and then by the war, and, second, thanks to the establishment by successive governments of state corporations—ESCOM (electricity supply), ISCOR (iron and steel), IDC (industrial development)—whose task it was to provide the infrastructure for the industrialisation of South Africa. Yet this industrialisation led to the formation of an urban black proletariat. The war years saw a wave of African labour disputes and the expansion of black trade unions as part of a broader movement of social and political protest—squatters' campaigns and bus boycotts in Johannesburg, peasant revolts in the Reserves, and the revival of the quiescent African National Congress.

The scale of the challenge to the system represented by the black working class was brought home in 1946, when the African Mine Workers Union called a strike around demands which amounted to the destruction of the migrant labour system. It was ruthlessly crushed by the employers and the state.

Repression was, of course, nothing new. The Hertzog government had mounted a brutal offensive against African trade-union and political organisation in the late 1920s and early 1930s, while Smuts had used troops and planes to crush resistance in the Reserves. But secondary industrialisation, and the urban black working class it had created, posed a new set of problems. The ruling United Party, reflecting manufacturers' worries about the scarcity of skilled labour, advocated a gradual relaxation of the pass laws and the colour bar.

Such a policy would, however, conflict with the interests of both mining capital, which still depended on the migrant labour system, and the white farmers, who were losing workers to the towns—partly because wages were higher there, partly because labour-tenants reacted to attempts by their employers to cut down the land allocated to them by abandoning the countryside. It was challenged by the opposition National Party, formed in 1934 in protest against Hertzog's decision to fuse with Smuts, and committed to reversing the defeat of 1902 and establishing an Afrikaner republic independent of Britain.

The Nationalists' power base lay in the Afrikaner farmers of the Cape and the financial institutions—notably the SANLAM and SANTAM insurance companies—which they created, but increasing influence was exercised by the Afrikaner Broederbond, a secret society dominated by middle-class intellectuals from the northern provinces and especially the Transvaal. Their solution to the challenge of the black working class was the systematic extension of the migrant labour system to the whole of the African population, in other words, an intensification of labour repression rather than its relaxation. They called this policy *apartheid* (separation).

The Nationalists won the election, thanks chiefly of their capture of seventeen extra seats in the Transvaal—six in white working class constituencies on the Witwatersrand, where the Broederbond had just taken control of the white Mine Workers Union, the rest in rural areas where white farmers were worried about the labour crisis. The Nationalists have held office ever since.

Their policies proceeded along two lines. First, Afrikaner domination of the state was institutionalised, symbolically through South Africa's withdrawal from the Commonwealth and the declaration of a republic in 1961, practically by the promotion of Afrikaner economic interests. Second, successive governments set out to generalise the migrant labour system and thereby to break the African working class.

The cornerstone of apartheid is a piece of legislation inherited from Smuts, the Blacks (Urban Areas) Consolidation Act of 1945, first introduced in 1923. Under section 10 (1) of this Act no African may remain in a prescribed (urban) area for more than 72 hours unless s/he produces proof that (a) s/he has, since birth, resided continuously there; or (b) s/he has worked continuously there for one employer for not less than 15 years; or (c) is the dependent of any African with rights under (a) or (b); or (d) has been granted permission by a local labour bureau.

The Nationalists strengthened the pass laws and applied them to women for the first time; expelled black 'squatters' from white farms and 'surplus' Africans from the towns; enforced stringent geographical segregation between the races under the Group Areas Act. A network of labour bureaux was created to police the movement of Africans between country and town. Under the Black Labour Act of 1964, every African authorised to be in a prescribed (urban) area must register at his or her local labour bureau.

To administer these laws a vast bureaucracy was created around the Department of Bantu Administration and Development (BAD), which progressively assumed total control of urban African life, notably after reponsibility for the black townships was transferred from the white municipalities to 22 regional boards subordinate to BAD in 1971. There thus took shape a massive engine of repression and control designed to atomise the African working class and prevent any organised workers' movement developing.[2]

The ideological rationale of apartheid was provided by the notion of separate development, according to which there exist a number of distinct *nations* in South Africa—the whites and the various African tribes. Legislation was passed conferring powers of self-government upon the (government-appointed) tribal authorities in the Reserves, renamed Homelands but more usually known as Bantustans. Under H F Verwoerd, prime minister 1958-66 and the main architect of apartheid, the Nationalists adopted a policy of self-determination for the Homelands whose ultimate implication was that of granting independence to them. This policy justified the enforcement of apartheid and the denial of political rights to Africans, since they were, it could be argued, in the same position as, say, a Spanish immigrant worker in West Germany, with citizen rights in their own Bantustans but the status only of aliens in the white areas (some 87 per cent of the country).

This policy was summed up by the Minister of Bantu Administration and Development, Blaar Coetzee, in 1972:

(1) Every Bantu person, wherever he may find himself, is a member of his specific nation;

(2) the Bantu in white areas, whether they were born here or allowed to come here under our control laws, are here for the labour they are here to perform;

(3) the fundamental citizenship rights may only be enjoyed by a Bantu person within his own ethnic context, attached to his own homeland;

(4) the maximum number of people must be present in their own homelands;

(5) the Bantu persons who are in white South Africa are treated by us as homogenous communities;

(6) insofar as the Bantu are secondarily present in white areas, we see to it in every possible respect that the neccessary liaison exists between them and their peoples in their own homelands.'

The administration led by John Vorster (1966-78) proceeded to carry separate development into practice. The first homeland to achieve (formal) independence was the Transkei in October 1976, and it was followed by Bophuthatswana and Venda. In each case the people belonging to the tribal groups concerned were deprived of their South African citizenship. Connie Mulder declared on taking charge of BAD in February 1978: 'If our policy is taken to its logical conclusion...there will not be one black man with South African citizenship.'⁴

The destruction of black political and trade union organisation was both the condition of apartheid's success and its objective. It took more than 15 years—from 1948 to the Rivonia trial of 1964—to crush black resistance, a process symbolised by the massacres of African demonstrators at Sharpeville and Langa in March 1960. The 1950s were a period of low and uncertain growth, a situation that in part reflected the doubts of foreign, and much local, capital about the Nationalists' strategy, but which also helped put black workers on the defensive, just as the 1934-45 boom fuelled African militancy.

Industrial capital, while critical of those aspects of apartheid which affected its interests, especially the introduction of the statutory colour bar, fell in behind the government during the Sharpeville crisis. South Africa's leading mining company, Anglo-American, despite the fact that its chief Harry Oppenheimer was one of the Nationalists' leading white critics, came to the rescue when money poured out of South Africa after the massacre. To stem the outflow of foreign capital (R200 million in 1960 alone), one Anglo subsidiary raised a $30 million loan, Oppenheimer's American associate, Charles Engelhard, launched a company to attract US capital back into the country and Anglo helped the government arrange a loan with the Chase Manhattan Bank.[5]

Once it became clear that the regime had been successful in crushing all black opposition, foreign capital poured into the country, attracted by the low wages and high profits, fuelling a prodigious boom. Between 1960 and 1970 the South African economy grew, in real terms, at an annual rate of 7 per cent.[6] During that same period South Africa's foreign liabilities almost doubled, while direct foreign investment rose from R1,819 million to R3,943 million.[7]

The initial conflict of interest between the Nationalists and manufacturing capitals should not, in any case, be over-stated. The Board of Trade and Industry had argued on behalf of private capital in 1945 that 'the extension of manufacturing industry can be stimulated...through increased mechanisation so as to derive the full benefit of the large resources of comparatively low paid non-European labour' while white workers should be 'raised to the status of an aristocracy of labour'.[8] As we shall see, precisely this pattern was to characterise capital accumulation under Nationalist rule. Capitalism and racial oppression continued to reinforce each other in South Africa after 1948.

Contradictions

The process of capital accumulation in the 1960s and 1970s proved to be highly contradictory. Four main contradictions developed in the course of the boom, and underlay the economic and political crisis which broke out in 1973: South Africa's continued dependence on primary exports, the tendency towards growing capital intensity in all sectors, the expansion of the economic role of the state, and, most fundamentally, the growing power of black labour.

Until the 1950s South African manufacturing industry was confined largely to the production of consumer goods; thereafter heavy industry—cars, chemicals, engineering—began to set the pace. The result was that manufacturing came to outdistance mining and agruculture, accounting for 28.1 per cent of gross domestic product in 1976 as compared with 8.1 per cent from mining and 7.3 per cent from agriculture.' However, the South African economy is still unable to provide all its physical constituents from its own output. In particular, it has not become self-sufficient in the production of means of production, with the result that the expansion of heavy industry has required a constant inflow of capital goods, which constitute South Africa's largest import item, averaging between 40 and 50 per cent of the country's annual import bill. Every phase of rapid growth has led to a balance of payment crisis caused by the rise in imports of plant and equipment.

Such a dependence on imported capital goods is characteristic of the middle-income 'newly industrialising countries' in the Third World (Brazil, Mexico, Argentina, Taiwan, Hong Kong, Singapore), to which category South Africa properly belongs.[10] As a consequence South Africa has a very open economy—one rand of goods and services must be imported for every four rand spent.[11] Foreign exchange must be found to purchase these imports. There have been two sources, foreign investment and export earnings, the latter making up no less than 29.6 per cent of gross domestic product in 1976.[12]

However, unlike the other 'newly industrialising countries', South Africa has not been able to become a significant exporter of manufactured goods. This reflects, in part, the fact that labour productivity in manufacturing industry is very low, and is rising only very slowly (0.6 per cent a year in 1970-78).[13] A 1979 study showed that the most competitive South African exports are principally raw materials, while of manufactured goods those produced in the capital-intensive chemicals and metal industries are the most competitive, those produced in certain labour-intensive industries the least.[14]

Among the reasons that can be given for this situation are: the inefficiencies caused by apartheid, which keeps skilled labour expensive and limits labour mobility; the restricted nature of the home market, caused in part by low African wages, which prevents firms, for example in the car industry, from exploiting economies of scale; and import controls, which have encouraged the growth of small and relatively inefficient labour-intensive firms. Furthermore, South African manufacturers' natural market in the rest of Africa have been largely closed to them for political reasons: 19 per cent of South African exports went to other African countries in 1964, 18.6 per cent in 1971, and only 9.3 per cent in the first nine months of 1977.[15]

The result is that South Africa is still heavily dependent for its export earnings on the more or less processed products of mining and agriculture.

Table 1: South African exports by types of production (percentages)[16]

	Primary	Processed	Manufactured
1969	38.7	37.5	23.8
1970	36.0	38.6	25.4
1971	36.9	37.1	26.0
1972	38.5	38.6	22.9
1973	36.0	39.0	25.0
1974	35.4	43.1	21.5
1975	39.5	39.7	20.8

As a consequence:

South Africa remains a peripheral economy, in spite of its considerable growth and in spite of its substantial capacity to attract foreign investment... Its expansion continues to be heavily import dependent, at the same time as its capacity to earn foreign exchange continues to be limited by the fact that its access to export markets is still largely confined to a restricted range of primary commodities.[17]

The South African ruling class, whatever their aspirations to autarky, remain dependent partners of Western capitalism. Furthermore, the country's economic prosperity is bound up with the fluctuations of the world economy. In particular gold remains of crucial importance to the South African economy. Gold exports are still the biggest earner of foreign exchange and play a crucial role in off-setting trade deficits and financing exports.

Table 2: Net gold output as a percentage of total foreign receipts[18]

1960	1965	1970	1971	1972	1973	1974	1975	1976
32.3	35.9	29.2	29.3	28.1	33.7	37.7	33.6	27.3

Moreover, these crucial export industries are particularly labour-repressive. This is most obviously true in the case of the mining industry, which continues to rely on the migrant labour system to provide and discipline its workforce. The massive state investment projects designed to extend South Africa's role as a producer and processor of raw materials, and the plans to transform it into a major exporter of coal (a commodity for which the world market is rapidly growing), expanding exports from 15.4 million tonnes in 1978 to 46 million tonnes in the mid-1980s,[19] will merely reinforce the country's subordinate position within the international division of labour and her rulers' dependence on highly repressive forms of labour control.

The second major feature of capitalist development in South Africa is that it has involved considerable mechanisation. The figures available suggest that what Marx called the organic composition of capital, the ratio between capital invested in plant and equipment and capital advanced to purchase labour power, has risen sharply as a result of the trend towards mechanisation.

Table 3: Capital-labour ratios in South Africa, 1946-77[20]

	Real fixed capital stock per economically active person (R at constant 1970 prices)			Annual rate of increase (percentage)	
	1946	1970	1977	1946-70	1970-77
All sectors	1,726	3,294	4,146	2.7	3.3
Manufacturing	1,216	2,689	3,818	3.4	5.4

This development has not been confined to manufacturing industry. In mining the capital employed per worker rose in real terms at an annual 3.2 per cent in 1946-70 and then jumped very sharply in 1973-76 when the real fixed capital stock rose by 28 per cent while employment fell by 2 per cent.[21]

Table 4: South African agricultural production, 1946-75[22]

Year	Production Units	Tractors	Value (Rm)	Volume (1960 = 100)
1946	112,453	20,292	252.5	53
1950	116,848	48,422	447.2	68
1955	105,859	119,196	698.5	84
1960	105,859	119,196	814.6	100
1965	95,438	138,422	1,039.9	119
1970	90,422	157,127	1,516.2	159
1975	77,591	167,981	2,729.0	170

As this table shows, similar trends have been displayed in agriculture where government tax policies encourage mechanisation and the centralisation and concentration of capital, leading to a fall in labour costs as a total proportion of farming costs from 68 per cent in 1948 to 29 per cent in 1973.[23]

One consequence is very high levels of African unemployment. A business economist estimated that there were two million black unemployed in May 1978, 20 per cent of the economically active population.[24]

The character of capital accumulation in South Africa bears a number of similarities to the pattern of development in the 'newly industrialising countries', where the rapid expansion of manufacturing industry has been secured thanks to considerable state intervention, wholesale repression and large scale foreign investment. But, as Nigel Harris explains, rapid capital accumulation in these countries does not prevent very high levels of unemployment:

> Today levels of labour-productivity, determined in technically advanced capitalism, ensure that industrial output can be expanded very rapidly without proportionately increasing the employment of labour... Instead of the industrial economy expanding to encompass the potential labour force of a whole country, it tends to remain limited to a small enclave of high growth with relatively few effects on the mass of the rural population.[25]

The migrant labour system is one method of sustaining this pattern of capital accumulation. The Bantustans are in no sense self-sufficient economic units. The Transkei government itself acknowledged that 'one can hardly speak of a Transkei economy in any meaningful sense; more properly one must call it a labour reserve.' The 'state' is forced to import some two-thirds of its food requirements and to export more than 60 per cent of its male labour force as migrant contract workers in the 'white' areas.[26] One study suggests that some 60 per cent of all rural households in the Transkei depend for their reproduction on the sale of labour power, leading to a situation in which the men go to work in the 'white' areas while women are responsible for the bulk of wage labour and subsistence agricultural production in the Transkei.[27]

The Transkei pattern was reproduced in other Bantustans. In 1980 Kwazulu was struck by one of the worst droughts in Zulu history. Cases of child malnutrition increased sharply; it was feared that as many as 500,000 cattle, one quarter of the Zulu herd which is the homeland's main source of internally generated wealth, might die. Nicholas Ashford wrote in **The Times**:

> The drive from the Indian Ocean coast through the European-owned sugar plantations up into the hills of Zululand provides dramatic evidence not just of the effect of the drought but of how the government's homeland policy is steadily debilitating the land and people of Kwazulu.
>
> Although European farmers have also been affected by the drought they have on the whole been able to compensate for the lack of rainfall by irrigation. The relative greenness of their sugarcane plantations contrasts starkly with the dry, burnt-out fields of the Zulus.

A church worker at Tugela Ferry, where only 4 per cent of the topsoil was left, attributed this to overcrowding caused by resettlement of blacks from white areas, which had trebled the local population.[28]

Disaster areas though they are, the Bantustans are essential to the reproduction of capitalism in South Africa. They act as a 'labour reserve', providing a pool of cheap black labour power for the white-owned factories, mines and farms, and at the same time serve as dumping grounds for 'surplus' workers and the 'superfluous appendages' of the workforce in white areas—the unemployed and the unemployable. In other words, the Bantustans provide the institutional framework through which the industrial reserve army generated by South Africa's highly capital-intensive pattern of growth is organised and controlled.[29]

The policy of resettlement fitted into this pattern. A government circular in 1967 declared that 'no stone is to be left unturned to achieve the settlement in the homelands of non-productive Bantu at present residing in the European areas.' The 'non-productive' included 'the aged, the unfit, widows with dependent children', 'Bantu on European farms who become superfluous as a result of age [or] disability', 'Bantu squatters', and 'professional Bantu'. By 1975 some three million Africans had either been resettled or scheduled for resettlement in the Bantustans. In 1978 the government took wider powers to deport 'idle or undesirable' blacks from the urban areas. Pass law arrests in the cities rose from 173,571 in 1977 to 272,887 the following year:

Exporting the unemployed to the Bantustans is a logical extension of the doctrine that the presence of Africans in the 'white' areas is to be tolerated only for so long as they are required to 'minister' to white needs. Indeed, influx control already serves as a means of confining unemployed Africans to the Bantustans in the sense that Africans living there are not allowed to enter the 'white' areas to look for work but must instead remain in the Bantustans in the hope that they will be requisitioned and recruited under the migratory labour system.[30]

The South African state has not only assumed responsibility for organising and regulating the supply of labour power. It has increasingly become a productive capitalist in its own right. State corporations dominate a number of sectors—ISCOR (iron and steel), ESCOM (electricity), Sasol (coal and oil), Natref (oil refining), Alusaf (aluminium), in addition to the Industrial Development Corporation (IDC), which has interests in a number of sectors. The share of the state in productive capital has been growing rapidly, notably in manufacturing, where in 1970-77 the real fixed capital stock of public corporations rose by nearly 17 per cent a year (compared to an annual rate of 9 per cent in the 1960s), while in the private sector the rate of growth of real fixed capital stock halved, from 9 per cent a year in the 1960s to 4.5 per cent a year in 1970-77.[31]

The rising gold price in the early 1970s encouraged Vorster and his finance minister, Nico Diedrichs, to undertake an ambitious programme of state-controlled investment projects, notably a series of coal-fired power stations (R5.8 billion), an increase in steel producing capacity to 6.5 million tons a year (R2.67 million), the deep sea harbour at Richards Bay (for the Natal coal mines) and the 861 kilometres Sishen-Saldhana railway to transport exports of iron ore (together R3 billion) and the nuclear power station at Koeburg in the Cape (R970 million).

These investments were financed by heavy foreign borrowing by the state and contributed to a sharp rise in the public sector's share of the economy.

Table 5: Total public spending as a percentage of gross domestic expenditure, 1960-76[35]

1960	1965	1970	1971	1972	1973	1974	1975	1976
17.2	22.3	23.7	25.9	27.9	24.7	26.1	30.1	31.8

Government expenditure doubled in the three years to 1976, leading to a huge increase in the money supply (which rose at an annual rate of 20 per cent in 1972-76)[32], and double digit inflation. The characteristic pattern of the business cycle in South Africa—rapid expansion, a sharp rise in imports, followed by a balance of payments crisis—combined with the government's inflationary policies and the abrupt fall in the gold price in 1974-75 to precipitate in 1976 what the **Financial Mail** called 'the longest and deepest recession in the South African economy for at least 45 years'.[33]

The Vorster-Diedrichs boom and its aftermath crystallised the fears of both Afrikaner and English-speaking businessmen that they would be suffocated by the ever-expanding state sector. Andreas Wassenaar, head of the Afrikaner business empire centred around SANLAM, and a member of the Broederbond, scandalised the Nationalist establishment by publishing a book denouncing the trend towards state capitalism. He wrote:

> Economic history in the Republic of South Africa has produced an officialdom—including a bureaucracy which is extremely Afrikaner-orientated—which is extremely lukewarm if not antagonistic in its attitude towards private enterprise and certainly vehemently opposed to the profit motive to a degree which, in the long run, threatens the future of capitalism.[34]

Most serious of all for the apartheid economy was its continued dependence on black labour.

Table 6: South Africa's economically active population, 1976.[35]

	(thousands)	percentage
Whites	1,802	17.9
Coloureds	809	8.0
Asians	229	2.3
African	7,216	71.8
Total	10,056	100.0

The expansion of manufacturing industry (whose output rose at an annual rate of 5.7 per cent in 1961-77) continued to suck blacks into the urban areas, while the attempt to transform the African working class into migrant labourers failed. In 1970 there were four million African workers in the 'white' areas, of which only 1.3 million were male migrants; settled black workers amounted to 1.1 million in the urban areas, 1.6 million in the rural areas. In 1970-77 the African labour force rose by 1.6 million (30.4 per cent), while the white labour force rose by 300,000 (21.7 per cent); the increase caused the proportion of whites in the total labour force to fall from 19.6 per cent to 18.7 per cent in the same period, while Africans' share rose from 68.8 per cent to 70.5 per cent.

The process of capital accumulation in the 1960s and 1970s did not merely lead to an increase in the numbers of black workers. It also involved a tranformation of the labour process, closely connected to the rising capital-intensity of production—'deskilling', the reduction in the skill content of work performed and the destruction of craft control over the process of production, together with an expansion in the numbers of the so-called 'new middle class'—white-collar, professional and supervisory workers—and of the semi-skilled workers performing such tasks as machine-minding. In South Africa whites have tended to move out of manual jobs into the 'new middle class', while Africans make up the bulk of semi-skilled as well as unskilled workers. Behind the apartheid legislation reserving skilled jobs for whites, a process known as 'fragmentation' or 'dilution' took place, involving shifting the colour-bar upwards as skilled jobs formerly held by whites were broken up into a number of simpler tasks performed by less skilled—and cheaper—blacks. The Wiehahn commission acknowledged that:

> a process of restructuring of work categories to utilise available skills better and to create semi-skilled tasks for relatively unskilled workers—mainly blacks... has become a permanent feature of the process of industrialisation in the country's main centres.

This process was stimulated also by an endemic shortage of skilled and white-collar labour. Only 16.5 per cent of the economically active population in South Africa were employed in professional and technical, administrative and executive, and clerical and sales jobs in 1970 compared to a norm of 18 to 20 per cent in other newly industrialising countries. This reflected a shortage of the white workers who monopolised these categories. On one estimate, if a 5 per cent growth rate were assumed, there would be 2,796,000 white employees in demand in 1990, but only 1,348,000 whites available. During the boom years of the 1960s and early 1970s this shortage was offset by the ready availability of foreign capital and by 'dilution', but as the crisis of the mid-1970s unfolded, it became clear that more radical solutions were necessary.

Ironically, then, the boom unleashed by the Nationalists' defeat of the black resistance led to the economy's *increased* dependence on African labour. The implications of this change were brought home to white South Africa in 1973 when a wave of spontaneous mass strikes involving some 60,000 black workers shook the Durban-Pinetown area. The response of the employers and the state to the strikers was quite mild: only 207 strikers, 0.2 per cent of the total, were prosecuted compared to 822—24 per cent of all those striking—in 1959,[43] and legislation was introduced conceding Africans the right to strike.

One study of the strikes offers these reasons for the comparative moderation of both government and bosses:

> One of the employers' representatives to whom we spoke explained the absence of massive arrests, and the fact that those firms who dismissed their staff re-engaged most of them, by saying that 'it is too jolly difficult to get a labour force as it is'. He pointed out that groups of unskilled workers can be sent back to the homelands, but this is impossible when there are strikes all over. Moreover, when workers are a bit more skilled employers no longer want a high labour turnover... The proportion of African workers in the workforce is increasing. The total number of African workers doing jobs that require some sort of training is increasing. The traditional artisan plus several unskilled labouring assistants is being replaced by the machine-minding operative who requires several weeks' training and several months' production in order to reach the normal level of production. All these factors mean that the potential bargaining power of African workers is increasing.[44]

The mid-1970s saw this bargaining power reflected at a number of levels. African trade unions, although they enjoyed only a twilight semi-legal existence, rarely recognised by the employers, never by the state, grew rapidly in this period. The Wiehahn Commission estimated that at the end of 1977 there were 27 black trade unions organising between 55,000 and 70,000 workers.[45] Their growth and the strike wave itself were stimulated by the rapid rise in prices, itself a result of the Vorster-Diedrichs boom.

Employers were quite ready to concede wage-increases—a shift in attitude reflecting the capital-intensity of industrial production, which meant that labour costs had fallen as a proportion of total costs—as well as the economic muscle their greater skill gave black workers. In 1970-75 African wages rose in real terms at an annual 6.6 per cent, while white wages rose by only 1 per cent. The black-white wage gap fell for the first time in 1973-75, from R2,815 to R2,724 (in constant 1970 prices), while the black share in personal income rose by 6 per cent in 1970-75, from 26 to 32 per cent.

These increases were unevenly distributed (the figures for wage rises exclude agricultural and domestic workers), affected migrant labourers far less than urban workers, and still left the white/black income ratio at 11.1 in 1975. However, as one economist pointed out, 'this is the first time in South Africa's economic history that such a redistribution has taken place'.[46]

The mines, still as we have seen central to South African capitalism's prosperity, were also shaken by black labour unrest which resulted in 178 dead and 1,043 injured in 1972-76.[47] Despite this brutal response, the Chamber of Mines, like other employers, was prepared to pay more: black miners' wages rose fivefold in 1970-75, increasing from 14 per cent of working costs in 1970 to 25 per cent in 1975.[48] This policy reflected in part the Chamber's worries about labour supplies, especially after the Malawian government banned recruitment of its citizens for the South African mines and the liberation movement Frelimo took over in Mozambique. The mining houses responded by stepping up recruitment among the unemployed and underemployed of the Homelands, especially the Transkei and Kwazulu, and of the rural 'white' areas, of the Cape and Natal in particular. South Africans rose from 20 per cent to 44 per cent of the black workforce in the mines between 1973 and 1975.[49]

The shift in the balance of power between white capital and black labour underlay the Soweto uprising, even if it was the victories of Mozambique and Angola that provided the inspiration, and the tyranny and inhumanity of 'Bantu education' the occasion of the school students' revolt. A number of very thorough studies of the uprising have now been published,[50] but its principal significance lay in the fact that, as John Rogers and I pointed out at the time, unlike Sharpeville—'simply the most prominent in a series of events in which a mass movement that had fought throughout the 1950s was crushed'—'Soweto... is the highest point reached so far in a *rising* wave of struggles' both within the country and elsewhere in the region. 'South Africa', we wrote, 'is clearly entering a period of massive confrontation between the regime and the oppressed black population.'[51]

And so it proved to be the case. The black youth revolt which began in Soweto on 16 June 1976 spread both geographically—to the rest of the Rand and then to the Cape—and socially—from the schools to the factories. No less than three stay-at-homes—political general strikes—occured in 1976, two in the Transvaal, on 4-6 August (100,000 on strike) and 23-25 August (132,000), and then in both the Transvaal and the Western Cape, where half-a-million African and Coloured workers downed tools on 13-16 September.[52] But the core of the revolt was the black youth of the townships, who sustained their movement throughout 1977, winning a signal victory in June, when they forced the stooge Soweto Urban Bantu Council to resign.

The eventual collapse of the revolt arose in part from the nature of its leadership—drawn largely from high-school students, a small and comparatively privileged minority of their age-group. The students only gradually groped towards a strategy connecting their demands to the conditions and grievances of black workers. The resulting failure to weld a lasting alliance between workers and students was to some degree related to the grim economic climate—wage rises, under the impact of the recession, began to slow down late in 1976,[53] while one in ten factory workers were laid off in 1976-77.[54] Its effect was to confine the revolt to the townships, which were comparatively easy for the regime's forces to isolate and surround. Moreover, the students' main weapon—the school boycott—deprived them of the most obvious means of bringing their supporters together, within the classrooms.[55]

These factors combined with sheer exhaustion, the effects of wholesale repression—700 publicly recorded deaths between June 1976 and October 1977, mass detentions and the suppression of the black consciousness movement on 19 October 1977—and an exodus of thousands of young blacks into exile caused the revolt to wind down early in 1978. As we shall see, this proved to be only a temporary respite for the regime.

Chapter 2:
Rationalising Apartheid
(April 1981)*

THE CRISIS IN South Africa is what Antonio Gramsci called an 'organic crisis':

> A crisis occurs, sometimes lasting for decades. This exceptional duration means that incurable structural contradictions have revealed themselves (reached maturity), and that despite this, the political forces that are struggling to conserve and defend the existing structure itself are making every effort to cure them, within certain limits, and to overcome them.[1]

We saw in the last chapter what these 'incurable structural contradictions' were in South Africa's case—her peripheral status in the world economy, the rising organic composition of capital in South African industry, the growing role of the state, and the revolt of the black working class. Since his accession to the premiership in September 1978, P W Botha has sought to 'cure' and 'overcome' these contradictions, 'within certain limits'—those set by the continued reproduction of capitalism in South Africa. In this chapter we shall consider his ambitious 'total strategy'.

Muldergate and the rise of P W Botha

To understand this strategy, we must first take account of the peculiar form of state that exists in South Africa. It is not a fascist state, but rather 'a racially exclusive bourgeois democracy', as one South African Marxist put it,[2] involving a parliamentary system

---

*First published in A Callinicos, **Southern Africa After Zimbabwe** (London 1981)

of government in which blacks are denied the vote. This situation reflects both the economy's continued reliance on 'labour repression' and influx control and the need for some framework within which the conflicting interests of particular fractions of capital can be expressed and to some degree reconciled.

Also represented in the state, and forming the popular base of the ruling National Party, is the white working class. The loyalty of white wage-earners to the status quo was secured through a combination of economic concessions ('civilised labour', job reservation), the incorporation of white trade unions in the state and the dense network of cultural and other associations built up under the aegis of Afrikaner nationalism.

The National Party, indeed, in its relation to the white working class offered an almost textbook illustration of Gramsci's notion of a hegemonic party ruling by consent as well as force. Its ideological domination of the white masses was organised through the Federasie van Afrikaanse Kulturverenigings (FAK), a front for the Broederbond, with over 2,000 affiliated cultural, religious and youth bodies, including the three main Afrikaner churches, the Voortrekkers (scouts), and cultural associations of nurses, the defence forces and white employees in the railways and post office. The FAK organised the *Volksfeeste*, like Republic Day (31 May) and the Day of the Covenant (16 December), at which the continuity of the Afrikaner struggle for national independence was reaffirmed. Afrikanerdom also had a powerful 'organic intelligentsia', charged with articulating and developing Nationalist ideology, based in the universities, churches and press. The crux of this ideology was the notion of national self-determination, which served to justify both the Afrikaner struggle for ethnic, political, and economic identity, *and* the denial of rights of Africans, since they had their own national homes in the Bantustans.'

Within this framework the nature of Afrikaner Nationalism has changed since the National Party came to power. In 1948 it was mainly an alliance of the rural bourgeoisie of the Cape with the northern petty bourgeosie against the domination of 'English-speaking' capital. Nationalist governments set out to build up Afrikaner capital, both by giving government accounts and contracts to Afrikaner firms and through the expanding role of the state corporations, all controlled by Afrikaners. State backing, combined with an economic enviroment favourable to growth, and plentiful cheap labour, caused the Afrikaner share of the private sector (excluding agriculure) to rise from 9.6 per cent in 1948-49 to 20.8 per cent in 1975.[5] The result was the rise of Afrikaner firms such as Federale Volksbeleggings (investments), General Mining (now the third largest mining finance house), Rembrandt (tobacco and drinks), Volkskas and Nedbank (banking), SANLAM (insurance). A powerful Afrikaner financial and industrial bourgeosie has come into being. A feature of this development has been that, as the *Financial Times* put it:

> the Afrikaner businessman now probably has as much, if not more, in common with his English-speaking counterpart in commerce, industry and mining as with the blue-collar workers, farmers, teachers and civil servants who have traditionally formed the power base of the National Party.[6]

This shared business interest was expressed after the Soweto uprising when both the Transvaal Chamber of Industries and the Afrikaanse Handelsinstitut (Afrikaans Chamber of Commerce) called on the government to accept the permanent presence of blacks in urban areas, while retaining influx control.[7]

The emergence of the Afrikaner bourgeoise also led to changes within the Nationalist establishment, a process typified by the transformation of the Broederbond. This secret society began life as the class organisation of the northern Afrikaner petty bourgeoisie, founded in 1918 by fourteen railway clerks, clergymen and policemen, and played a crucial role in the subjection of certain key white unions, notably the mineworkers, to Nationalist domination.[8] Under Verwoerd the Broeders, and their chairman, Piet Meyer, also head of the South African Broadcasting Corporation, enjoyed great influence, and came to occupy centre-stage in the mythologies of liberal critics of the regime.

Pride came before a fall. Vorster effectively transformed the Broederbond into a 'mere tool of the National Party', [9] forcing Meyer to expel the supporters of his old associate, Albert Hertzog, who in 1969 broke with the government to form the far-right Herstigte Nasionale Party (HNP). Hertzog and Meyer had directed the Nationalist takeover of the white unions, and were critical of measures such as the 1963 deal between the Afrikaner mining house Federale Mynbou and the Anglo-American which allowed the former to take over General Mining. Vorster resisted Broederbond-instigated moves to have the state break up Anglo-American as a step towards imposing Afrikaner economic domination.[10] The subordination of the Broederbond to the government was shown in 1974 when Professor Gerrit Viljoen, a prominent *verlig* (enlightened) intellectual, ousted Andries Treurnicht, the Broederbond's ultra-*verkramp* (reactionary) chairman.

The clash between Vorster and Hertzog was also a conflict between the Cape and the Transvaal. The National Party is a federal organisation, each province (Cape, Transvaal, Orange Free State and Natal) possessing its own congress, head committee and leader, while the parliamentary caucus of Nationalist MPs elects the party's national leader. When D F Malan formed the modern National Party in 1934 in protest against J B M Hertzog's decision to fuse with Smuts, it was the Cape alone that had an organisation, significant parliamentary representation (fourteen MPs, compared to four in the Orange Free State and one in the Transvaal) and a newspaper, **Die Burger**.

However, after 1948 the Transvaal party, representing the most populous and economically important province, claimed the dominant say in Nationalist counsels, with the Broederbond acting as a formidable pressure group for their interests. When Malan retired from the premiership in 1954 he was replaced by J G Strijdom, 'the Lion of the North', for many years the only Nationalist MP in the Transvaal, who had the backing of Verwoerd and Albert Hertzog, rather than by the Cape leader, T E Donges. Again, in 1958 it was the Transvaal candidate, Verwoerd, who became prime minister after Strijdom's death.

Thereafter, the Cape Nationalists sought to challenge northern dominance within the party. Their chief instrument was **Die Burger**, which campaigned successfully for the establishment of a parliamentary republic rather than one involving an executive presidency like the old Boer republics, the form favoured by the Broederbond. In 1965 Nasionale Pers, the Cape-based owners of **Die Burger**, established **Die Beeld**, a Johannesburg Sunday paper, against Verwoerd's wishes, in order 'to propagate Cape Nationalism in the Transvaal and undermine the ever-growing dominance of Transvaal Nationalists in the Government'. It was **Die Beeld** which opened the attack on Hertzog and the Nationalist far right in August 1966, closely followed by the rest of Nasionale Pers. Elaine Potter, in her study of the South African press, writes: 'There can be little doubt that the Afrikaans press brought about or, arguably, speeded up the first split in the National Party for 20 years.' **Die Beeld** and **Die Burger** even attacked Ben Schoeman, the leader of the Transvaal Nationalists, in 1967, with the backing of P W Botha. To quote Elaine Potter again: 'Nasionale Pers was trying to influence the selection of a future leader of the party, who in their terms was quite logically the leader of the Cape National Party—P W Botha'.[11]

This division between Cape and Transvaal within the National Party arose to some degree from differences in the party's power base in the two provinces. The wealthy Afrikaner farmers of the Cape had created the great SANLAM financial empire, backed Malan against J B M Hertzog, donated the funds for the Nationalist drive in the trade unions and provided much of the impetus behind the movement in the 1930s and 1940s to divert the savings of the *volk* into Afrikaner business interests.

The Afrikaner middle class in the Transvaal were confronted with an English-speaking business establishment and a white population that was rapidly being urbanised and proletarianised. Hence the greater importance in the north of the drive for ideological hegemony, to defend the Afrikaner working class from 'alien' and subversive influences and provide a base for attaining state power. Hence also the importance—after 1948—of the state apparatus for the Afrikaner establishment in the Transvaal, centred on Pretoria, the seat of administration.

> Whereas in the north the bureaucratic strata predominate in Afrikaner life, the salient feature in the south is the more established Afrikaner bourgeoisie of the Cape, based, more characteristically, on private wealth or professional qualifications.[12]

It was indeed the hypertrophy of the Nationalist-controlled state bureaucracy, denounced by Andreas Wassenaar on behalf of the Cape business establishment, that lay behind the Muldergate scandal. This affair centred on the use of R64 million of state funds by Eschel Rhoodie, the secretary for information, chiefly to finance an English-speaking pro-Nationalist daily paper, **The Citizen**. Despite desperate efforts by the government to limit the damage caused by revelations of Rhoodie's activities, a number of leading Nationalist figures were implicated. Most important among them were Connie Mulder, leader of the Transvaal Nationalists and Minister of Information, General Hendrik Van Den Bergh, the widely feared chief of BOSS, the Bureau of State Security, reputed to be Vorster's *eminence grise*, and, finally, prime minister John Vorster himself. The scandal compelled Vorster to announce in September 1978 his resignation to stand for the ceremonial post of state president.

In normal circumstances Mulder could have expected to defeat the other main candidate, P W Botha, since the Transvaal had 80 votes in the Nationalist caucus, compared to the Cape's 55, Natal's 13 and the Orange Free State's 24. However, Pik Botha, the immensely popular *verligte* foreign minister, ran and split the Transvaal vote, preventing any candidate winning on the first ballot, when P W Botha got 78 votes, Mulder 72 and Pik Botha 22. In the run-off, with Pik eliminated, Botha won 98 votes, Mulder 74. For the first time in nearly 25 years the Cape had won the party leadership.

Botha's control of the government was strengthened when subsequent revelations forced Mulder to resign from the government and parliament and to give up the Transvaal leadership. Finally Vorster himself was thrown to the wolves, resigning from the state presidency in June 1979 after the Erasmus commission appointed to investigate the scandal confirmed that he too had been aware of Eschel Rhoodie's activities.[13]

Muldergate, culminating as it did in the disgrace of three of the most powerful figures in the Nationalist establishment, including 'Honest John' Vorster himself, had a traumatic effect on Afrikanerdom, in whose ideology Calvinistic rectitude plays a significant part. The affair somehow summarised the changes that had occured in Afrikanerdom.

For a start it symbolised the squandering of state money to the detriment of national capital. When Wassenaar, before the scandal broke, wrote that 'the national crisis which the RSA faces is a direct consequence of overspending by the state',[14] he could have been describing the actions of the free-spending Rhoodie. Then there was the sheer corruption of the business: it was claimed that Rhoodie and his two brothers, Nico, a prominent intellectual apologist for apartheid, and Denys, deputy secretary for information, had misappropriated state funds for their own benefit, running up huge bills on expenses. And there seemed to be more dirt beneath the surface—Robert Smit, former South African representative to the IMF, and his wife were murdered in November 1977 because, it was alleged, he had uncovered the illegal transfer of funds abroad by prominent Nationalists.

Finally, it brought home that the Afrikaners were no longer a rural people but part of an urban, industrialised, class-divided society. As the **Financial Mail** put it, 'the Nats are no longer the party of the *volk*. They are the better-dressed, affluent members of the *volk*.'[15] The malaise of the Afrikaner people after 30 years of Nationalist rule was diagnosed with irony and precision by Andre Brink, in novels such as **Rumours of Rain**, a study of the moral nullity of one of the new generation of Afrikaner businessmen.

The 'Brazilian model'

P W Botha was nobody's idea of a liberal. His political career began in 1936, when he was appointed a full-time organiser of the Cape Nationalists. Although a protege of Malan's, as a back-bench parliamentarian in the 1950s he supported the hardliner Hendrik Verwoerd first for the post of minister of native affairs (as BAD was then known), then for prime minister. He became leader of the Cape party in 1966.

But before coming to the premiership Botha was known chiefly for his role as Vorster's minister of defence. When he took on this portfolio in 1966 the South African Defence Force (SADF) occupied a relatively lowly position in the state apparatus, since the principal coercive role, that of suppressing internal black opposition, was performed by the South African Police (SAP). The outbreak in 1967 of liberation wars on South Africa's borders in Zimbabwe and Namibia, and the changed situation brought about in the region by the Portuguese coup of 1974, led to a reversal of positions, with the SADF assuming an increasingly important role both inside and outside the country.

Botha's years as minister of defence (1966-80) saw a prodigious expansion of the armed forces and of South Africa's military-industrial complex. The defence budget rose from R36 million in 1958-59 to nearly R2 billion in 1979-80, while the turnover of the state Armaments Development and Production Corporation (Armscor) increased in 1968-78 from R32 million to R979 million. By the end of that period 800 private companies employing 100,000 workers were involved in Armscor contracts, helping South Africa to become largely self-sufficient in arms production. Thanks to the introduction of compulsory military service for white males between 18 and 45 (two years' initial service, three-month call-ups thereafter), the standing operational force rose from 11,500 in 1960 to 180,000 in 1979, and total SADF manpower from 78,000 to 494,000.[16]

Muldergate involved a struggle for power between two different branches of the repressive state apparatus. Vorster as minister of justice and police had, with the help of Van Den Bergh, then head of the security branch, crushed the black resistance in the early 1960s. After Vorster's rise to the premiership, BOSS was created with Van Den Bergh acting as his closest political adviser, for example representing him in negotiations with President of Zambia Kenneth Kaunda and other black leaders during 'detente', Pretoria's ill-fated policy towards the 'front line' states in the mid-1970s. Van Den Bergh, however, antagonised P W Botha by opposing the SADF invasion of Angola in October 1975. On becoming prime minister Botha wasted no time in clipping BOSS's wings, renaming it first the Department of National Security and then the National Intelligence Service, and placing it under his control along with its rival, the Department of Military Intelligence.

Now it was the turn of the SADF, with its chief, General Magnus Malan assuming a position similar to that of Van Den Bergh under Vorster. The rise of the military was reflected in the enhanced role of the State Security Council, a committee of senior ministers, civil servants and generals, which under Botha (who initially retained the defence portfolio) became a sort of super-cabinet, meeting on Mondays, the day before the cabinet's weekly meeting, and effectively pre-empting the latter's decisions. In September 1979 Botha reduced the number of cabinet committees from forty to five—internal affairs, social affairs, economic affairs, foreign affairs and state security. The five committee chairmen—Piet Koornhof, Fanie Botha, Owen Horwood, Pik Botha and Alwyn Schlebusch, respectively ministers of co-operation and development, manpower utilisation, finance, foreign affairs, and interior and justice—formed with Botha an inner cabinet, by-passing both the bureaucracy (there were plans afoot to reduce the number of departments from thirty nine to eighteen) and the Nationalist Party machine, especially the disgruntled Transvaalers.

This centralisation of power and militarisation of the state apparatus was justified by the claim that South Africa was fighting a 'total war' which required a 'total strategy'. Botha has as minister of defence presided over the emergence of a new generation of senior officers, who made the study of counter-insurgency operations in other parts of the world—Malaya, Indochina, Algeria (where Malan actually served), Latin America—one of their main pre-occupations. They were especially interested in the case of Brazil, where after the 1964 coup the army had created a 'national security state' committed to the promotion of growth and the suppression of disorder and based on two premises:

> The first stressed the fact that national security and economic development were inter-dependent, and that since the fighting of a modern war required the active consent of the whole nation, means must be found of mobilising its will, its unity and its productive capacity. Thus in addition to its traditional requirements, national security implied planning of the national life so as to optimise production and the economy while minimising internal tensions... According to the second concept, part of the economic backwardness found in under-developed countries was due to internal pressures resulting from the world-wide ideological struggle [between capitalism and communism] and these pressures represented a serious threat to national security.[17]

The second element, the 'total assault' against South Africa was defined by Magnus Malan in a 1977 speech as involving 'diplomacy, industry, trade, technology, the written and spoken word, the public media, demonstrations, strikes, boycotts, subversion and so on'. The enemy, then, was perceived as being, not only black nationalism and the Soviet Union, but also Western capital, which showed itself ready to back an arms boycott against South Africa in November 1977. Professor Jan Lombard, an Afrikaner economist close to Botha, summed up the Nationalists' fears: 'If the present regime should become the target of liquidation by the Western powers themselves, in the hope that they could replace it by a more acceptable anti-communist regime, the nature of the security problem becomes something of a nightmare'.[18]

Certainly Botha adopted a less cooperative stance towards the West. What the *Economist* called 'the biggest diplomatic operation ever to be mounted in southern Africa',[19] the visit by the foreign ministers of the US, West Germany, France, Britain and Canada to Pretoria in October 1978, ended in failure when Botha and Malan refused to accept the 'contact powers' proposal for a Namibian settlement involving the liberation movement SWAPO and instead held 'internal' elections in December, which led to the installation of the stooge Democratic Turnhalle Alliance. Pretoria also backed the internal settlement in Zimbabwe and only reluctantly acceded to the Lancaster House agreement. In April 1979 three US military attachés were expelled from South Africa after being caught looking for secret nuclear installations (Pretoria and Washington had already had a major row in 1977 over the former's reputed possession of atomic weapons).

The rift between South Africa and the West should not, however, be exaggerated. The Reagan administration adopted a policy of 'constructive engagement' which involved tacit support for Botha. Similarily, despite the regime's attempts to make the economy more self-sufficent—in November 1977 the National Supplies Procurement Act was activated, empowering the government to assume direct control of the economy in the event of sanctions being imposed—South African capitalism remained heavily dependent on Western imports of capital goods and on foreign investment to help finance them. Western assistance for the apartheid regime continued to be forthcoming. It was suggested, for example, that the CIA, State Department and Pentagon were involved in the supply of long-range 155mm howitzer shells to South Africa by an American firm, Space Research.[20]

Nevertheless, the notion of a total assault against South Africa served to justify the enchanced role of the military. Lieutenant-General J R Dutton, SADF chief of staff operations, wrote that 'in the new perspective...civil riots, strikes accompanied by violence and urban terrorism are seen as part of the total assault' and could no longer be left to BOSS and the SAP to deal with. Therefore:

> the military role in National Security can no longer be confined to the employment of armed force. It is broadened to include contributory roles in virtually every other sphere of strategic action and specifically in the psychological, economic and political spheres.[21]

The 1979 Defence White Paper provided for the establishment of a 'national strategic planning process' involving all departments and directed by the State Security Council and the Prime Minister's Department.[22]

Interestingly enough, Andreas Wassenaar was an advocate of South African adoption of the 'Brazilian model', and in particular the military regime's recruitment of ministers from the private sector, funding of private enterprise and encouragement of partnerships involving the state, local capital and multinationals.[23] Unlike Vorster, who had been infuriated by Wassenaar's book, Botha agreed with the criticisms it contained of the over-inflated public sector. He encouraged Owen Horwood, the minister of finance, who had already implemented an austerity programme in 1976-77, to adopt monetarist policies designed to reduce the economic role of the state. After rising at an annual rate of 10 per cent in 1973-76 real government expenditure increased by only 1 per cent in 1977, by half a per cent in 1978 and was static in 1979.[24] Horwood's 1980 budget, which gave away R1.5 billion to whites in tax cuts, was greeted by the **Financial Mail** as giving 'substance to prime minister P W Botha's promises to revitalise the free market economy and switch resources to the private sector'.[25] Plans were announced to convert Sasol into a holding company owned 70 per cent by private shareholders, 30 per cent by the state.[26]

The Wiehahn and Riekert Reports

It was, however, less Botha's economic policies than his plans for rationalising apartheid that won him the support of big business. These plans were unveiled when the reports of two government commissions, chaired by two of the Afrikaner intellectuals whose influence increased under Botha, were published in May 1979. The more fundamental of the two documents was the Riekert report, concerned with the machinery of influx control. The thinking behind it was spelled out by Jan Lombard in a paper already quoted:

> South Africa must 'normalise' the character of its socio-economic regime in terms of the concepts used in the debate between the forces of individual liberty, on the one hand, and communism, on the other hand... If, in other words, the maintenance of order requires discriminatory provisions in our legal system, these provisions must be defined in terms of the maintenance of order. To declare or imply that racial differences as such are, in themselves, a threat to political order and socio-economic stability is simply no longer accepted.[27]

Apartheid, then, could no longer be justified, either to foreign opinion or indeed to the black middle class on which the regime increasingly rested its hopes, in racial terms. Indeed, P J Riekert, the chairman and sole commissioner (again, no liberal— he had served a spell in internment camps during the second world war along with Vorster and Van Den Bergh for supporting the pro-Nazi Ossewa Brandwag) was highly critical of aspects of the migrant labour system: the massive BAD bureaucracy and the arrest of vast numbers of Africans for minor breaches of the pass-laws (278,887 in 1978 alone) had become counter-productive, helping to provoke the Soweto uprising and severely limiting the mobility of labour power. However, Riekert did not advocate the abolition of influx control:

> Owing to the potential extent and the nature of the migration of blacks from rural areas to urban areas, serious social and sociological welfare problems would arise in urban areas in South Africa... Control over the rate of urbanisation is, in the light of circumstances in South Africa, an absolutely essential social security measure.[28]

In other words, the Bantusans should continue to perform their function of a dumping ground for 'non-productive' blacks. Riekert actually advocated tightening up influx control by making employers, rather than the Africans themselves, liable for breaches of the pass laws. This measure along with the abolition of the old rule that blacks should have to prove their right to be in a prescribed (urban) area for more than 72 hours would end the mass arrests of pass law offenders and mean that the demand for passes, Riekert told an academic audience, 'which causes so much bitterness to blacks, will not take place in public, as at present, but in the secluded office of the employer's personnel office. We must get the thing off the streets.'[29]

At the same time, Riekert abandoned his earlier opposition to the right of a minority of Africans to reside in urban areas under section 10 (1) of the Blacks (Urban Areas) Consolidation Act as 'in conflict with the accepted policy that every Bantu in South Africa belongs to a people with a political home of its own'.[30] These rights should be retained, not abolished, and 'influx control should be linked only with the availability of work and of approved housing'.[31] 'Section tenners' should be guaranteed the right to have their families with them—hitherto, not always the case—and the right to move from one urban area to another provided that jobs and approved housing were available, increasing labour mobility. These proposals were based on the premise, stated explicitly by the commission on labour law chaired by Professor Nic Wiehahn, that 'black workers are a permanent part of the South African economy' and 'are no longer..."mainly unskilled" ' but 'have achieved a far greater degree of employment stability and industrialisation'.[32]

In line with this thinking, Wiehahn recommended that Africans should be permitted to form trade unions registered under the Industrial Conciliation Act, which, *inter alia*, makes strikes effectively illegal, bans shop stewards and the involvement of unions in political activity and has encouraged the development within the white labour movement of a trade-union bureaucracy incorporated in the state machine.[33] The commission complained that the existing unregistered black unions 'in fact enjoy much greater freedom than registered [white] unions, to the extent that they are free if they so wished to participate in politics'. The report warned that 'the influence of this extra-statutory segment could well undermine the statutory systems' and argued that permitting the registration of black trade unions:

> would have the beneficial effect of countering polarisation and ensuring a more orderly process of collective bargaining, in addition to exposing black trade unions in South Africa's trade-union tradition and the existing institutions, thus inculcating a sense of responsibility and loyalty towards the free market system.[34]

The **Financial Mail** commented:

> It would be wrong to dismiss either the Riekert or the Wiehahn report as merely advocating cosmetic change. The change is real—but central to both documents is the replacement of crude racial discrimination by more sophisticated techniques of control. Also central to both reports is the idea of building up a privileged labour aristocracy among blacks in the urban area.

Sheena Duncan of the Black Sash, which seeks to help the victims of the pass laws, was quoted as saying:

> Isolating a privileged group of blacks in the urban areas is going to take place at the expense of a vast number of people in the homelands, whose only safety net up to now has been the inefficiency of the influx control system, which has enabled them to survive by getting jobs, albeit illegally, in the informal sector of the urban areas. Now this avenue will be closed to them and starvation appears to be the inevitable result.[35]

The government's initial response to the two reports narrowed the margin of change proposed. The Industrial Conciliation Amendment Act implementing Wiehahn excluded migrant and foreign workers from trade union rights, gave the government registrar wide powers to grant and withdraw registration and forbade mon-racial unions.[36] As the **Financial Mail** pointed out, 'the new system is there to control, not to strengthen the unions'.[37]

The government white paper following Riekert's report rejected his proposals to scrap the 72-hour rule and end the prosecution of blacks breaking the pass laws. However, a law was speedily passed raising the maximum fine per worker from R100 to R500 for the illegal employment of Africans. Sheena Duncan commented that these stiffer penalties for employers 'are so severe that there will be no more illegal employment'.[38] The Black Sash advice centres in Johannesburg and Cape Town were soon flooded with Africans sacked by employers fearful of the new fines and Piet Koornhof, minister of co-operation and development (as BAD was renamed), was forced to announce a moratorium until 31 October 1979 on the R500 penalty. But by the following January Sheena Duncan reported that prosecution and sackings of 'illegal' Africans were 'worse than ever before. Cases which we would expect to win five years ago are now just not succeeding'.[39]

This did not prevent the employers giving Botha their support. The president of the Transvaal Chamber of Industries, Jack Holloway, responded to the new fines by saying: 'we are in favour of influx control because it protects the entire society'.[40] And Harry Oppenheimer, patron of the liberal white opposition, had said even before Botha took office:

> I would handle influx control quite separately. I think we certainly need it in the sense of providing a service to black people, because it is certainly true that if you had no machinery for directing people to where jobs are, you would get too many swamping the urban areas, where there are neither jobs nor housing to cope with them.[41]

At the same time, the employers were given what they wanted in other respects. By the late 1970s the acute shortage of white labour and the militancy of the black working class had made imperative both the intensified rationalisation of production, which would, by deskilling labour, reduce white workers' bargaining power, and an assault on job reservation.[42] A major victory was won by the employers when an industrial council agreement involving the white unions in July 1978 opened all job categories to Africans in the crucial iron, steel, engineering and metallurgical industries.

The offensive against white labour was not so peaceful in the mines, where since the 1920s white workers had been able to retain significant control over the labour-process by insisting that blacks not be issued with blasting certificates, which entitled the bearer to head an underground gang (although in the rapidly expanding open-cast coal mines, where blasting was replaced by the use of walking dragline scrapers driven by Africans, the basis of white bargaining power had been undermined). Resistance to change was spearheaded by the Mine Workers Union (MWU), led by Arrie Paulus, who came to power as part of an Action Committee which had successfully blocked an 'experiment' in the 1960s by the Chamber of Mines designed to reduce the role of the white gangers.[43]

On 5 March 1979 MWU members went on strike at the American-owned O'Kiep mine at Nabapeep in protest against the transfer there of three Coloured artisans. By 7 March 7,500 white miners were on strike nationally. The MWU leadership seem to have seen this as a one-day protest action, but the Chamber of Mines decided to provoke a confrontation, scrapped the closed-shop agreement with the union and sacked the strikers. The Minister of Mines, Fanie Botha, refused to intervene and even threatened to introduce legislation banning protest strikes. The Chamber's threat to make the strikers pay an 'economic rental' of R6 a day for their company houses forced the MWU executive to call the strike off.

Paulus described the government's support for the mine owners as 'the biggest treason toward the white workers in white South Africa since the days in 1922 when white mine-workers were shot down in the Rand by General Smuts'.[44] Fear of a white backlash did not prevent Botha accepting Wiehahn's proposals that the statutory colour bar be scrapped (although job reservation imposed by collective agreement with registered unions or by the employer's choice was still permitted) and that the training of black apprentices in white areas be allowed.

One final ingredient of Botha's strategy also had the support of big business, and indeed had been advocated by its representatives for some time—namely, the encouragement of an urban black middle class. Separate development had blocked the achievement of an African bourgeoisie outside the Bantusans. The frustrations of the business and professional classes that did develop in the townships was well expressed by Dr Ntatho Motlana, chairman of the Soweto Committee of Ten:

> *I* get frequently stopped in the middle of the day, in the middle of Johannesburg, in my professional safari suit—and I buy them expensive—with the words, '*Jou pas, jong*' [Your pass, man].[45]

After the Soweto uprising, both Afrikaner and English-speaking capital swung behind the notion of a black middle class that would act as a buffer between the white minority and the African masses. The Urban Foundation was launched to tackle the problem of urban blacks. At its founding conference in November 1976, Anton Rupert, head of the Afrikaner multinational Rembrandt's, said: 'a prerequisite for achieving our overall objectives should be the adoption of free enterprise values by the urban blacks'.[46]

Gradually, and in the face of opposition from within the National Party and BAD, reforms were introduced to make life easier for the urban blacks, notably when in December 1978 blacks were permitted to buy 99-year leaseholds in urban areas, an admission that they were more than 'temporary sojourners' in the 'white' areas. However, by June 1979 only one such leasehold had been granted—to the Soweto millionaire Richard Maponya; financial institutions were reluctant to lend to potential African home-owners unless the latter had full ownership rights.[47] At the same time, moves began to be taken in the direction of permitting black firms to operate outside the townships and Homelands. Piet Koornhof told the National African Federated Chambers of Commerce in July 1979 that 'by 1982 the black businessman would have arrived in South Africa and taken his rightful place in the economy'.[48]

However, there were real differences of interest between white and black business. Many South African industries—notably food, clothing and footwear—were basing their hopes of expansion on the growth of the African market. Already the rise in blacks' share of personal income (22.5 per cent in 1970, 25.4 per cent in 1975, 28.9 per cent in 1980) and the flight of whites to the suburbs meant that the central business districts were becoming more and more dependent on African consumers;[49] 44 per cent of Johannesburg central business district income (excluding the motor trade) came from blacks.[52] The director of Ford South Africa's parts and services division predicted that black car ownership would rise from

8.2 per cent in 1977 to 25 per cent nine years later.[51] He explained that:

> the white market is close to saturation point and we must look to the rest of the population for an increase in volume to the 500,000 units a year the industry requires to utilise production to its maximum and to reduce production costs.[52]

Other industries also had their eyes fixed on the African market, which some economists expected to account for half the total spending by the end of the 1980s. Thus the electrification of Soweto, financed by government and private loans, would lead, according to the **Financial Mail**, to 'a mini-boom in black spending in consumer durables'.[53] The 6,000 black retailers in the townships were, not unreasonalby, afraid that this market would be snapped up by the white-owned chain stores. The National African Federated Chambers of Commerce demanded protection against 'unfair competition' and a monopoly of trading in the townships. This did not prevent plans being made to establish a central business district at Jabulani in Soweto, in which a number of big retailers—Checkers/Greatermans, Southern Sun, Ster Kniekor—showed an interest, despite the protest of African businessmen.

At no point did either the government or big business consider extending the economic concessions they had offered to significant political reforms. Jan Lombard, one of the theorists of the new strategy, wrote:

> The replacement of colour discrimination by classical norms of competition and democracy in the production and distribution of goods and services, both in the private and the public sector, does not automatically imply the subjugation of the sovereignty of the state to the whims of simple majorities in the total population... Under present circumstances, that would be tantamount to the destruction of all freedom in southern Africa.[54]

Proposals were published in May 1980 for the establishment of separate parliaments for whites, Coloureds and Indians, each of which would be represented on a President's Council with a white chairman (Alwyn Schlebusch, author of these proposals, was nominated for the post). Africans, however, would be excluded from this 'dispensation'. The homeland leaders would form a separate council, while the townships would be conceded greater powers of self-government within the framework of the Community

Councils Act 1977. In the meantime, neither Afrikanerdom nor English-speaking capital would even consider black people's basic demand—universal suffrage. Here again, the difference between the 'liberal' capitalist Harry Oppenheimer, and Broederbond chairman Gerrit Viljoen was very slight. Oppenheimer said:

> It may well be that we should have Soweto organised on a canton or several cantons and that they should govern themselves in the local sense and then should be represented in some central parliament.[53]

This did not seem so far from Viljoen's concession that:

> in the long run certain black areas, such as the large complexes of the Witwatersrand, will in the long run have to attain some sort of city state independence... Through separation one could develop a confederal system, which in time to come could develop into a federal one and maybe in the next century into a union.[56]

The Limits of Change

In the course of 1979 euphoria steadily built up in white business circles about Botha's new course. In contrast to the inertia of Vorster's later years here seemed a leader who was ready to push through the reforms necessary to stabilise South African capitalism. Botha unveiled a 12-point programme for change at the Natal congress of the National Party, defended his policies before a hostile audience at the Transvaal congress and told Afrikaners to 'adapt or die'. His minister of co-operation and development, Piet Koornhof, a former chief secretary of the Broederbond, even claimed, in Miami of all places, that 'apartheid as the world knew it was dead'.

The high point came when Botha and his cabinet met 250 businessmen at the five-star Carlton Hotel in Johannesburg on 22 November 1979. This meeting—Botha's 'most spectacular coup since reaching the premiership', the **Financial Mail** called it—saw Harry Oppenheimer give the government his critical support.[57] Botha's aim seemed to be to isolate, and if necessary force out, the Nationalist far right, at the same time drawing English-speaking capital behind him.

There followed a series of major setbacks for Botha. In February 1980 he seemed all set to sack Andries Treurnicht, the chief hardliner in the cabinet, who had succeeded Connie Mulder as leader of the Transvaal Nationalists, but occupied the minor government post of Minister of Public Works, Statistics and

Tourism. At the last moment, Botha backed off in the face of opposition within the cabinet and caucus. Vorster emerged from retirement to denouce him, and the victory of ZANU-PF in Zimbabwe delivered an apparently fatal blow to his plan to create a 'constellation of states' dominated by Pretoria in southern Africa.

The basis for resistance to reforms could be counted under three heads. First, there was the opposition within the National Party itself. Although the initiative lay firmly in the hands of the cabinet, whose proposals the parliamentary caucus normally accepted,

> power has come increasingly to rest on a provincial rather than an ideological base. The provincial parties have become personal fiefdoms of their respective leaders, with enormous patronage, including cabinet posts, at their disposal as well as the power to protect followers.[58]

The Transvaal party, whose MPs were in any case more *verkrampte* than the rest of the caucus,[59] were infuriated by their loss of the premiership in September 1978. Treurnicht had their support less as the upholder of unmitigated apartheid than as the standard-bearer of Transvaal interests within the Nationalist establishment. The **Financial Mail** reported after Vorster's fall that 'party divisions are now grouped along provincial lines—Transvaal versus the rest'.[60] The Transvaal congress in September 1980 cheered Treurnicht when he declared that 'any political planning aimed at getting white and black nations to grow together politically or socially is unacceptable to whites' and gave Botha a rough ride when he spoke. As **The Times** put it, the congress 'regards him as the Cape Nationalist leader who is a temporary tenant of the premier political position'.[61]

The second focus of opposition lay in the bureaucracy centred around BAD (now the Department of Co-operation and Development):

> Verwoerd [as minister of native affairs in the 1950s] embarked on the elaboration of the apartheid policy and the creation of a vast bureaucratic structure. Just before he became prime minister in 1958 he was under fire within the party for creating 'an empire of unprecedented scale out of his own department—a state within a state.' Verwoerd more than any other prime minister before or after him imbued the bureaucracy with his particular political vision. 'He attracted not pliable servants but like-minded ideologues', a top

bureaucrat who worked in close association with him would later recount... Today the apartheid bureaucracy is staffed mainly by men dedicated to the ideology of separate development. They form the resident opposition in the National Party to any attempts at reforms of the Verwoerdian blueprint.[62]

The white civil service, with a vested interest in the maintenance of apartheid, and enjoying the advantage of knowing their way around the vast network of statutes and regulations created by the Nationalist regime, were a formidable obstacle to change, resisting every reform, and taking full advantage of the cabinet's method of modifying apartheid through administrative actions rather than amendments of the law.

Finally, there was the white working class. Afrikaners in particular are entrenched within the public sector. In 1977 30 per cent of economically active whites were employed in this sector—35 per cent of Afrikaners as opposed to 25 per cent of English speakers, who occupy only 10 per cent of the top positions.[63] White public sector employees, guaranteed well-paid jobs by successive Nationalist governments, would obviously resist any attempt to introduce large numbers of Africans. In general, white workers were being squeezed. Their wages were rising more slowly than those of blacks while they were vulnerable to the employers' offensive. Women—their proportion of the white workforce was expected to rise from 29 per cent in 1969 to 37 per cent in 1981, no less than 83 per cent of them working in nursing, teaching and clerical and sales jobs—would be especially likely to suffer with the rationalisation of office work (the value of computer equipment installed rose by 55 per cent in the eighteen months to mid-1979).[64]

White workers were in no sense the autonomous initiators of racial oppression South Africa, as some bourgeois commentators have claimed.[65] In general, they accepted political subordination to the Afrikaner bourgeoisie and petty bourgeoisie in exchange for economic privileges within the framework of South Africa's 'racially exclusive bourgeois democracy'. Arthur Grobelaar, leader of the main white trade union federation, TUCSA, expressed the class-collaborationist politics of the white labour movement when he said: 'Co-operation with management is the crux of industrial relations. I hope TUCSA unions are collaborating with management. This falls within the ambit of partnership in industry'.[66] Even the far-right

Confederation of Labour rather grudgingly accepted the Wiehahn report, despite the opposition of the MWU.

Nevertheless, as the government aligned itself more closely to a capitalist class engaged in the erosion of white economic privileges, a white backlash could not be ruled out. Disgruntled white miners voted for the ultra-*verkramp* HNP in a series of by-elections in 1979, and the Transvaalse Onderwysersvereniging, 'the most powerful body of teachers in South Africa', threatened to go on strike if Treurnicht was sacked.

For support Botha could rely on the military and big business, both English-speaking and Afrikaans. His problem lay in the narrowness of his popular base among Afrikaners. In response to opposition within the National Party, he sought to detach the executive from parliamentary control, moving towards what a senior government MP called 'a civilian-military junta'.[67] This involved in part the 'coalition government with private enterprise' advocated by Wassenaar.[68] In June 1979 Botha appointed some business leaders, notably Dick Goss of South African Breweries and Wim de Villiers of General Mining, to the Public Service Commission in an effort to streamline the administration and break down bureaucratic obstruction. The constitution was changed to permit the appointment of ministers from outside parliament.

This move was followed by a cabinet reshuffle in August 1980, which brought General Magnus Malan and Gerrit Viljoen into the government as ministers of defence and of national education respectively. It was only then that Botha felt confident enough to press ahead with implementing the Riekert report. Proposals linking influx control to the availability of jobs and housing and scrapping the 72-hour rule were published in October 1980.

One of Malan's generals had written in 1978:

> Two requirements for the application of total strategy would appear to favour a system of unified command, joint central planning, decentralised execution and sustained vertical and horizontal organisation... Conventional organisations in democratic systems do not as a rule lend themselves to these procedures. Therefore organisational changes or adaptations would appear to be imperative.[69]

Was Botha moving towards an 'exceptional state' which would dispense with the need for securing the consent of even the white population? The conditions for such a '*veligte* dictatorship' certainly existed—a crisis of ruling-class hegemony, serious divisions within the power bloc, a serious challenge from the popular masses.[70]

Yet there were perhaps insuperable obstacles on the road to such an 'exceptional state'. Short of a military coup, impossible because it might involve armed conflict between whites which could provoke a successful black uprising, there seemed no easy way to remove the Nationalist opponents of change in parliament and the bureaucracy. They remained well entrenched: Gerrit Viljoen was replaced as chairman of the Broederbond by Carel Boshoff, author of a preposterous plan to preserve the purity of apartheid by setting up a white 'homeland' in the eastern Cape. Attempts to fuse Afrikaner and English-speaking interests had led to the political destruction of earlier Afrikaner leaders—Jan Smuts and J B M Hertzog. Such might be Botha's fate.

In any case, Botha's aim was to rationalise apartheid, not abolish it. The proposals of the Wiehahn and Riekert commissions were designed to adjust the system of influx control to the needs of South African capitalism in the 1980s. These needs involved demand for more differentiated forms of black labour—to the old roles of unskilled contract labourer (still crucial in industries such as mining and textiles) and semi-skilled operative were added those of skilled worker, technician and even foreman. The division at the heart of Riekert between section-tenners and migrants was designed to provide a more flexible system of labour control and supply that would be capable of responding to these needs. Influx control would remain at its basis, both as a 'social security measure' to shunt the unemployed off to the Bantustans and as a means of moulding the black workforce to capital's needs. Neither it nor the white monopoly of political power were regarded by Botha as negotiable.

Pace Piet 'Promises' Koornhof, apartheid was far from dead.

Chapter 3:
Between reform and revolution?
(September 1985)*

IS SOUTH AFRICA entering a revolutionary situation? Lenin said that a revolution happens when the ruling class can't go on in the old way, and the masses won't. By this criterion the question of revolution is at least posed in South Africa today.

The last time the regime was forced to impose a state of emergency was after the Sharpeville massacre in March 1960. But it faces a far more dangerous challenge now than it did a quarter of a century ago.

The township revolt which began, again in Sharpeville, twelve months ago, has now spread throughout the country. Two developments in August confirmed this. Riots erupted in Durban. The area has been quiet over the past decade largely thanks to the political machine of Chief Gatsha Buthelezi, ruler of the KwaZulu Homeland, which incorporates most of the city's black townships. A curfew was imposed in Soweto, hitherto quiescent since the great 1976-77 uprising.

However, what qualitatively distinguishes the present situation from 1960 is the strength and militancy of the black working class, increasingly organised in the independent unions. The two main union federations, FOSATU and CUSA, participated in a two-day stay-away by 800,000 black workers in the Transvaal last November.

So the mass movement in South Africa has reached

*First published in Socialist Worker Review, September 1985.

unprecedented proportions. What about the other side of the equation, the state of the ruling class? President P W Botha's speech to the Natal Congress of the ruling National Party on 15 August was highly revealing. The speech received huge advance publicity, largely thanks to the promises by Foreign Minister Pik Botha to Western governments and journalists that it would announce major reforms.

From this point of view it was a damp squib. Botha stuck to generalities, but firmly ruled out majority rule, continued to endorse the policy of conceding 'independence' to the tribal Bantusan regimes, and refused to release Nelson Mandela. What was striking about Botha's speech was its defensiveness. There was no ringing defence of apartheid, no pretence that it is a viable way of running South Africa. Botha conceded that the swelling numbers of urban blacks have no representation in the present political system, and that 'a solution will have to be found for their legitimate rights'.

The regime no longer believes in the ideology of 'separate development' which has guided its policies for the past 37 years. It is forced therefore to offer reforms, however inadequate, if only to stave off the threat of revolution.

The situation—mass revolts, ruling class disarray—reflects the deep-seated structural crisis of South African capitalism. South Africa has failed to become a significant exporter of manufactured goods. Its relation to the world economy remains that of a producer of primary commodities (above all, gold) while it depends on the Western bloc for the capital and technology without which its industries could not survive. At a time of acute trade rivalries, South African firms are under increasing pressure from foreign competitors. This explains the flow of capital, both local and Western, out of the country.

At the same time, capitalism in South Africa is increasingly reliant on a black working class which can no longer be confined to the lowest paid, least skilled jobs best performed by migrant labourers. Even in the mining industry, heart of the migrant labour system, blacks are moving into jobs hitherto monopolised by whites. The legal colour bar banning them from skilled work in the mines is being abolished, while some owners have moved towards employing a settled workforce housed with their families rather than in all-male compounds.

The greatly strengthened *objective* position of the black working class is the fundamental cause of the upsurge which began with the Durban mass strikes of 1973 and has now attained such a colossal scale. The crucial question is how much room for manoeuvre the regime has in dealing with this very acute crisis.

The ruling class in South Africa retain one decisive advantage, succinctly stated recently by the **Economist**: 'The whites have the guns, the blacks do not: and Mr Botha's army and police force, though they have a growing black component, will not turn their guns on the big white chief.' Although some townships, especially in the ultra-militant Eastern Cape, may have become effectively no-go areas for the security forces, the white monopoly of armed force has not been seriously dented.

A sobering fact which every opponent of apartheid should remember is that South African capital has proportionately a much larger popular base than virtually any other ruling class in the world. The five million middle and working-class whites' huge material privileges are inseparable from white supremacy. Apart from the massive private ownership of arms by whites, all adult male whites are closely intregrated into the South African Defence Force. The state therefore has considerable repressive resources which it has scarcely mobilised.

The regime's military strength means that in all likelihood it will ride out the present crisis. But even much greater doses of repression will only buy Botha a limited amount of time. The Soweto uprising was finally broken by mass arrests and bannings which smashed the black consciousness movement in October 1977. Within less than three years a new wave of strikes and school boycotts erupted, to be followed after an interlude by the struggles of the past year. Repression alone cannot save the regime.

This explains all the talk of reforms. While the tempo of change has become much faster as a result of the township risings, P W Botha has made the 'modernisation' of the regime his main policy plank ever since he became leader of the National Party in September 1978. What is at stake in the various concessions touted around in ruling South African circles?

The migrant labour system at the core of apartheid evolved at the end of the last century to provide the gold mines with the ultra-cheap workforce their profitability required. Apartheid proper, introduced by the Nationalists after 1948, was a response to the emergence of a militant urban African working class during the Second World War. The entire black proletariat was to be reduced to the status of migrant labourers with no citizenship rights in the 'white' areas which make up nearly 87 per cent of South Africa. The creation of black 'states' in the remaining 13 per cent—the Homelands or Bantustans—provided a spurious rationale for this set-up. Urban Africans would be citizens of their respective Homelands, even if they had never set eyes on them.

The struggles of the mid-1970s blew this system to bits. The Durban strikes and the Soweto uprising showed that the urban black working class could not be treated as 'temporary sojourners' in white South Africa. As one government commission acknowledged: 'Black workers are a permanent part of the South African economy.'

Botha sought to evolve a strategy based on recognition of this fact. A variety of concessions were made to urban blacks, notably the legalisation of African trade unions. The aim was to divide the urban proletariat between the 'section tenners'—the usually better paid and more skilled workers with the right to live in 'white' cities—and the mass of unskilled migrant workers. Influx control—the system buttressed by the pass laws which controls Africans' movements—was tightened up. At the same time a number of political concessions were made to the black middle class. The minority Coloured and Indian communities were each given their own chamber of parliament and ministerial posts. Africans (73 per cent of the population) were not offered any share in central government. However, new town councils with increased powers to run the black townships were set up. The general thrust of Botha's reforms was to preserve white supremacy while incorporating privileged layers of middle-class blacks and labour aristocrats.

This strategy is now largely in ruins. It is now acknowledged, even by Botha, that urban blacks have somehow to be incorporated within the political system. The question is how to do this without threatening the survival of capitalism in South Africa. More specifically, the institutions of white rule have served to create a low wage economy. The economic crisis places enormous pressure to reduce labour costs even further. To what extent can capital secure the cheap labour it needs without the apartheid institutions?

One major issue is influx control. The basis of current policy is the 1979 Riekert report, which argued that 'control over the state of urbanisation is, in the light of circumstances in South Africa, an absolutely essential social security measure'. The pass laws have been used to keep unemployed and underemployed in the Bantustans, which have functioned in practice as dumping grounds for 'superflous' Africans. One wing of the ruling class now wants to scrap influx control. It is identified with the Urban Foundation, headed by two key capitalists, Harry Oppenheimer and Anton Rupert. The Foundation's researchers estimate the pass laws would only reduce the urban black population projected for the year 2000 by two million, a relatively marginal amount. Why antagonise both the black masses and foreign opinion by holding onto a set-up which no longer makes that much economic difference?

The bulk of South African capital still takes a much more cautious line. But big business is united in demanding reforms from the goverment. The two main employers' organisations issued a joint statement after Botha's speech, expressing regret that 'at this time of crisis, the state president…was not more specific in pointing the nation more positively in the direction of reform and national reconstruction'. Adverse reaction to the speech by both local and Western capital pushed the rand down at one point to the all time low of 38.5 US cents.

The sticking point for all wings of the ruling class remains African majority rule. They fear that black rule will mean the dismantlement of capitalism. Professor Jan Lombard, a leading Afrikaner intellectual and key government adviser recently appointed deputy governor of the Reserve Bank, spelled it out:

> If an unqualified one-man one-vote election was held today in the Republic, a non-white leader with a communistic programme would probably attain an overall majority on a pledge to confiscate and redistribute the property of the privileged classes.

What alternative is there to such an unpleasant outcome? Here the ruling class seem generally agreed in advocating a federal system which would respect what Botha calls 'the multi-cultural and polyethnic nature of South Africa's population'. A recent article in the excellent **South African Labour Bulletin** argues that 'regionalisation-federalism…could provide the basis for a long-term strategic offensive aimed at reconstituting the relations of exploitation and domination in South Africa.'

Already government planners have redrawn the country into

eight 'development regions' which are soon due to replace the four provinces into which the country has been divided since Union in 1910. These regions reflect the socio-economic patterns which have developed since the late 1960s. 'White' metropolitan areas have tended to draw specific Bantustans into their labour markets, with a rapid growth in the number of 'commuters', blacks living in Homelands who go to work daily in a 'white' area. The result is, the **South African Labour Bulletin** article argues, 'the formation of regional proletariats'. These developments provide the basis for multiracial regional governments incorporating, alongside white politicians and administrators, black Homeland bosses and urban petty bourgeois politicians. Jan Lombard advocated such a solution for Natal back in 1980, winning the support of both Buthelezi and the local sugar planters. What seems now to be envisaged is a generalisation of this 'KwaNatal' set-up, but with control over the state apparatus nationally still in white hands.

This sort of federal solution could only work with the cooperation of far more significant black leaders than have yet been prepared to collaborate with Botha. At the very minimum it would require the involvement of Butelezi, very much a national figure thanks to his Zulu political movement Inkatha yeSizwe. He endorsed a 'KwaNatal' solution in 1982, but the political situation has changed dramatically since then. Buthelezi has no desire to share the fate of the black mayors and town councillors burned to death as quislings. His price will be a high one, in all likelihood a share in the central government. Even then Buthelezi is too shrewd a politician to accept a settlement which would allow him, like Bishop Muzorewa in Zimbabwe, to be outflanked from the left, pilloried as a black stooge.

This raises the question of the African National Congress. There is considerable support in the ruling class for including the ANC in negotiations—an issue posed by the demands for Mandela's release. Leading industrialist Tony Bloom of Premier Milling put it succinctly when he wrote in the **Financial Mail**: 'There is an historical inevitability about talking to the ANC—it is not a question of if, but rather when.'

The likelihood that the regime will eventually be forced to negotiate with the ANC poses the question of whether or not South African capital might not be able to co-exist with majority rule. The ANC is no more radical an organisation than ZANU-PF in

Zimbabwe. Could there not be a South African version of the 1979 Lancaster House settlement which ended the Zimbabwean war?

The Marxist Workers' Tendency, a group of supporters of the British Militant group expelled from the ANC, are absolutely emphatic that this is impossible. In a closely argued document, 'South African Perspectives: Workers' Revolution or Racial Civil War', they declared: 'We cannot conceive of conditions which would permit the creation of an ANC government on a bourgeois basis.'

The reasoning behind this analysis centres on two claims. First, that the depth of the economic crisis means that the material basis for a peaceful transition to majority rule does not exist. Secondly, that the interests of capital in South Africa, as elsewhere, depend ultimately on the repressive state apparatus, which is in this case inseparable from white supremacy. Thus, says the MWT document, the ruling class

> are caught on the horns of a contradiction from which there is no escape...Because of the challenge of the black proletariat from below, the ruling class have to try to reform the state system; they have to try to change the state itself. But they cannot afford to weaken the repressive power of the state in the face of this black challenge. To the limited extent that they can 'blacken' the state forces, they render the state potentially unreliable to them; and at the same time this drives to disaffection the reliable white forces they have. With everything in turmoil around them, they have no choice but to keep the snarling wolf-hounds of the white state apparatus in readiness for action, and again and again unleash their ferocity against the people.

This analysis is undoubtedly a cogent one. It captures quite well the zig-zags described, not just by Botha, but by Anglo-American, whose bosses one minute are calling for reforms, the next minute calling in the police to break strikes.

Nevertheless, the MWT's assertion that majority rule is impossible on a bourgeois basis is far too unconditional. It is worth remembering that ten years ago the entire European revolutionary left argued that there could be no peaceful and capitalist 'rupture' with the Francoist dictatorship in Spain. We argued for precisely the same reasons that are now given out in South Africa's case, namely the economic crisis and the dependence of the bourgeoisie on the reactionary 'bunker' controlling the army and police. We were wrong.

The past few years have also seen the establishment of bourgeois parliamentary regimes across large portions of Latin America (Peru, Argentina, Brazil, Uruguay), at precisely the time when the debt crisis and IMF-imposed austerity programmes were immiserising hundreds of millions of people. These examples underline the importance of not trying to read off political developments directly from the economic situation. Politics played the decisive role in all these successful transitions to something at least approximating bourgeois democracy. The success of, for example, the Spanish bourgeoisie's liquidation of Francoism depended on two factors: a governmental team with the necessary skill and room for manoeuvre; and an opposition dominated by reformist parties who were able to short-circuit working class militancy.

Are there counterparts present in contemporary South Africa? The ANC is considered in the next chapter: suffice it to say that nothing in its politics or leading personnel rules out it participating in a settlement which would save South Africa for capitalism. To suggest, as the MWT do, that the logic of the situation will somehow drive the ANC to make a socialist revolution is to capitulate to the sort of vulgar Marxism for which the overthrow of capitalism is predetermined.

It doesn't follow that a Zimbabwean-style solution is likely. The fact that the repressive power of the state depends on the white population does impose distinct limits to the ruling class's room for manoeuvre. In the short term it has imposed on the regime the policy of piecemeal reform combined with large scale repression that has become Botha's hallmark.

The National Party depends for its parliamentary majority on the votes of the white working class and petty bourgeoisie. Botha, a veteran of 50 years of Afrikaner politics, must well remember the fate of the party's founder, General J B M Hertzog, who was outflanked on the right when he threw in with Jan Smuts' South Africa Party, the representatives of English-speaking capital. Ex-cabinet minister Andries Treurnicht and his breakaway Conservative Party are waiting in the wings for swelling white popular reaction to allow them to do to Botha what the Nationalists did to Hertzog. The belligerence of Botha's Durban speech, its reassertion of Afrikanerdom's contempt for world opinion and opposition to black rule, were undoubtedly very much for domestic white consumption. It is difficult for the regime to offer more than limited changes at any one time, even if it alienates even the most reactionary black leaders.

The pressure of the white electorate on the regime has contributed to a longer-term tendency to detach the state apparatus from any sort of parliamentary control. The new constitution, with its enormous concentration of power in the hands of an executive state president, has encouraged speculation that Botha is driving towards a Bonapartist regime in which he can balance between black and white masses, enforcing a programme of reforms from above.

But there are limits to this process. One of Botha's main bases of support is the military. Between 1966 and 1978 he was Minister of Defence. Since 1978 the State Security Council has largely replaced the cabinet as the key decision-making body. Nevertheless, Botha and his generals could not impose black rule on South Africa through military dictatorship even supposing they wanted to, for the simple reason that their repressive forces are and will remain predominantly white. Any white political split which disorganised the armed forces would be catastrophic for capital, since it would give the black masses the opportunity to unleash a genuinely revolutionary situation.

The roads before both the ruling class and the black proletariat are, therefore, neither of them straight ones. The white state's monopoly of force will buy the regime time to pursue reforms. But at the same time, concessions which do not involve seeking a political accommodation with the main forces of black resistance, above all the ANC, with all the difficulties which this involves, will not stabilise the situation. It follows that, even though the regime will in all probability survive the present crisis, the respite will only be temporary. The immense problems involved in detaching capitalism in South Africa from apartheid put socialist revolution on the agenda in an exceptionally direct way. The need for a revolutionary party which could provide the political leadership in the struggle for state power is very urgent.

Chapter 4:
Working-class politics in South Africa
(April 1986)*

SINCE SEPTEMBER 1984 the eyes of the world have been fixed on South Africa. For the third time in a decade a wave of uprisings in the black townships has shaken the apartheid regime. The present revolts have achieved a scale and intensity and persisted for a length of time even surpassing the great Soweto uprising of June 1976. Moreover, the present unrest has a number of features which make it especially threatening for white power in South Africa.

First, the revolts have been at least in part precipitated by an acute economic recession. They have helped to exacerbate South African capitalism's difficulties by encouraging a flight of capital from the country. The government of President P W Botha has faced unprecedented pressures from local and foreign capital to accelerate his programme of reforms.

Secondly, the African National Congress has, despite losing its bases in Swaziland and Mozambique, succeeded in escalating its military campaign within the country. The number of armed actions, usually involving the ANC's military wing, Umkhonto we Sizwe (MK), rose by 309 per cent in 1985.[1]

Thirdly, the black working-class movement, organised increasingly through the independent unions, has emerged as a formidable power in its own right. The unions have been drawn into the township revolts, participating in a number of stay-aways

---

*First published as 'Marxism and Revolution in South Africa', in **International Socialism** 31, Spring 1986.

(political general strikes), notably in the Transvaal in November 1984. The threat they pose to the regime was underlined in December 1985, when the bulk of the unions merged into a new 'super-federation', the Congress of South African Trade Unions (COSATU), organising half a million workers.

These developments should not be allowed to obscure the obstacles which lie in the path of a successful revolution in South Africa. The regime has at its disposal enormous repressive forces, being able to mobilise the entire adult white male population in its defence. Neither the risings nor MK have inflicted a serious dent in the ruling class's monopoly of armed force. The workers' movement, as we shall see, has developed primarily within the limits of trade unionism. It is likely to take years of future struggle, with both advances and retreats, to overthrow the apartheid state.[2]

The scale of the present struggles and the distance the movement has yet to travel pose very sharply questions of analysis and strategy. For a number of years we have argued that the struggle in South Africa is concerned with more than national liberation and the establishment of political equality. So intertwined are apartheid and capitalism that only a socialist revolution can uproot the system of racial domination in South Africa, and in this revolution the cental role will be played by the black working class.[3]

Very similar arguments have been raised by activists in the unions and township organisations over the past five years. A polarisation has developed between 'workerists' and 'populists'. The former have emphasised the significance of independent working-class organisation, especially in the unions. The latter have instead argued that the unions, like other popular organisations, should see themselves as part of a broad democratic alliance of all the oppressed. Underlying this debate has been the question of whether workers' power is on the agenda today, or whether the South African masses must confine themselves to achieving black majority rule, as the ANC and its supporters, heavily influential in the United Democratic Front (UDF), argue.

These are the questions, of the utmost importance for the South African revolution, which this chapter will try to address, through a survey of the different political currents within the resistance to the apartheid state. My focus will be on the left, by which I mean those activists and organisations who believe that the struggles against apartheid and capitalism are inseparable, but inevitably the programmes and practice of the main populist currents, especially the ANC/UDF, cannot be ignored. It should go without saying that any criticisms I make of South African activists is made on the basis of admiration for their courage and solidarity with their struggle, and only in order to help render that struggle more effective.

The dominant populist tradition:
1: The UDF and the Congress tradition'

The African National Congress was founded in 1912. For its first thirty years of existence it was a timid and reformist organisation, dominated by the respectable African middle class— clergymen, teachers and the like. It underwent a process of radicalisation in the 1940s for a variety of reasons—the development of mass workers' and township struggles culminating in the 1946 miners' strike, the formation in 1943 of the militant nationalist ANC Youth League, and the coming to power in 1948 of the National Party with its apartheid programme designed to intensify the system of racial domination.

The ANC organised a variety of forms of mass resistance to the Nationalist regime, before being banned in the wake of the March 1960 Sharpeville massacre. Its leadership subsequently went underground, formed MK and launched a sabotage campaign. The MK high command were captured at Rivonia in July 1963 and sentenced—along with their chief, Nelson Mandela—to life imprisonment. The ANC then became effectively an exile organisation, with its headquarters at Lusaka in Zambia. MK guerrillas have been steadily infiltrated into South Africa, especially since the mass influx of young recruits into the ANC after the 1976 Soweto rising.

The 1970s were a difficult period for the ANC, during which the Black Consciousness movement appeared to be gaining in influence. ANC supporters did not play the leading role in the Soweto uprising. Subsequently, however, the ANC enjoyed a remarkable revival in support, for a variety of reasons. Among them were the temporary eclipse of the main Black Consciousness organisations after the bannings of October 1977, the incoherence of Black Consciousness ideology, the ANC's international support—it has governmental status in much of Africa, the campaign launched in 1980 for Mandela's release, and last but not least the ANC's possession of an increasingly active military wing.

The ANC's hold on the masses has been greatly strengthened as a result of the emergence of the United Democratic Front. This is not to say, as the regime claims, that the UDF is merely an ANC front. The surges in mass resistance since June 1976, and the regime's strategy of creating 'autonomous' Black Local Authorities to run the African townships as a means of incorporating the black middle class into the state, have encouraged the formation of a dense network of local civic organisations.[5] These 'civics', as they are called, have played an active role in a variety of struggles around rents, rates, transport and education, helping to create a high level of popular mobilisation.

Two initiatives by the regime helped to give these localised resistances a national focus. First there was the appearance in 1982 of three Bills, known as the Koornhof Bills, after the minister then in charge of apartheid, which greatly tightened up the system of influx control over Africans' movement to and from the cities.[6] The second was the new constitution, approved by the white electorate in November 1983, which concentrated executive power in the hands of the state president and conceded to Coloureds and Indians their own parliamentary chambers—though no share in effective power. Africans were offered nothing: their political needs outside the Bantustans would be catered for by the Black Local Authorities.[7]

These state initiatives were widely seen as requiring a coherent national response. The call for a national united front against Botha's 'new deal' was first publicly made by Dr Alan Boesak in Johannesburg at the beginning of 1983. Although the idea had already been suggested by forces which were later to form the National Forum Committee, it was now 'hijacked' by ANC sympathisers.[8]

A number of regional UDFs were then formed, culminating in the launch of the national alliance at Rocklands outside Cape Town on 20 August 1983. The UDF committed itself to 'uniting all our people, wherever they may be in the cities and countryside, the factories and mines, schools, colleges and universities, houses and sports fields, churches, mosques and temples, to fight for our freedom.'[9]

The UDF claims to be a broad front of autonomous

organisations, rather than a political movement in its own right. Nationally some 600 organisations were affiliated in early 1985. Special emphasis, however, is placed on the role of the working class. The inaugural conference proclaimed its faith in 'the leadership of the working class in the democratic struggle for freedom.'[10]

The reality is rather different, as the following assessment of the UDF in Cape Town suggests:

...the organisations which have joined the UDF...can be divided into three groups:

1. 'Non-mainline' organisations (eg church groups, trade organisations, etc). These clearly are petty bourgeois in membership and programme.

2. Student/youth organisations. These are mixed in membership and programme, with the radical petty bourgeoisie probably dominating working-class elements.

3. Community organisations . . . :

a. The organisations are locally very weak with a small membership mostly confined to people with experience of other opposition organisation.

b. Their programmes are generally limited, eg agitation around the issue of rents without drawing out clearly the link to wages and hence economic exploitation at the site of production.

c. Within the organisations attempts are made to blur class distinctions and consequent differences in approach—'We are all oppressed women' or 'We are all oppressed residents' approach . . .

d ...the leadership is on the whole dominated by intellectuals with a reformist ideology.

We cannot leave the question of the UDF without looking briefly at the pervasive attempts to smother progressive opposition to its central propositions. The line of the UDF, emanating from somewhere, is not to be opposed, we are told. To criticise the UDF is tantamount to being an *impimpi* [informer], to running with the Nationalist government. Former friends cross the road when they see a 'workerist' approaching; a series of pitched battles is being fought in academic circles and even on committees only marginally political in operation.[11]

The depth of popular organisation beneath the UDF varies considerably in different parts of the country. In the Eastern Cape, a traditional ANC stronghold, the UDF undoubtedly has a formidable mass base. For example, the Cradock Residents' Association (Cradora), formed in October 1983 as a result of struggles against rent rises, built youth and student wings and organised a network of elected street committees. No doubt their success in creating popular structures explains the brutal murder of Matthew Goniwe and three other Cradora leaders in June 1985.[12]

Nevertheless, the character of the UDF as a broad alliance was clearly expressed by the Front's publicity secretary, 'Terror' Lekota: 'we are non-racial, which means that we embrace all races, and . . . we bring together all classes.'[13] Underlying this conception of the UDF is a view of the nature of the South African revolution which is central to the ANC tradition. For the Congress, its allies and offshoots, the objective of the struggle is national liberation—the elimination of apartheid and the establishment of black majority rule, and not socialist revolution—the destruction of capitalism and the seizure of power by the black working class.

The ANC has two main programmatic documents. The first is the Freedom Charter, adopted by the ANC-convened Congress of the People in 1955. There was some discussion of the Charter in 1985, its thirtieth anniversary. One leading Marxist intellectual, Duncan Innes, argued that there is 'a large measure of ambiguity in the document as a whole—an ambiguity which lends itself to different political interpretations, with some people wanting to interpret it in a capitalist direction and others in a socialist direction.'[14]

This ambiguity is reflected in the fact that much of the Charter is an impeccably bourgeois-democratic programme, summed up by its famous opening words, 'South Africa belongs to all who live in it, black and white,' and its first main demand, that 'the people shall govern'. However its third demand, 'the people shall share in the country's wealth', goes on to call for the nationalisation of 'the mineral wealth beneath the soil, the banks and the monopoly industry [sic].'

However, shortly after the Charter was adopted, Nelson Mandela ruled out socialist interpretation of this clause:

Whilst the Charter proclaims democratic changes of a far-reaching nature it is by no means a blueprint for a socialist state but a programme for the unification of various classes and groupings amongst the people on a democratic basis... Its declaration 'The

People Shall Govern!' visualises the transfer of power not to any single social class but to all the people of this country, be they workers, peasants, professional men or petty bourgeoisie.

As for the nationalisation demand:

> The breaking up and democratisation of these monopolies will open fresh fields for the development of a prosperous non-European bourgeois class. For the first time in the history of this country the non- European bourgeosie will have the opportunity to own in their own name and right mines and factories, and trade and private enterprise will boom and flourish as never before.[15]

Similarly, the ANC's other programmatic document, adopted at the Morogoro Consultative Conference in May 1969, emphatically asserts: 'We in South Africa are part of the zone in which national liberation is the chief content of the struggle.'[16] For the ANC the struggle for socialism is a matter for the future. The immediate question is that of constructing an alliance of all the classes of black society in order to establish a bourgeois-democratic regime in South Africa.

The dominant populist tradition:
2: The SACP and Two-Stage Revolution

It might be argued that the ANC is a multi-tendency organisation, in which a right wing espouses the strategy outlined above, but is challenged from the left. However, the most articulate champion within the ANC and UDF of an approach whose objective is national liberation but not workers' power is the South African Communist Party (SACP).

The Communist Party of South Africa was founded on 29 July 1921.[17] Its origins lay in the International Socialist League, formed in 1915 as an anti-war breakaway from the racist South African Labour Party. Like the Labour Party, the International Socialist League and early Communist Party were very much products of a certain milieu, the white labour aristocracy of craft workers, many of whom were British in origin and brought with them to South Africa the traditions of pre-1914 syndicalism and Marxism.

Although the Communist Party's most creative leaders, such as Sidney Bunting and David Ivon Jones, were insistent that it should relate to black workers, the party tended to regard the white labour aristocracy, with its record of craft organisation and militancy, as the vanguard of the South African proletariat. This led it to support the Rand Revolt of January to March 1922, a reactionary strike of white miners to stop the erosion of the colour bar banning blacks from skilled jobs in the mines. In the subsequent 1924 general election the Communist Party supported the pact uniting the National and Labour Parties on an explicitly racist programme.[18]

However, under the influence of Bunting and others, and with prodding from the Communist International, the party shifted towards an orientation on the black working class. This process was sidetracked by the Stalinisation of the Comintern. In the wake of the Comintern's Sixth Congress in August and September 1928 the party was instructed to 'combine the fight against all anti-native laws with the general political slogan in the fight against British domination, the slogan of an independent native South African republic as a stage towards a workers' and peasants' republic, with full equal rights for all races, black, coloured and white.'[19]

The 'Native Republic' slogan was merely the application to South Africa of the general strategy evolved for the colonial and semi-colonial countries by Stalin in the mid-1920s. This envisaged a revolution in two stages—first a struggle for national liberation, uniting workers, peasants, intellectuals and the 'national bourgeoisie', and only then, after imperialism had been expelled and national independence achieved, should the proletariat launch its own struggle for socialism.

This strategy was applied with disastrous consequences during the Chinese revolution of 1925-7: the Chinese Communist Party subordinated itself to the bourgeois-nationalist Kuomintang, restrained the independent struggles of workers and peasants in order to avoid antagonising the 'national bourgeoisie', and was rewarded by the bloody massacre of its militants once the warlords had been defeated by Chiang Kai-Shek's armies. Trotsky subjected this strategy to ruthless criticism. It was in this period that he formulated his general theory of permanent revolution, arguing that the bourgeoisie had ceased to play a revolutionary role in the backward countries, and that therefore only the working class could lead a successful struggle for both national liberation and socialism.[20]

The Stalinist strategy of a two-stage revolution has shaped the strategy of the South African Communist Party ever since 1928.

Subsequent to the Comintern's Sixth Congress, the party was 'Bolshevised', and critics of the new strategy, Bunting included, expelled.[21] The party's policies have faithfully followed the twists and turns of Moscow's line ever since. This subservience to the Kremlin bureaucracy has survived even Stalin's death and Khrushchev's secret speech: from Hungary to Afghanistan the SACP has toed the line. The party also cultivates, notably in its theoretical quarterly, **African Communist**, a style of debate with other socialists which preserves in aspic the good old traditions of fraternal argument perfected by Vyshinsky and Zhdanov.[22]

One consequence of the SACP's two-stages strategy has been its gradual fusion with the ANC. The party's central committee, faced with legal prohibition under the new Nationalist government's Suppression of Communism Act, voted to dissolve the party on 20 June 1950. Secretly reconstituted in 1953, the party kept its identity secret for a decade. A party conference in 1958 was deeply split over whether to resume open mass work.[23] Instead the party increasingly operated through its activists' presence in other organisations, especially the ANC itself and other components of the Congress Alliance, notably the white Congress of Democrats.

This mode of operation—the SACP working through the ANC and its affiliates—developed further subsequent to Congress's banning and move into exile. SACP members have taken on major leadership positions. A notable example is Joe Slovo, a white barrister who has been for many years a member of the MK high command, who served on the Revolutionary Council set up to direct the armed struggle in 1969, and who was the first white elected to the ANC executive at Congress's consultative conference at Kabwe, Zambia, in June 1985. Some observers have claimed that the SACP was very heavily represented on the new expanded executive chosen at this conference.

The SACP's influence has been as much political as organisational. It has been the most coherent force defending the two-stage strategy. The SACP programme, **The Road to South African Freedom**, adopted in 1962, declares that 'the immediate and imperative interests of all sections of the South African people demand . . . a national democratic revolution which will overthrow the colonialist state of white supremacy and establish an independent state of national democracy in South Africa.' The document acknowledges that the ANC's Freedom Charter, in which 'the main aims and lines of the South African democratic revolution have been defined'...'is not a programme for socialism'. The SACP document nonetheless 'pledges its unqualified support for the Freedom Charter.' Similarly the programme declares approvingly: 'As a national liberation organisation, the ANC does not represent any single class, or any one ideology. It is representative of all the classes and strata which make up African society in this country.'[24]

Three particular problems arise in this context for the SACP: the nature of South African society, the question of the black middle class, and the role of the working class and its struggle for socialism within the broad alliance.

The first issue arises in the following way. The two-stage strategy was formulated for colonies and semi-colonies. In these cases the nature of the first stage was reasonably clear, namely the elimination of foreign domination. But how does this analysis apply to South Africa, with its own well-entrenched ruling class? The answer that the SACP came up with was that in this case the colonial relationship is internal to the South African social formation. This is the celebrated theory of 'internal colonialism' or 'colonialism of a special type':

> On one level, that of 'White South Africa', there are all the features of an advanced capitalist state in its final stage of imperialism...
> But at another level, that of 'Non-White South Africa', there are all the features of a colony. The indigenous population is subjected to extreme national oppression, poverty and exploitation, lack of democratic rights and political domination by a group which does everything to emphasise and perpetuate its alien 'European' character ...Non-White South Africa is the colony of White South Africa itself.[25]

This theory was later adopted by the ANC.[26] It was recently re-affirmed by Slovo, who underlined the theory's political significance:

> A grasp of the institutionalised national oppression which characterises South Africa is the starting point for elaborating the perspectives of our revolutionary practice, and leads to the conclusion that the main content of the immediate struggle is to achieve complete national liberation for the racially dominated and racially exploited black communities.[27]

In other words: since black South Africa is a nation colonised by the whites, then all its classes should unite to win their political independence.

Convenient though these political implications may be, the theory of 'internal colonialism' is a piece of bizarre fantasy. South Africa is the most highly industrialised country in Africa, whose population, black and white, has been progressively proletarianised and urbanised over the past century. The SACP invite us to view this capitalist social formation as in fact two societies, one white, the other black, each with its distinct class structure, related primarily politically through whites' colonial domination of blacks. Not only is the suggestion intrinsically preposterous, it flies in the face of the past fifteen years' research by South African Marxists, which has showed how the institutions of racial domination were first created and have since been reshaped over the years in order to meet the needs of the different fractions of South African capital.

Defenders of the theory of internal colonialism often accuse its critics of having an 'abstract' conception of capitalism.[28] Yet it is they who are guilty of this error. They assume that because Marx's analysis in **Capital** abstracts from the relationship between capitalist exploitation and racial oppression, this relationship is always a contingent one, such that apartheid can be eliminated without threatening the survival of capitalism in South Africa. But Marx in **Capital** is concerned with the capitalist mode of production as such: the particular form it takes in particular societies varies according to concrete circumstances: for example, prevailing class relations, the country's historical development and place in the world economy, and so on. Apartheid is no mere aberration which can be easily removed allowing capitalism to continue and prosper.

The second issue concerns one component of the oppressed black 'nation', namely the black bourgeoisie and petty bourgeoisie. The SACP programme is emphatic about their progressive role:

> The special character of colonialism in South Africa, the seizing by whites of the opportunities which, in other colonial countries, have led to the growth of a national capitalist class, have strangled the development of a class of African capitalists . . . The interests of the African commercial class lie wholly in joining the workers and rural people for the overthrow of white supremacy.[29]

In the first place, this analysis underestimates the degree to which a black commercial bourgeoisie has succeeded in developing in the townships; this phenomenon may not have been so evident in 1962, but it cannot be ignored today, particularly in the light of the way in which a similarly oppressed black business class emerged in Zimbabwe after independence to buy into the previously purely white sectors and to exercise a significant influence on the ruling party.

Secondly, a main thrust of Botha's strategy is precisely to incorporate the black middle class into the state through a variety of economic concessions, the new constitution, and revamped Black Local Authorities. Already a layer of collaborators has emerged in the townships and Bantustans with a material interest in the status quo. The SACP notes this phenomenon, but insists:

> ...the fate of the majority of the black middle strata is more closely connected to the black workers than to their white counterparts ...the destruction of the system of national domination is in their interests...the winning over to our side of larger and larger groups from amongst the middle strata remains a revolutionary necessity.[30]

Now it is undoubtedly true that insofar as they are racially oppressed, black capitalists, lawyers and other professionals have an objective interest in the removal of white domination. It is also true that any serious revolutionary party in such circumstances would, at the very minimum, seek to neutralise such elements, and, if possible, to win their active support. However, the situation in South Africa is a dynamic one. On the one hand, the regime, under pressure from big capital, is likely to offer further reforms, including at some stage 'power-sharing' at the national level, in the hope of winning over wider layers of the black middle class to its side. On the other hand, the black working-class movement is likely to take its own struggles and demands further. The crucial question is whether it should at some future stage abandon these struggles and demands in order to avoid alienating the vacillating black middle class. In other words, will the proletariat neutralise the middle strata, or vice versa?

Clearly the answer to this question depends crucially on whether or not the working class possesses its own independent political organisation. This takes us to the third problem facing the SACP, namely the role of the proletariat within the broader national alliance. In principle, the answer is perfectly clear:

> The working class seeks a close alliance with the rural people, and with the urban middle classes and intellectuals in the national

democratic revolution. Only under its leadership can the full aims of the revolution be achieved.[31]

This theme is closely connected to another, which might seem to undercut criticisms of ANC strategy. Its defenders often claim that the two-stage revolution will in fact be an uninterrupted process, so that 'it is false to counterpose national liberation and socialism, for they are part of a single process.'[32] Joe Slovo spelt out the logic of this position thus:

If . . . the liberation struggle should bring to power a revolutionary democratic alliance dominated by the proletariat and peasantry *(which is on the agenda in South Africa)*, the post-revolutionary phase can surely become the first stage in a continuous process along the road to socialism: a road that ultimately can only be charted by the proletariat and its natural allies.[33]

And so the SACP's critics might seem to be disarmed: the working class and its interests will after all be central to the struggle for national liberation.

Viewing the two-stage revolution as an uninterrupted process in fact goes back to Stalin's first formulations of the theory.[34] What on this account guarantees the continuous character of the revolution? The leading role of the working class. And how is this secured? Why, through the role of the SACP, 'the party of the working class', whose 'central and immediate task...is to lead the fight for national liberation of the non-white people, and for the victory of the democratic revolution.'[35]

The leading role of the black proletariat over other layers of the oppressed population could only be secured by encouraging every initiative by workers, every struggle which allows them to strengthen their organisation, to develop their consciousness, to increase their confidence. However, the record of the SACP is one of greeting forms of working-class organisation and struggle which fall outside the Congress Alliance with profound suspicion and often hostility.

This was especially true of their attitude to the independent unions, which emerged outside the control of the exiled, ANC-aligned, SACP-dominated South African Congress of Trade Unions (SACTU). Thus the claim by Joe Foster of the main union federation, FOSATU, that the union movement was necessary to provide working-class leadership in the national liberation struggle, was greeted with blind rage by the SACP, which accused FOSATU of challenging the party's right to speak for the working class:

> Dare FOSATU ignore this? And dare it ignore the confusion and
> division it will sow in the ranks of the working class if it sets up a
> new 'workers' movement' in competition with or alongside the still
> living Communist Party?[36]

The SACP's conception of working-class leadership of the
national liberation struggle is thus a substitutionist one, in which
the party represents and acts on behalf of the proletariat. It serves
to justify the party's influence within the ANC. This presence is
supposed to act as a guarantee of the struggle's socialist future,
but the nature of the broad alliance and the tactics it pursues are
calculated to prevent any transition from the 'national-democratic'
to the 'socialist' stages. This is clear when we consider Congress's
actual strategy.

The dominant populist tradition:
3: Guerrilla warfare and community struggles

Since 1961 the ANC has pursued a strategy of armed struggle
through MK. Its early efforts were amateurish and led to the
Rivonia debacle, which cost MK its underground high command.
However in the following two decades the ANC's approach became
a highly professional one, and it was able to build up, especially
in the wake of the Soweto uprising, a trained guerrilla force some
6,000 to 10,000 strong according to one usually well-informed
source.[37] Starting in the late 1970s, MK launched a guerrilla
campaign consisting primarily of the sabotage of buildings and
installations, and the assassination of government personnel.

Guerrilla warfare typically involves political rather than military
objectives, and the ANC's strategy is no exception. Its campaign
has been well described as the 'construction of a mass political
following through armed propaganda'.[38] In other words its aim
has been to build up popular support rather than inflict military
defeats on the vastly superior security forces.

Such methods have been perfected in guerrilla struggles
elsewhere in Africa and in other parts of the world. But these have
almost invariably been peasant wars, in which guerrillas were
infiltrated into isolated rural areas and gradually built up popular
support, allowing them slowly to create 'liberated zones' outside
government control and to encircle the urban centres of state power.
But South African conditions are very different. One of the

peculiarities of capitalist development in the country has been the virtual destruction of the peasantry as an independent social class.³⁹ A majority of the population still live in the countryside: indeed, in 1980 only a third of Africans were urbanised,⁴⁰ but peasant production has long ceased to support those living in the countryside. Thus in the predominantly rural Transkei Bantustan, gross income from farming is less than 20 per cent of total household income.⁴¹ The mass of the rural population are either wage-labourers or their dependents, often living in conditions of abject misery in the resettlement camps created in the Bantustans to provide the 'white' cities with a readily accessible workforce of migrant workers and commuters.

This means that the social and economic base for a classical guerrilla strategy does not exist in South Africa. Enormous popular struggles did indeed shake rural South Africa for a generation, culminating in the great Pondoland revolt of the late 1950s, yet despite the appalling conditions in which most rural blacks live there has been no repetition of these struggles in the past decade. This suggests that South Africa's social structure has in the past generation been drastically skewed in the direction of mass urbanisation and proletarianisation—indeed one estimate suggests that 75 per cent of Africans will live in the cities by the year 2000.⁴² It is there that the fate of the South African revolution will be settled.

The ANC tacitly acknowledges this fact. The bulk of MK's armed actions have taken place in urban areas. But urban guerrilla warfare has proved historically very unsuccessful, to judge by the experience of Algeria, Brazil, Argentina, Uruguay and Italy, to take some recent examples. Urban populations, highly concentrated as they are, are much easier for the security forces to monitor and control. Urban guerrillas are therefore forced rigorously to isolate themselves through secretive cell structures if they are to survive. It is therefore very difficult for them to stimulate mass struggles, let alone to organise the development of a genuine people's war in the towns. Usually they have been eventually picked off and crushed by the security forces.

South Africa represents somewhat more favourable conditions than many other cases of urban guerrilla warfare: MK clearly enjoys widespread popular support, and arguably the township revolts have created a political terrain in which armed struggle can assume a mass character. That, at any rate, is the belief of the ANC leadership, who have sought since 1984 to turn the MK campaign into a people's war.

This strategy has three elements. First, there has been the call to 'render South Africa ungovernable'. This has involved the use of a variety of tactics—for example, school boycotts—to bring the state's administration of the townships to a halt. Secondly, there has been an attempt to turn the townships into 'liberated zones', where 'people's power' prevails. Thus ANC acting president Oliver Tambo declared at the beginning of 1985:

> In the course of our mass offensive, we have, from time to time and with increasing frequency, created the situation in various localities such that the democratic forces challenged the apartheid authorities for control of these areas, emerging as the alternative power. With regard to the perspective of people's war, this means that we forged the conditions for us to transform these areas into mass revolutionary bases from which Umkhonto we Sizwe must grow as an army of the people.[?]

Thirdly, for MK to become 'an army of the people' rather than merely a guerrilla elite, the masses themselves must be armed. There is some evidence of weapons—grenades and even AK-47 automatic rifles—reaching the townships. But the ANC does not regard this as the main means of arming the people. An ANC broadcast on 22 February 1985 asked:

> Where are the weapons to destroy this regime? They cannot be found anywhere else countrymen. They can only be found in our country itself. The weapons are there in front of you. They are in the hands of the policemen themselves. Some of these policemen are coming back to sleep within our midst in the townships. We know where they live. Let us break into their houses and take those guns that the apartheid regime gives them to kill us and turn those guns against them. Let us break into their barracks and take those guns and machine guns... We should attack the police station[s] and army barracks and capture those weapons.[?]

This call has been repeated in leaflets distributed within the country, which have also appealed to 'white democrats and . . . anti-apartheid whites' in the security forces to mutiny against their commanders:

> Within the army and police we must refuse to shoot our fellow countrymen, and turn our weapons against the sadists who order us

to kill and maim."[45]

Now this general approach would make perfect sense in a revolutionary situation where popular insurrection against the apartheid regime were immediately on the agenda. But such a situation does not exist in South Africa today. The balance of military power is still overwhelmingly in the ruling class's favour. There is absolutely no sign of serious unrest in the armed forces even on the relatively modest scale of the drug-taking and fragging (blowing up of officers) which afflicted US troops in the latter years of the Vietnam war, let alone the beginnings of mutinies.

Attempts to take on the security forces militarily would in present circumstances be suicidal (and are studiously avoided by MK, whose escalation of the armed struggle since the June 1985 ANC conference has taken the form mainly of attacks, hitherto rare, on 'soft' targets—in other words white civilians).

ANC supporters defend these calls by arguing that armed struggle is a process, and that unsuccessful battles are a necessary condition for the development of a trained popular army. But what the ANC's call to arms is leading to is heroic young blacks squandering their lives in hopeless assaults on the security forces. Such episodes—which were occurring with increasing frequency in late 1985 and early 1986—will train no-one in anything except (with luck) the bankruptcy of the ANC's entire strategy.

Similarly the call to build 'revolutionary mass bases' in the townships is unlikely to be effective. Undoubtedly some areas, especially in the Eastern Cape, have become no-go areas for the security forces. But it does not follow that they can become secure bases for armed struggle. The townships have been designed so that the army can cordon them off and if necessary starve out the population. The experience of the struggle in the north of Ireland shows that urban no-go areas can only be sustained if the level of mass mobilisation remains high—once it had receded after the imposition of British direct rule in March 1972 the army was able to re-occupy areas such as Free Derry.

The experience of the 1976 and 1980 revolts in South Africa shows that township risings tend, under the weight of repression, eventually to exhaust themselves. While the present upsurge has had a greater duration and intensity, it too will in all likelihood run aground on the rocks of state violence and popular exhaustion. Indeed, the ANC strategy of 'ungovernability' may help to bring this result. In the light of this strategy, the ANC tended to treat the school boycotts which spread through the country in 1984-85 as a matter of principle. Its activists put forward the slogan 'liberation before education', implying that the schools should be closed until white power was overthrown. This approach only made sense on the assumption that insurrection was the order of the day.

The effect of the long school closures was to deprive the township population of one of the few focuses of collective organisation and activity they possessed (all significant workplaces are outside, in the 'white' areas). The result was that mass participation in the student struggles declined, with only a small and very brave minority taking to the streets to engage in unequal battles with the security forces.

The same sort of dynamic had helped to dissipate the student movement which led to the 1976 risings.[46] In 1985 the left drew the lesson and called for tactical retreat. Thus Socialists of Young Azania, an affiliate of the Cape Action League, argued at the end of 1985:

> The absence of our soldiers (the student mass) at our training centres (the schools) has put us at a great disadvantage. We've reached a situation where very few students pitch up at schools. As serious revolutionaries we know that there is no point in having ten generals but no soldiers in our army. SRCs [Student Representative Councils] therefore need to examine the material conditions in their schools in order to win a decisive victory.[47]

Under pressure from right and left, the ANC executive backed a call from a conference convened by the Soweto Parents' Crisis Committee on 29-30 December 1985 temporarily to end the school boycott.

But behind these weaknesses of ANC strategy lies a deeper one.

Typically, guerrilla warfare has succeeded in a colonial or semi-colonial context. It does so not by inflicting military defeat on the enemy but by breaking the will of the metropolitan power by making the price of hanging on unacceptably high. It was thus that the struggles in Vietnam, Algeria and the Portuguese colonies succeeded.

But South Africa, contrary to ANC and SACP theory, is not a colonial situation. There is no metropolitan power to throw in the towel. Instead there is a local bourgeoisie displaying all the features of modern finance capital.[48] The South African ruling class is interwoven with and dependent on Western capital, but its economic base and control over the state apparatus are such as to allow it to resist outside pressures. The relative independence of South African capitalism was shown in August and September 1985, when the Botha regime defied the demands of foreign and local big business that it speed up the reforms, and effectively defaulted on its debt to the Western banks.

It is with this powerful and entrenched ruling class that the South African resistance has to contend. This class's interests are dependent on its control over the South African economy—there is no 'home' where it can fly. This is true even of the Anglo-American Corporation: despite its considerable international interests, Anglo's dominant position in virtually every sector of the South African economy binds its fate to that economy.

Defenders of the ANC may argue that nevertheless South African capital may be forced to negotiate with the liberation movement, leading to a transition to majority rule comparable to the Lancaster House agreement which ended the Zimbabwean war of independence in 1979. Indeed the willingness of one wing of the ruling class to negotiate was shown by the September 1985 meeting in Lusaka between ANC leaders and Gavin Relly of Anglo and other white bosses.

But in the first place, even this liberal wing of South African capital has rejected black majority rule—all Relly and company are willing to contemplate is 'power-sharing', the involvement of black leaders in a central government which would still not be chosen by one person one vote.

Secondly, the obstacles to even this arrangement are formidable, since they would meet with massive opposition from the white petty bourgeoisie and working class, whose material privileges are closely bound up with white rule.

Thirdly, assuming that these obstacles were removed and Relly and company accepted black majority rule, they would do so only on terms highly unfavourable to the mass of the population. The Lancaster House agreement is hardly an auspicious precedent, since it left the economic power of capital intact, with the result that in Zimbabwe the black middle class now manage the state apparatus while all the phenomena of low pay, unemployment and landlessness—which led to the peasant war in the first place—remain.

Yet such an outcome is probably the best that ANC leaders can hope for. Their strategy of guerrilla warfare and township risings can serve, at its best, as a means of pressurising the South African ruling class into negotiations. The result of this would indeed involve dismantling the institutions of white political domination, but would leave little altered the low-wage economy they helped to create. The choice facing the ANC is thus that of betrayal or defeat.

The minority populist tradition: Africanism and Black Consciousness

The ANC has never gone unchallenged by other political forces—from the left, for example, by the SACP in its revolutionary days, and by the Non-European Unity Movement in the 1940s and 1950s. But the most serious challenge has come from a form of politics which offers a variant of rather than an alternative to the ANC's strategy. Black exclusivism, at certain points in the struggle—the late 1950s and mid-1970s—threatened to eclipse Congress. Its influence today is on the ebb, so I shall deal with it comparatively summarily.[49]

Africanism emerged within the ANC itself, after the formation of the Youth League in 1943. The dominant influence in the Youth League was Anton Lembede who, affected by the current of Pan-Africanism then sweeping through Britain's colonies, wrote in 1946:

> Africa is a black man's country... The basis of national unity is the nationalistic feeling of the Africans, the feeling of being Africans irrespective of tribal connection, social status, educational attainment or economic class.[50]

The Africanists, whose leadership was taken over by Robert Sobukwe after Lembede's death, thus followed ANC orthodoxy in seeing the struggle as a multi-class one for national liberation. The only difference of substance was that they opposed the involvement of whites in this struggle.

The matter came to a head over the influence of white SACP members over Congress policy in the 1950s. In 1959 the Pan-Africanist Congress (PAC) was formed as a split from the ANC. It proceeded to lead a campaign against the pass laws; the regime's response was the Sharpeville massacre and the banning of both the ANC and the PAC.

In exile the PAC moved to the left, abandoning its anticommunism, which undoubtedly was a factor in the original split, for a Maoist strategy of peasant war. This approach was no more successful than MK's campaign; moreover the ANC, partly through the connections it enjoyed through the SACP and its Russian backers, was able to build up a far more effective network of international support. The PAC went into an organisational decline from which it has yet to recover.

The ideology of Africanism retained an influence, however, and enjoyed a major revival in the 1970s. In 1969 black radicals broke away from the predominantly white National Union of South African Students (NUSAS) to form the South African Students Organisation (SASO) and later the Black People's Convention (BPC). The new movement, like the Pan-Africanist Congress, refused to work with whites. Its leaders, notably Steve Biko, went on to formulate the ideology of Black Consciousness.

This involved a number of elements. First, heavily influenced by the black power and black theology movements in the US, there was an assertion of black pride and a stress on the importance of black self-consciousness in the liberation process. This required a rejection of co-operation with whites: 'Black man, you are on your own!' Secondly there was a nostalgic invocation of the communal virtues of the allegedly classless pre-colonial African societies.

Thirdly, there was the rejection of class analysis and class politics. Biko dismissed white Marxists who 'tell us that the situation is a class struggle rather than a racial struggle. Let them go to Van Tonder in the Free State [in other words the typical poor Afrikaner] and tell him this.'[51] And fourthly it involved a view of change as the result of the gradual building up of black bargaining power, for example through the development of a stronger African business class. Biko wrote: We should think along such lines as the "buy black" campaign once suggested in Johannesburg and establish our own banks for the benefit of the community.'[52]

Black Consciousness ideology thus contained some highly reactionary elements.[53] In the short term, however, its impact was positive, helping to rebuild black confidence after the despair and apathy produced by the defeats of the early 1960s. Black Consciousness ideas undoubtedly had a major influence on the Soweto uprising, and its activists bore the brunt of the repression that followed, culminating in the banning of the BPC, SASO and other Black Consciousness organisations in October 1977 and the murder of Biko himself by the security police.

Under the hammer of the state, and in the face of a revived ANC, Black Consciousness was forced to adapt and regroup. It re-emerged openly with the formation of the Azanian People's Organisation (AZAPO) in May 1978. This represented a certain leftward evolution. AZAPO laid stress on the role of the black working class—a shift reflecting the emergence of Black Consciousness-aligned unions which were later to form the Council of Unions of South Africa (CUSA). However this orientation was undermined by an underlying populism—a black worker was defined as 'any black person irrespective of professional status'.[14]

AZAPO has been heavily involved in the struggles of the past few years [up to 1986]—it has, for example, considerable influence in the Vaal Triangle where the current [1986] wave of township risings began in September 1984. Moreover, it seems that AZAPO activists took the initiative in proposing in November 1982 a national united front against Botha's 'new deal'. Pipped to the post by the UDF, but re-invigorated by the release from Robben Island in December 1982 of a number of BPC and SASO leaders, AZAPO helped to launch an alternative broad front, the National Forum Committee, on 11-12 June 1983. Two hundred organisations took part in the founding conference.[15]

There were two elements to the National Forum opposition to the UDF. The first was a traditional black exclusivist rejection of alliances with 'white democrats'. Thus AZAPO objected to the involvement in the UDF of predominantly white organisations such as the student body NUSAS and the Johannesburg Democratic Action Committee. Secondly there was a new factor in the political equation: the influence within the National Forum Committee of a non-racial left wing which rejected any 'stages' strategy.

The Cape Action League (CAL), of which more below, played a major part in the formation of the National Forum. Its leading theorist, Neville Alexander, read a paper at the 1983 AZAPO conference which was greeted with a standing ovation. CAL's hand was evident in the Manifesto of the Azanian People adopted by the National Forum Committee. This declared that:

> ...our struggle for national liberation is directed against the system of racial capitalism... Only the eradication of the system of racial capitalism can put an end to apartheid. The black working class

inspired by revolutionary consciousness is the driving force in our struggle... [whose objective is] the socialist republic of Azania.

The Manifesto proclaimed four principles:

Anti-racism and anti-imperialism; Non-collaboration with the oppressors and their political instruments; Independent working-class organisation; Opposition to alliances with ruling-class parties.[56]

The Manifesto represented a significant theoretical break with the populism hitherto characteristic of Black Consciousness. To what extent it involved a real political shift on the part of the dominant forces within AZAPO was another matter, however. One source reported after the National Forum's founding meeting that 'a number of black exclusivists confided disatisfaction with the new left-wing emphasis, but said the "moment" was not right for a counter-offensive.'[57]

It is likely that for many AZAPO leaders the alliance with the left was more a tactical expedient to counter the UDF juggernaut than a genuine political break. It is however significant that one of the two main populist currents should feel itself obliged, even verbally, to adopt a form of socialism. This indicates the degree to which the situation within the country has placed working-class politics on the agenda. Let us therefore turn to consider those forces actively and consciously committed to such politics.

The intellectual left

Marxism can be said to have been born in South Africa at the beginning of the century with the appearance of the local versions of the Social Democratic Federation and the Socialist Labour Party, the two main revolutionary currents in the English-speaking world.[58] However for much of its early history the South African revolutionary left was crippled by its failure to confront the reality of national oppression weighing down upon the black majority.

As we have seen, the International Socialist League and the early Communist Party regarded the white working class as the vanguard of the proletariat. They expected economic pressure to bring about the unity of white and black workers, constantly predicting the collapse of South African capitalism even when, as in the 1930s, the economy was booming. In all this, South African Marxism was a reflection of the milieu from which it sprang, that of the white artisans, militant on trade union issues but treating black workers as at best irrelevant, at worst a threat.[59]

The influence of the Comintern, with the emphasis at the Second Congress in 1920 laid on the need for Communists to support national liberation movements, was at first beneficial. However once the international Communist movement had been Stalinised, the Communist Party's contribution to South African Marxism consisted entirely in elaborating and applying the two-stages theory. The **African Communist** reeks of the vulgarised 'Dialectical Materialism' of Stalin's heyday.

Nor did the Trotskyist movement in South Africa break out of the mould of abstract Marxism typical of the International Socialist League and the early Communist Party.[60] The local supporters of Trotsky and the Left Opposition emerged publicly in 1932 with the formation of the Lenin Club in Cape Town. In 1934 the group split into the Communist League (later the Fourth International Organisation) and the Workers Party of South Africa. The latter managed to produce a monthly paper, **The Spark**, until the group collapsed in 1939; the former had more enduring influence through the Unity Movement.

Both groups perpetuated the abstract Marxism of the earlier socialist organisations. Thus **The Spark** declared in October 1938:

> Workers of South Africa! You are all bound together by the same bonds of oppression! Forget your different colours, your races and nationalities! You are all alike workers, exploited by the same oppressor, the capitalist![61]

In line with this, both Trotskyist organisations denounced the Communist Party's slogan of a 'Native Republic' because 'it is bound to antagonise one section of the working class against another. Instead of uniting the workers it again splits them on racial grounds.'[62]

Trotsky, in his only intervention on South Africa, challenged this approach. Commenting on theses submitted by the Workers Party of South Africa, he wrote in April 1935:

> When the theses say that the slogan of 'black republic' is *equally* harmful to the revolutionary cause as the slogan of a 'South Africa for the whites', then we cannot agree with the form of the statement. Whereas in the latter there is the case of supporting complete oppression, in the former there is the case of taking the first steps towards liberation.
>
> We must accept decisively and without any reservations the complete and unconditional rights of the blacks to independence.

Only on the basis of a mutual struggle against the domination of the white exploiters can the solidarity of the black and white toilers be cultivated and strengthened...

The proletariat of the country consists of backward black pariahs and a privileged, arrogant caste of whites...the worst crime on the part of the revolutionaries would be to give the smallest concessions to the privileges and prejudices of the whites. Whoever gives his little finger to the devil of chauvinism is lost.[63]

At the same time Trotsky emphasised that only workers' power could solve the national question:

Insofar as a victorious revolution will radically change the relation not only between the classes but also between the races and will assure to the blacks that place in the state that corresponds to their numbers, thus far will the *social* revolution in South Africa also have a *national* character.

We have not the slightest reason to close our eyes to this side of the question or to diminish its significance. On the contrary, the proletarian party should in words and in deeds take the solution of the national (racial) problem into its hands.

Nevertheless, the proletarian party can and must solve the national question by *its own* methods.

The historic weapon of national liberation can be only the *class struggle*.[64]

Trotsky thus placed the South African struggle within a perspective of permanent revolution. But it was only nearly forty years later that a new generation of South African Marxists were fully to pursue this insight. The 1960s and 1970s saw the radicalisation of NUSAS, the predominantly white liberal student movement in the English-speaking universities. A variety of factors was to push these white radicals in the direction of Marxist theory and working-class politics.

In the first place, the development of Black Consciousness and its break with NUSAS in 1969 undermined the possibility of a broad democratic movement uniting both blacks and whites against the regime. A new strategy was needed.

Secondly, the beginnings of the black workers' movement in the early 1970s involved, among other things, the formation by NUSAS of Wages Commissions to work around the issues of black poverty. In this way some white radicals helped to establish the first independent unions after the 1973 Durban strikes.

Thirdly, many white radicals went to study abroad and became involved in the student movement and the revival of Marxist theory in the West after 1968. Many returned, some to take up academic posts in the English-speaking universities, spreading the new theories they had discovered overseas, and began to apply them to South African society.

The result was the emergence of a new Marxism, or Marxisms, based on the attempt systematically to reinterpret South African history, and above all to grasp the peculiarities of the social formation. Crucially, this meant analysing the relation between capital accumulation and racial domination. While it is invidious to select individual names from so gifted a group of scholars, two articles by Harold Wolpe and Martin Legassick[65] have rightly been called 'seminal'.[66] Legassick's essay in particular challenged the orthodoxy common to both liberals and the ANC/SACP that there was a contradiction between capitalism and apartheid, boldly asserting in a rich interpretive essay that 'the specific structures of labour control which have been developed in post-war South Africa are increasingly functional to capital.'[67]

The new South African Marxism was not free from the faults of the Western Marxism on which it drew. The writings of Althusser and his followers undoubtedly encouraged tendencies towards academicism and dogmatism. (Their influence spread far: it is a bit alarming to learn that Barry Hindess and Paul Hirst's **Precapitalist Modes of Production** 'dominated' the 'Workshop of Precapitalist Social Formations and Colonial Penetration in South Africa' held at the National University of Lesotho in 1976!)[68] However, political conditions in South Africa—the absence of bourgeois democracy and the rise of the workers' movement— meant that even most Marxist academics could not simply remain closeted in their studies. The theoretical debates among South African Marxists often had important practical implications. I shall give two examples.

The first debate turned around Wolpe's work. He drew on Althusserian writing which treated social formations as 'articulations' of different modes of production in order to explain the role of racial domination in South African capitalism. Wolpe argued that the tribal Reserves remained essentially pre-capitalist economies in which the relations of production prevailing before the colonial conquest still survived. They thereby helped to support the migrant labourers working in the 'white' economy, keeping wages very low:

> The crucial function thus performed by the [pre-1948] policy of Segregation was to maintain the productive capacity of the pre-capitalist economies and the social system of the African societies in order to ensure that these societies provided [a] portion of means of reproduction of the migrant working class."

Wolpe argued that this policy was undermined in the 1930s and 1940s as a result of the growing economic collapse of the Reserves, the increasing class differentiation within them, and the emergence of a black industrial proletariat. However, the policy of Apartheid which replaced Segregation after the Nationalist victory in 1948 'must be seen as the attempt to retain, in a modified form, the structure of the traditional societies'." Thus, in South Africa,

> the tendency of capital accumulation to dissolve the very relationship (with the non-capitalist economies) which makes that accumulation possible (at a particular rate) is blocked by the contradictory tendency of capital to conserve the relationship and with it the non-capitalist economies, albeit in a restricted form."

The effect was to rehabilitate the theory of internal colonialism. Wolpe was critical of the SACP's formulation of the theory, but sought to offer his own, much more rigorous version. Now the relationship between white and black 'societies' was explained in terms of 'the extraction of labour-power by a capitalist mode of production from non-capitalist productive systems.'" With admirable clarity Wolpe pointed out that for the theory to be tenable in Marxist terms, 'we must think of each such group [white and black society] as having a "specific structure, in particular because of the existence of classes with contradictory interests".'" And Wolpe concluded:

> The uniqueness or specificity of South Africa, in the period of capitalism, lies precisely in this: that it embodies within a single nation-state a relationship characteristic of the external relationship between imperialist states and their colonies (neo-colonies)."

Wolpe's Althusserian reconstruction of ANC/SACP orthodoxy was forcefully challenged by Michael Williams and others. Williams argued that the very measures which consolidated the migrant labour system, for example the 1913 Native Land Act setting aside less than 13 per cent of the country for the African Reserves, involved the collapse of the pre-capitalist societies:

> The very restructuring of African society entailed its destruction. This much is clear, especially if we have understood that what was at stake for the African people was nothing less than the untrammelled use of land indelibly interwoven into the entire fabric of their society. Take away from that use of land and the entire edifice collapses.[75]

Behind the debate over Wolpe's work was the question of whether, as Williams puts it, 'the dominant contradiction of South African society is . . . yet to be found within the capitalist mode of production.'[76] The second debate which I wish to discuss concerns the nature of the contradictions of South African capitalism. The work of Nicos Poulantzas had a major influence on South African Marxists, and in particular on some of those who spent some time during the 1970s in Britain at the Institute of Development Studies at Sussex University.

The 'Sussex School' were especially taken with Poulantzas's stress on divisions within the ruling class:

> Differences in the *form of state* are determined firstly, by the composition of the power bloc and its allied and supportive classes, and secondly, by changes related to which class/fraction is hegemonic.[77]

The Poulantzians developed on this basis an interpretation of South African history prior to 1948 which focused on the conflict between imperial and national capital. The Nationalists' victory in 1948 was seen as the attaining of hegemony by the latter 'fraction'. This account was challenged in a formidable assault mounted first by the British Marxist Simon Clarke, but supported by many South African scholars sharing the same approach, for example Martin Legassick and Duncan Innes.[78] Clarke and others made a variety of criticisms, challenging the Poulantzians' interpretation of particular episodes, and pointing out that 'fractions' looked suspiciously like the interest groups of orthodox bourgeois social science.

But the critics' fundamental point was that it was absurd to offer a Marxist account of South African history which ignored the struggle between capital and labour, treated the 'dominated class' as a passive object, and instead focused exclusively on divisions within the bourgeoisie.

Despite the justice of this criticism, there were some points to be made in the Poulantzians' favour. Clarke in particular espoused another variant of Western Marxism, the German 'capital-logic' school, whose tendency is towards an extreme form of reductionism in which social relations become merely an expression of the conflict between capital and labour."[79] Competition between capitals is a fundamental dimension of capitalist relations of production, and any Marxist account of South Africa which is not sensitive to the historic divisions within the ruling class is likely to be highly misleading. The work of one of the 'Sussex School', Dan O'Meara, shows that it is possible to develop an integrated analysis of both contradictions—that between capital and labour and that among capitalists.[80]

O'Meara's book **Volkskapitalisme**, a study of the class basis of Afrikaner nationalism, is one of a number of works to appear in the first half of the 1980s which showed the intellectual maturing of South African Marxism. These books—apart from O'Meara's there were Jeff Peires' **The House of Phalo**, Jeff Guy's **The Destruction of the Zulu Kingdom**, Duncan Innes's **Anglo-American and the Rise of Modern South Africa**, and Eddie Webster's **Cast in a Racial Mould**—all displayed both theoretical sophistication and a sensitivity to empirical sources which underlined the academic revolution they had wrought. The challenges from bourgeois scholarship seemed feeble by comparison with the weight and range of these works, extending as they did from the precapitalist social formations destroyed by colonial conquests to the divided working class produced by South Africa's specific patterns of capital accumulation.[81]

Political circumstances meant that, as I have already emphasised, the new South African Marxism could not merely sink into the academic subculture which its Western counterparts had shaped for themselves. And here the debates of the 1970s were important. They revealed a progressive polarisation into two camps.

There were those who used Western Marxism to provide a more sophisticated rationale for ANC/SACP strategy. Wolpe, himself a figure from an older generation and an ex-member of the MK high command who had made a sensational escape from prison in the early 1960s, was a prime example. Many of the Poulantzians followed in his footsteps. Poulantzas himself had been a member of the Greek Eurocommunist party, and at times was explicit about his commitment to a version of Stalinist stages theory in which a Popular Front confronted monopoly capital.[82] Important figures in the Sussex School, Rob Davies and Dan O'Meara for example were to follow in Poulantzas's footsteps, translating his theoretica and political presuppositions into support for the ANC/SACP strategy of a 'national democratic revolution' in South Africa.

The second current consisted of those who saw South Africa as a capitalist social formation, albeit one shaped by the peculiarities of its historical development, and concluded that the task of socialists was to organise the working class.

Legassick had concluded his path-breaking essay on South African history by rejecting the theory of internal colonialism and arguing that 'national liberation could be achieved only co-terminously with the abolition of capitalism in South Africa'. He suggested that socialists should 'return to the pre-1928 attempt to develop proletarian class consciousness amongst workers in industry'.[13] Legassick himself was one of the group later to become the Marxist Workers' Tendency.

Some Marxist academics, such as Eddie Webster, were to play an important role in building the new independent unions. The admirable **South African Labour Bulletin**, founded in 1974, has provided a forum in which analysis, information, and discussion relevant to the revived workers' movement could be found.

In these ways, the renaissance in South African Marxism began to develop into practical activity, and thus to help to create the 'workerist' tendency which is the most serious political challenge to both prevailing populist traditions yet to have to developed.

The trade union left

The emergence of independent unions in the early 1970s did not represent the first attempt to organise African workers. There had been a succession of previous waves of unionisation, notably in the 1920s, during the Second World War, and in the 1950s and early 1960s.[14] However, these earlier black workers' movements had been crushed by state repression.

The greater success and stability of the contemporary union movement reflect changes in the structure of South African capitalism, whose development created a racially divided working class: white workers monopolised skilled jobs, enjoying high wages, and trade-union and political rights, the price of which was their integration in the state; African workers were concentrated in unskilled jobs usually filled by migrant labourers. This division of labour was undermined by the prodigious expansion of South African capitalism after 1945, and especially during the 1960s and 1970s.

The rapid growth of mass production industries led to the deskilling of the work hitherto performed by the white labour aristocracy. White workers increasingly moved into supervisory positions, occupying a contradictory class location between bourgeoisie and proletariat where they exercised the function of surveillance and control over the production of surplus value on behalf of capital. White workers have, in other words, tended to move into the new middle class.[15] Productive labour, meanwhile, was progressively 'fragmented' and 'diluted', creating a mass of semi-skilled jobs performed by black workers, who thus ceased to be merely unskilled labourers.[16]

These changes were reflected in the quantitative growth of the African proletariat: between 1951 and 1980 the number of Africans employed in manufacturing rose from 360,000 to 1,103,000, and in mining from 449,000 to 768,000. In 1980 there were 2,304,000 African production workers.[17] South African capitalism, today based on many of the manufacturing industries characteristic of an advanced capitalist country, is therefore dependent on a predominantly black working class.

It is this structural shift which explains the rise of the independent unions. Their birth can be dated from the Durban mass strikes of January and February 1973, when 60,000 black workers spontaneously went on strike to demand higher wages. The employers and the state, taken by surprise, did not react simply by resorting to repression. However, they sought initially to head off the pressure for African unions by encouraging the formation of management-controlled works and liaison committees.[18]

The late 1970s saw a marked shift in ruling-class strategy. The Soweto uprising of 1976-77, the rise of the black unions, and the collapse of white power throughout the rest of the region, these underlined the bankruptcy of the policy of 'separate development', which denied blacks any rights outside the Homelands. After P W Botha's accession to the premiership in September 1978 the regime changed to a new course, summarised by the Wiehahn and Riekert reports published the following year.

The changes they proposed have been described as ' "deracialisation" of the workplace . . . without an accompanying "deracialisation" in society at large."[89] The white monopoly of political power was to be preserved, but at the same time made more secure through a widening of the regime's base. Economic and political concessions were to be made to the black middle class. More to the point, a black labour aristocracy was to be created by driving a wedge between the 'section tenners', Africans with the right to live in urban areas under section 10(1) of the Blacks (Urban Areas) Consolidation Act, and the mass of migrant workers and commuters (workers living in a Bantustan but travelling daily to work in a 'white' area) without this right. Thus Africans were to be permitted to form trade unions and to participate in the state-controlled system of collective bargaining based on Industrial Councils embracing employers and unions, but initially the regime sought to exclude migrants and commuters from these rights.

Wiehahn-Riekert was, in many respects, an attempt to extend the strategy of incorporation, so successfully pursued towards the white working class between the 1920s and 1940s, to include the better-paid and more highly skilled sections of the black proletariat. It backfired as spectacularly as Botha's attempts at political reform. African trade union membership more than trebled in 1980-83, from 220,000 to 670,000. In 1983 Africans represented 43.4 per cent of all trade union members, compared to whites (33.9 per cent), and Coloureds and Asians (22.7 per cent). For the first time white predominance in the South African working-class movement has been broken. Fifteen per cent of the economically active population was now organised in unions, twice the 1970 figure.[90]

At the heart of this growth were the independent unions. By late 1985 their signed-up membership was estimated to be 795,000, of whom 520,000 were paid-up members. In some ways more significant was that twenty-three unions, representing 363,000 paid-up members, had 12,462 shop stewards, more than double the 6,000 stewards that the entire independent union movement was estimated to have in 1984.[91]

The state's attempt to restrict union membership to section tenners wholly failed: indeed, many of the most important unions, for example the National Union of Mineworkers (NUM) and the Metal and Allied Workers Union (MAWU), are composed largely of migrants, reflecting the conditions of production in these industries—thus migrants made up 80-90 per cent of the workforce in basic metals.[92]

This new black workers' movement represents a militant form of trade unionism. Strikes rocketed in the late 1970s and early 1980s. The years 1981-82 saw two strike waves in the metal industry of the East Rand, a process through which MAWU grew enormously: membership trebled in 1981, and almost doubled the next year, to reach a total of 36,540. The same period saw fierce battles between labour and capital in the car industry of the Eastern Cape and the textile industry of Natal. Workers took political action as well: there was a wave of protest strikes against proposed government pensions legislation, and a half-hour strike by 101,000 workers on 11 February 1982 after union organiser Neil Aggett had been murdered by the security police.[33]

Working-class militancy was only interrupted, rather than broken, by the onset of recession in 1982. After a pause in 1983, the struggle resumed in 1984.

There were two very threatening features for the ruling class in this new strike wave. First, the emergence of the NUM as a powerful force in the country's most important industry led to the first legal strikes by black mineworkers, in September 1984 and 1985. Secondly, the independent unions and community organisations jointly called a stay-away in the Transvaal on 5-6 November 1984 which won the support of between 300,000 and 800,000 workers in the Pretoria-Witwatersrand-Vaal (PWV) area, the industrial heart of the South African economy.[34] Already by late 1983, Mike Rosholt, boss of Barlow Rand and a leader of the 'liberal' wing of South African capital, complained that the independent unions were threatening the 'private enterprise system' and the 'right to manage'.

The emergence of a powerful and militant black working-class movement in South Africa is an event of world-historic importance. It is one of the major developments in the worldwide struggle between capital and labour of the past fifteen years. Those who have built the independent unions require our praise and solidarity. However, the question of how the workers' struggle relates to the broader movement against apartheid is a vital, and as yet unresolved issue. To understand why this is so, we must consider the various forces within the workers' movement.

On the eve of the popular upsurge of 1983-84 there were three main currents in the independent union movement.[35] The first was the Federation of South African Trade Unions (FOSATU), with

106,000 members and nine affiliated unions. Highly structured and centralised, FOSATU was committed to building a non-racial union movement based on industrial unions and strong shop stewards' organisation. Apart from the metal workers' union MAWU its main affiliates included the National Automobile and Allied Workers' Union and the National Union of Textile Workers. White radicals played a crucial part in building individual FOSATU unions as well as in launching the national federation in 1979.

The role of white organisers was one crucial point of difference between FOSATU and the other main federation, the Council of Unions of South Africa (CUSA), formed in 1980. This much looser grouping of ten unions, with 148,000 members, had been heavily influenced by black consciousness, and so insisted on a black-led union movement. The most important CUSA union was the National Union of Mineworkers. A smaller Black Consciousness grouping, the Azanian Confederation of Trade Unions (AZACTU), emerged in 1984.

The third current were the seven so-called community or regional-general unions. The most important of these were perhaps the South African Allied Workers Union (SAAWU), the General and Allied Workers Union, and the Motor Assemblers and Component Workers Union (MACWUSA). These unions were, informally at least, politically aligned, supporting the ANC and its trade union front, SACTU. They stressed the unity of economic and political struggles, and argued that unions should organise around township as well as workplace issues.

These unions were much more unstable than the FOSATU and CUSA affiliates. SAAWU, the strongest of them, based in East London, claimed a membership of 50,000, although the real figure was estimated to be closer to 20,000:

> All seven of the regional-general unions emerged in the late 1970s when industrial relations reforms coupled with a sharp economic upturn provided uniquely favourable conditions for rapid union growth. Organising through strike waves and mass meetings in the townships, some of these unions gained large followings in a short space of time. But they failed to match their rapid gains in signed-up membership with consolidation on the factory floor. With the onset of recession in mid-1982, weaknesses in this method of organising workers began to show. In the face of retrenchments and mounting state attacks, all experienced heavy erosion of factory membership

and a weakening of worker participation in union activities.[96]

The community unions were at first the main obstacle to moves to form a united 'super-federation' of all the independent unions. One major question concerned whether unions should register under the state's new Industrial Conciliation Act extending trade union rights to black workers. SAAWU and some other unions, for example the small Western Cape-based General Workers Union, were opposed to registration on the grounds that it would lead to the independent unions becoming as incorporated and bureaucratised as their white counterparts. FOSATU, however, decided in 1980 to register, arguing that the unions could exploit the tactical advantages of state recognition without sacrificing their independence. Subsequent experience has tended to bear out FOSATU's case.[97]

Increasingly, however, the central question for the independent unions became that of their involvement in the political struggle, especially after the formation of the UDF and the National Forum. The community unions affiliated to the UDF, CUSA joined both the UDF and the National Forum, but FOSATU, the General Workers Union and another unaffiliated Western Cape union, the Food and Canning Workers, all refused to identify with either of the broad populist fronts.

It was here that the political polarisation between 'workerism' and 'populism' crystallised into an open division, with the leaders of FOSATU and its allies arguing a coherent, and effectively syndicalist strategy based upon the independent unions.

This strategy involved two elements. First, the trade union left (as I shall call those who identified with FOSATU's broad approach) developed a critique of ANC/UDF politics. The most developed version of their arguments was provided by a Sybilline paper by Alec Erwin, FOSATU's founding general secretary and later national education officer.

Erwin analysed what he called 'liberation politics', whose most relevant form to South Africa was 'populism', 'an alliance of classes whose economic interests differ but who find common cause against the regime'. In the 1950s and 1960s liberation politics had prevailed because 'apartheid was so abhorrent that it provided a very simple and powerful basis for mobilisation. So powerful that it strongly reinforced the momentum toward subsuming class interests.' However, in a period such as the present, one of structural crisis and reform from above, liberation politics tends to become 'no longer liberation politics but rather a process of negotiating.'[98]

Erwin argued:

the economy has profound structural problems which require substantial transformation if the working class both urban and rural is to improve its material and humanitarian position. Yet the imperatives imposed [by liberation politics] do not encourage or facilitate political practices that address transformation and transformation would focus attention on differing class interests.

Indeed, 'if the economic crisis is not cyclical but profoundly structural then any regime which works within existing parameters and structures'—by implication even the ANC after the triumph of the 'national democratic revolution'—would reject workers' 'justifiable demands' as 'irresponsible and inimical to economic recovery'.[99]

The experience of Zimbabwe, immediately to South Africa's north, where the Mugabe regime has ruthlessly suppressed independent workers' organisation, undoubtedly influenced the trade union left's critique of populism. FOSATU president Chris Dlamini visited Zimbabwe and returned shocked by what he saw. He concluded: 'Worker liberation can only be achieved by a strong, well-organised worker movement.[100]

But the left were also influenced by the experience of the workers' movement in South Africa itself, and in particular by what happened to SACTU during its period of open operation between 1955 and the repression of the early 1960s. The trade union left pointed to SACTU's submersion within the Congress Alliance. Rob Lambert wrote:

the essence of SACTU's failure . . . lay in [its] subordinate position within the alliance. The ANC and SACP leadership decided on the pace of events and SACTU followed as *the means* of realising long-term strategy. SACTU had no independent leadership. . .

Because of SACTU's subordinate position, decisions to launch national strike campaigns were taken with little reference to the level of preparedness and maturity of working-class organisation. It was the dominance of the ANC and the SACP in the alliance that finally led to the smashing of SACTU, at the very point when it was both developing a mass base and an experienced leadership. I refer here to the SACP-led decision to embark on the sabotage campaign against the state.[101]

There are two conclusions which can be drawn from this essentially correct analysis. The first is that the subordination of working-class interests within the Congress Alliance was a consequence of the influence of ANC/SACP *politics* on SACTU. The second is that the leadership of *any* political organisation is likely to involve the submersion of workers' specific interests and struggles. Lambert himself seems to have drawn the second conclusion:

> If SACTU had established its hegemony and independence within the alliance, it could have, within limits, dictated the pace of events and possibly steered clear of the mistakes of the SACP.[102]

Implicit in this passage is the second element of the FOSATU strategy, namely that a strong and democratic trade union movement is both a necessary and a sufficient condition of working-class independence. This position was apparently rejected by FOSATU general secretary Joe Foster in his very important keynote address to the 1982 Congress of the federation. Here he insisted on the necessity of an independent working-class movement, even in 'socialist' countries such as Poland, and certainly in South Africa, where

> it is...essential that workers must strive to build their own powerful and effective organisation even whilst they are part of the wider popular struggle. This organisation is necessary to protect and further worker interests and to ensure that the popular movement is not hijacked by elements who will in the end have no option but to turn against the worker supporters.

However,

> FOSATU as a trade union federation will clearly not constitute the working-class movement nor would this place FOSATU in opposition to the wider popular movement or its major liberation movement. FOSATU's task will be to build the effective organisational base for workers to play a major political role as workers. Our task will be to create an identity, confidence and political presence for worker organisation.[103]

Foster's formulations seemed to envisage a working-class politics based on a movement broader than the unions. Indeed, there was some discussion of forming a workers' party based on the unions. FOSATU **Worker News** carried two articles on the Brazilian Workers' Party in July and August 1985. However, in practice the FOSATU leadership identified the unions with the workers' movement. In the paper cited above, Erwin pointed to the need for a 'politics of transformation' which went beyond 'liberation politics' to meet the needs of workers. However he dismissed the idea of a party, telling **Socialist Worker**: 'We are not considering a workers' party. It would be premature and unwise.'[104]

The FOSATU leadership had a variety of reasons for pursuing this strategy. One was simply caution—the need to avoid destroying the infant workers' movement by a confrontation with the state or the Congress and its followers. No doubt also the monolithic and Stalinist conception of political organisation applied by the SACP, and the propagandism and sectarianism of the Trotskyist left, made the idea of a party unattractive to many union activists. Understandable though these reasons are, their effect was quite damaging, for the following reasons.

In the first place, as Eddie Webster, one of the trade union left's main theorists, himself pointed out: 'Attempts at deracialisation in the workplace, unless they are accompanied by deracialisation in the society at large, will lead to a widening, and not a narrowing of demands in the workplace.'[105] In the conditions of economic and political crisis of South Africa in the 1980s, a powerful workers' movement would willy-nilly be drawn into confrontation with the state.

Secondly, trade unions are workers' basic defensive organisations. This means that they reflect much of the unevenness of political consciousness in the class. In South African conditions this means that the unions' membership embraces political ideologies that range from tribalism to socialism. Gatsha Buthelezi's Inkatha ye Sizwe Zulu tribalist movement has considerable support among trade unionists in the Durban area. Indeed, FOSATU leaders gave this as a reason for not joining the UDF.

However, they did not face up to the contradictory character of trade-union consciousness. Militant workers are likely in present South African conditions to be both 'workerists' and 'populists', and, furthermore, to see no contradiction between these attitudes. In other words, they see themselves as militant trade unionists, committed to independent workers' organisation, but also support the ANC/UDF. At work they would participate in the independent unions, but their political loyalties would be to the old Congress Alliance. Politically, therefore, the influence of the ANC/UDF within the independent unions was likely to be greater than the relative weakness of the community unions might suggest.

These two factors made it inevitable that the independent unions would be drawn into wider political struggles once the townships began to explode in September 1984. In the absence of any coherent strategy on the part of the trade-union left, they vacillated between tailing and abstaining from the township-based, populist-dominated popular struggles.

One indication of the dangers involved in what some leftists acknowledged to be a 'political vacuum'[106] came in July 1984, when the United Metal, Mining and Allied Workers (UMMAWSA) was formed as a breakaway from MAWU.

MAWU's rapid period of growth had ended after the second great strike wave in the East Rand metal industry was broken when the management of Scaw Metals in Germiston, an Anglo-American subsidiary, sacked the entire workforce in April 1982. The onset of recession allowed employers to retrench many shop stewards. Increasingly, surviving stewards found themselves cut off from the demoralised rank and file, and more power was concentrated in the hands of full-time organisers. MAWU temporarily abandoned its demand for plant bargaining, joining the Industrial Council for the metal industry in February 1983.[107]

It was in these circumstances that David Sebabi, the MAWU general secretary, launched UMMAWSA, denouncing what he called a 'white bureaucratic elite'. While the split obviously had much to do with the demoralisation which followed defeat and retrenchments, the question of political trade unionism was a major issue. Sebabi said:

> We don't want to be told by white intellectuals that we should not join UDF, Inkatha or AZAPO. We are firmly committed to the national democratic struggle for the liberation of this country. If an organisation does this, we will support it.

One leading steward who joined the new union complained: 'In FOSATU and MAWU workers have been openly discouraged from taking up these [community] issues and political organisations have been openly criticised.' A MAWU steward dismissed the breakaway: 'They are interested in political trade unionism. They want to take up politics in the community.'[108]

The dangerous consequences of such a polarisation between community unionism and narrow economism were no doubt in

union leaders' minds when the township struggles exploded in the
Vaal Triangle a few months later. As the turmoil increased, and
especially after troops were used to search the Vaal townships house
by house in October 1984, calls for a stay-away mounted.

> With growing polarisation in the townships, the unions have been
> under pressure to give a political direction to their members... Unable
> to resist this pressure, intensified in the Transvaal with the entry of
> the Defence Force in the townships, these unions were catapulted
> into a central role in the stay-away. Thus when these trade unions
> were finally to move beyond the factory floor it was to be on terrain
> not fundamentally different from that criticised by Foster as non-
> worker controlled.[109]

Indeed the initiative for the November 1984 stay-away came
not from the unions but from the UDF-affiliated Congress of South
African Students. As in 1976, the school students demanded
solidarity from their parents. Three local stay-aways, in the Vaal
Triangle, Soweto and Kwa Thema, showed that the call had
support from many rank-and-file unionists.

In response to shop floor opinion, FOSATU and CUSA unions
participated in a meeting of 37 organisations, mainly youth and
community groups, on 27 October 1984 which called for a two-
day stay-away and set up a committee of four (including MAWU
steward Moses Mayekiso) to co-ordinate the action. The stay-away
was a success, and the state's attempts at retaliation by detaining
trade union and student leaders and sacking 5,000-6,000 workers
at the Sasol 2 and 3 coal-into-oil plants at Secunda were only
partially effective.

However the unions had been drawn into community action
on terms dictated largely by the populists. The stay-away was, like
its predecessors in the 1950s, the early 1960s, and 1976, an
extension of community action, based on township organisation
rather than workplace discipline and solidarity.[110]

If the November 1984 stay-away was an example of tailism on
the unions' part, the stay-away in the Port Elizabeth/Uitenhage
area on 18-22 March the following year was an instance of
abstentionism.[111]

The area is one of the main centres of the South African car
industry. It is also, like the Eastern Cape generally, a traditional
stronghold of the ANC. The Port Elizabeth car factories were
devastated by the recession: 31,000 workers in motor and related

industries lost their jobs in 1982-85. Black unemployment in Port Elizabeth was estimated at 56 per cent in August 1985.

The car-workers were a traditionally militant group, but there had been a history of divisions in the area. A bitter strike at Ford's in October-December 1979 led to a three-way split, between the FOSATU-aligned car unions, later to form the core of the National Automobile and Allied Workers Union, but dominated by the National Union of Motor Assembly and Rubber Workers, a Coloured union which had broken away from the white-dominated Trade Union Council (TUCSA); the more militant Ford Workers' Committee, led by Thozamile Botha, president of the Port Elizabeth Black Civic Organisation, and which was later to form the UDF-aligned Motor Assemblers and Component Workers; and more right-wing and middle-class elements who won control of the Port Elizabeth Black Civic Organisation (PEBCO).[112]

These divisions revived in a somewhat different form in 1985. PEBCO had by then become militant and UDF-aligned, but the running in the townships was made by the Port Elizabeth and Uitenhage Youth Congresses, which had been inspired by the Congress of South African Students. These groups were able to mobilise unemployed youth as well as school students: among the former were the 'guerrillas', who 'tend to be younger, less educated and less politically conscious than the average Congress member. They move around the townships in large groups and attack police and army vehicles, as well as councillors and black policemen.'[113]

The precise events leading up to the stay-aways are disputed. It seems that PEBCO called for a stay-away without consulting the unions. The idea was rejected by FOSATU and the other in dependent unions, as well as by the Black Consciousness movement. The unions were highly critical of PEBCO's demands, which were national, opposing increases in petrol prices and general sales tax; they also objected to the fact that no attempt was made to mobilise Coloured workers, and at the failure of PEBCO to do anything to protect unorganised workers from sacking.

The community organisations went ahead anyway and 90 per cent of African industrial workers joined the strike in Port Elizabeth on 18 March. Union leaders claimed that the high turn-out was a result of intimidation by PEBCO and the 'guerrillas'. The aftermath of the stay-away was even more bitter: the Motor Assemblers and Component Workers Union accused FOSATU of being indirectly responsible for the massacre by police of residents of Uitenhage's Langa township on Thursday 21 March as they made their way to a funeral which had been banned, allegedly as a result of union pressure to have funerals scheduled for the following weekend unbanned. A week later, however, 8,000 workers in FOSATU-organised factories stopped working in memory of those killed.

Whatever the rights and wrongs of the affair, the polarisation which it involved between workplace and community, workers and unemployed, was disastrous. It is difficult to disagree with Devan Pillay:

> Union leaders...were unable to appreciate the potential for a powerful united front to develop between the youth and organised workers. The youth had energy, courage and militancy. Workers had organisation, consistency and access to the means of production. By dwelling on the shortcomings of the call for a stay-away without posing alternatives, union officials and shop stewards missed an opportunity to take the struggle further.[114]

The danger of open political warfare between the 'unity unions', chiefly FOSATU and CUSA, both of which were then committed to a new 'super-federation', on the one hand, and the community unions and the UDF, on the other, was very real. Alarming rumours spread of plans to revive SACTU within the country.[115]

Three factors prevented this new and very serious split from developing, and led to the formation of COSATU at the end of November 1985.

First, the ANC/SACP leadership in exile appear to have intervened to prevent the community unions from launching SACTU. They must have recognised the distinct possibility of the most powerful unions merging anyway, and preferred to be in a position to influence them rather than base themselves on the much weaker community unions.

Secondly, the CUSA and its affiliates, with one exception, had second thoughts about unity, ostensibly because they objected to one of the five principles adopted as a basis for unity in May 1985, namely non-racialism (the others were one union-one industry, workers' control, representation on the basis of paid-up membership, and co-operation at a national level in the new federation). CUSA withdrew, to form with AZACTU a loose grouping of Black Consciousness unions representing between 100,000 and 150,000 paid-up members.[116]

The third factor was the one CUSA union to join the new federation, the National Union of Mineworkers. CUSA's annual congress voted in August 1982 to launch the NUM. The previous month 100 miners had been killed and thousands deported when the mines were hit by strikes and riots over pay increases. This explosion was the culmination of ten years' of labour unrest in South Africa's key industry as the mines' predominantly black migrant workforce rebelled against the conditions of near-slavery to which they are subject—all-male compounds, company police, the tribalist *induna* system—and were able to exploit the gradual erosion of whites' monopoly of skilled jobs to win higher wages. The 1982 struggles pushed one wing of the Chamber of Mines, notably Anglo-American and Rand Mines, into encouraging the formation of black unions as a means of stabilising the workforce.

The chief beneficiary of this change of tack was the NUM, which grew astonishingly fast, till by late 1985 it was claiming 230,000 signed-up members, and had signed 52 recognition agreements.[117] The NUM pursued a distinctive strategy. Whereas MAWU had adopted a methodical approach, trying to build up support carefully in an individual plant before pressing management for recognition and only then moving to the next factory, the NUM built by mass mobilisation, mounting big rallies in order to generate enthusiasm for the union and sign workers up. Despite the use of radical rhetoric, the NUM leadership, headed by general secretary Cyril Ramaphosa, adopted a cautious strategy towards the Chamber of Mines.

In both 1984 and 1985 the union's annual pay claim involved a carefully orchestrated campaign following the collective bargaining procedures laid down by law, and involving strike ballots. In September 1984 a strike in Anglo gold mines was called off at the last minute, but not before 70,000 workers took part in industrial action.

A year later the Chamber of Mines split, with one group of hard-liners headed by the great Afrikaner house Gencor refusing to follow Anglo and the others in improving their offer. The NUM reacted by calling out only its members in the comparatively weakly organised mines owned by the hard-liners. Between 10,000 and 30,000 workers responded to the call. The strike was rapidly smashed by state and company security forces. Ramaphosa reacted by taking Gencor and its allies to the Industrial Court, set up in 1979 as part of the Wiehahn reforms in order to supervise collective bargaining on behalf of the state.[118]

NUM's break with CUSA came in August 1985, at a special conference which called the second of the union's abortive strikes. The decision by NUM, now probably the largest union in the entire African continent, to throw its lot in with FOSATU guaranteed that the new federation would be a formidable force.

COSATU, at its launch, embraced 34 unions organising 450,000 paid-up members and 565,000 signed-up members.

The NUM leadership seems to have played a crucial role at the founding congress as arbiters between the 'workerists' and the 'populists', FOSATU and the community unions. Both sides made significant concessions. By accepting the principle of one union, one industry, SAAWU and the other UDF-aligned general unions voted for their own eventual dissolution. On the other hand, UDF supporters were heavily represented in the COSATU leadership: they included the new federation's president, Elijah Barayi (NUM), general secretary, Jay Naidoo (Sweet, Food and Allied Workers Union), and assistant general secretary, Sydney Mafumadi (General and Allied Workers Union). The most clearly aligned 'workerist' office-holder was COSATU treasurer Maxwell Xulu (MAWU).

Although COSATU remained unaffiliated to either the UDF or the National Forum, the new federation seemed immediately swept into an overtly political orientation. Barayi addressed a mass rally at the founding congress. He called for the nationalisation of the mines and other major industries, backed the international disinvestment campaign, and threatened a mass pass-burning campaign unless the pass laws were repealed within six months. A few days later Jay Naidoo met ANC leaders in Harare, capital of Zimbabwe.

Neither of these political initiatives had been sanctioned by the COSATU central executive committee. The fear was naturally expressed on the left that the new federation had been hijacked by the populists. Defenders of the 'survivalist' strategy of the old FOSATU left were more sanguine. They argued that the UDF unions lacked a shopfloor base, and that their official machines would soon disintegrate once they were merged with the industrial unions.

Certainly COSATU itself was a historic achievement, even

though the withdrawal of CUSA and its alliance with AZACTU left major unions outside the new federation. It was also far better to have 'workerists' and 'populists' united in the same federation, creating the possibility of open debate on the basis of united action, than to risk more damaging polarisations between unions and UDF like that in Port Elizabeth.

At the same time, the trade union left continued to underestimate the political threat from the Congress and its allies. The mass support which the ANC and UDF enjoy means that they can exercise an influence within COSATU out of proportion to their organisational muscle. The workerists could, in a political confrontation with the populists, find the rank-and-file organisation they have painfully built up taken away from under them.

It is true that the more powerful industrial unions, above all the NUM, would probably call the shots in COSATU and resist a UDF takeover. But the NUM leadership has built through a strategy of mass mobilisation combined with the avoidance of confrontation with the Chamber of Mines. Sooner or later there would have to be a reckoning, not just with Gencor and the other hard-line mining houses, but also with such 'liberal' employers as Anglo-American. Anglo still maintains a highly repressive labour regime in the mines, helping to provoke a wave of struggles in early 1985, culminating in the sacking of 14,000 workers at Anglo's Vaal Reefs mine at the end of April.[119]

Only determined leadership and strong shaft organisation could permit the NUM to win the inevitable trial of strength. But despite an emphasis on shaft stewards as the basis of the union, it was not clear how solid NUM's roots were. There have been other black unions in South African history which have grown fast only to vanish under the hammer of repression, for example the African Mine Workers Union and the Non-European Confederation of Iron, Steel and Metal Workers Unions in the 1940s. The latter soared to 35,000 members during the Second World War, only to sink to 96 by 1950.[120] It remains to be seen whether NUM will avoid this fate [see Chapter 5].

The basic failure of the trade union left is that they do not recognise that an independent and class-conscious proletariat depends on more than strong workplace organisation. It also requires an organised political alternative to populism, a revolutionary workers' party. What then of those sections of the left which have placed the main emphasis on political organisation?

The political left:
1: The Marxist Workers' Tendency of the ANC (MWT)

Trotskyism, as we have seen, has been an open force in South Africa since the early 1930s, and the three organisations considered here all derive from this tradition. The Marxist Workers' Tendency is considered here first, not because it is the oldest, but because it represents an intermediate position between building an independent organisation and working within broader fronts.

The MWT is perhaps the best-known far left group in South Africa, even though it is not clear how much support it has within the country. It originated among some of the most talented white radicals to emerge in the late 1960s and early 1970s, including David Hemson, an early organiser for the textile union in Natal, and the brilliant historian Martin Legassick. Exiled in Britain, they joined the ANC and began to work with SACTU. They also fell under the influence of the Militant Tendency which operates inside the British Labour Party. One of them, Robin Petersen, was editor of SACTU's paper, **Workers' Unity**.

In July 1979 Petersen was sacked from this job. Subsequently he was suspended from the ANC, along with Hemson, Legassick, and Paula Ensor. The 1985 ANC conference voted to confirm their expulsion. The group's crime was to have argued for a serious orientation on the black working class, and to have protested against SACTU's traditional role as a recruiting ground for MK.[121]

At the beginning of 1981 the MWT surfaced publicly, launching a magazine intended for circulation inside South Africa and called **Inqaba ya Basebenzi**. Its orientation was spelled out in the first issue:

> We will do our utmost to build up the ANC as a mass revolutionary organisation of the working class that can show the way forward to the socialist revolution.[122]

The MWT were already involved in a British-based organisation, the South African Labour Education Project, which seeks to build direct links between rank-and-file trade unionists in the West and the independent unions in South Africa, organising a tour by a striking British miner, Roy Jones, for the South African NUM. The project also established itself in Zimbabwe, and became involved in the local union movement, activities which led to the arrest and deportation of Hemson, Darcy du Toit and Anneke Poppe in April 1985, and the detention and torture of a number of Zimbabwean trade union activists.[123] The project is currently [1986] being witch-hunted in Britain by the Labour Party national executive.

Enemies such as these are an excellent recommendation. The MWT is indeed a serious organisation which has produced some of the best recent analysis of the struggle in South Africa. Its basic perspective is very similar to that developed in this book: like the Socialist Workers Party in Britain, the MWT sees a process of permanent revolution at work in South Africa which can only be accomplished by the working class seizing power to achieve both national liberation and the overthrow of capital.

Moreover, the MWT is not just a South African version of Militant. Thus Militant has traditionally argued that a successful socialist revolution in South Africa requires the unity of white and black workers—a position typical of the old Marxist left in South Africa and one which involves the same sort of abstract class politics which leads Militant to deny the existence of national oppression in Ireland and to refuse to side with the IRA against British imperialism.

The Inqaba group's approach is much more subtle and realistic than that of their British co-thinkers. Thus they recognise that because of the ruling-class offensive which has driven down white as well as black living standards,

> the era of the tame white working class is coming to an end. But, because an *independent class movement* is impossible among a privileged aristocracy of labour seeking to defend their position *against* the demands of the low-paid and oppressed mass of workers, this revolt among the whites inevitably falls at first into the clutches of the most reactionary bourgeois and petty bourgeois Nationalist politicians... The overall line of development [among whites] will be towards the right.[124]

At the same time, the MWT point to the material advantage which the ruling class derives from its popular base among whites—a factor crucial to its monopoly of physical force:

> Unless we can break the ability of the state to rely on the support of the white workers and middle class we shall leave a monstrous apparatus of repression in the hands of the ruling class, ready and able to wreak savage destruction upon our people... Of course it would

be Utopian to imagine that the mere proclamation of a socialist programme could lead to any significant number of white workers crossing to the side of the black workers and social revolution. *It is the organisation of the black workers as the decisive, conscious force of revolution, the arming of the mass movement and its adoption of a socialist programme, which alone can draw the white working class and middle class in any significant numbers to our side.*[125]

This orientation—a class appeal to white workers on the basis of the independent and leading role of the black proletariat—corresponds to the practice of the FOSATU unions. Thus the car union NAAWU was able to win over about twenty-five white workers from the traditionally ultra-racist Yster en Staal union in the Volkswagen plant in Uitenhage.[126] The two main white federations, TUCSA and SACOL, are both in a state of acute crisis, caught between employers intent on deskilling, Botha's reforms and the independent unions, and have suffered a series of breakaways to both left and right.

There are other respects in which the MWT has developed a cogent analysis of the current situation: it is, for example, firmly opposed to the ANC/UDF's adoption of tactics based on the assumption that the question of state power is on the agenda. Inqaba has argued correctly, drawing on the experience of the revolutionary movement internationally, that 'a victorious insurrection is not possible immediately or even in the relatively short term.'[127]

Nevertheless the MWT's strategy is crippled by certain errors which do derive from the version of Marxism which they share with Militant. These derive ultimately from a tendency mechanically to derive political developments from economic processes. Two examples are worth noting.

The first is the MWT's catastrophism, its denial that a bourgeois solution to South Africa's crisis is possible. Thus: 'We cannot conceive of conditions which would permit an ANC government on a bourgeois basis.'[128] Though Inqaba cannot conceive of such an outcome, it is clear that South African capital and its Western counterparts can do so very easily.

The MWT's reasons for denying such a possibility are, first, the depth of South Africa's economic crisis, and, secondly, the difficulties of reconstructing a capitalist state apparatus based on the white masses, whose privileges an ANC government would threaten. Both these obstacles are real enough, and make a Lancaster House-type deal much less likely than it was in Zimbabwe. However they are not insuperable, given that one major political condition is met, namely the absence of an independent working-class movement. Were the ANC able to dominate the workers' movement politically, they could impose a capitalist solution in the same way that, after the collapse of fascist rule in the 1970s, the Spanish and Portuguese Communist Parties were able to prevent socialist revolutions throughout the Iberian peninsula.

This brings us to the other main difficulty with the MWT's strategy, which is, of course, its entrist approach to the ANC. This is a mirror image of Militant's orientation on the Labour Party in Britain. **Inqaba**'s main slogan is 'Build a mass ANC on a socialist programme!' They were among the few on the non-Stalinist left to call for the unions to affiliate to the UDF (a demand which even Congress supporters have dropped as part of the deal involved in the creation of COSATU).

The MWT are adamant:

> The revolutionary workers' party and workers' leadership which is needed in South Africa can be created successfully in a struggle of organised workers and youth to build and transform for their purposes the ANC itself.[129]

To support this claim they point to the undoubted popular support the ANC has within the country:

> There are a number of factors combining to produce support for the ANC. But at the root of it all is an historical law which is working itself out also in most, if not all, capitalist countries. This is that, when the mass of workers turn to struggle, they turn first to the established, traditional organisations associated with their struggle in the past.[130]

As a general proposition this is undoubtedly true. But from the fact that workers 'turn first to the established traditional organisations' does it follow that they will stick with them? The MWT assume that they will, and that they will transform the ANC into a revolutionary socialist workers' movement. Behind these claims lie a view of history as an automatic process whose forward march is irresistible: the masses will simply flock to the ANC and force it to the left.

Also involved is an overestimation of the extent to which

workers have already been won to socialism:

> Nine-tenths of a revolutionary consciousness is already provided in
> the experience of life of the oppressed working people. The remaining
> one-tenth…is a clear grasp of the necessity to dismantle the entire
> machinery of the capitalist state and replace it with democratic organs
> of a workers' state, resting on the power of an armed people.[131]

This assertion ignores the contradictory character of working-
class consciousness, the fact that, as I have already pointed out,
wide layers of the class are both workerists and populists, and see
no contradiction between these attitudes. Workers believe that their
class demands will be realised under an ANC regime. This belief
is mistaken, and there is thus a contradiction between the workerist
and populist elements of mass consciousness. This conflict is only
likely to become conscious as a result of workers' own experience
of struggle—for example, if the ANC leadership, once engaged in
negotiations with the regime, were to restrain strikes.

The MWT believe that this conflict can be acted out and
resolved within the framework of the ANC. This leads them, in
rather familiar terms, to 'denounce all sectarian splitting of the mass
organisations.'[132] Like the Militant, they encompass under 'mass
organisations' both trade unions and political organisations. This
leads them to dissolve the difference between the unions—workers'
basic defence organisations—and the ANC, which is a bourgeois-
nationalist movement run along extremely undemocratic lines.

The MWT's insistence on being a 'tendency' within the ANC
is especially Quixotic in the light of their summary treatment at
the ANC's hands. There are no signs of the ANC's internal regime
being liberalised as a result of the recent upsurge. Indeed, the
formal expulsion of Hemson and company in June 1985 was used
as the occasion for lengthy and widely publicised denunciations
of the MWT.[133]

Nor was there any evidence of the situation being any better
inside South Africa. According to unconfirmed reports, **Inqaba**
supporters were recently [1986] purged from the UDF in the
Eastern Cape. It was also reported that a popular slogan in the area
was 'Kill the Marxists!' It would be a mistake to regard this call
as mere words. Stalinism is alive and well in South Africa.

This is not to say that there is not a 'rational kernel' in the
MWT strategy. The UDF rank and file will have to be won to the
cause of socialist revolution. **Inqaba**'s mistake has been to believe

that this can occur only within the framework of the ANC/UDF, rather than through united action between socialists and populists around concrete questions of struggle, especially within the unions. But a precondition of the latter approach succeeding is that socialists should organise independently of the populists. Let us look then at those left organisations which work outside the Congress and its allies.

The Political left:
2 The Unity Movement

South Africa is an enormous country where regional differences are of great political importance. No one could understand the National Party unless they appreciated the long-standing conflict between its Transvaal and Cape affiliates. Regional factors are not relevant only to ruling-class politics: South African Trotskyism was born in the Western Cape, which remains the stronghold of the left. The area's peculiarities have placed their stamp upon the various left organisations, and on the milieu in which they operate.

The Cape is, in the first place, the region which has been subject to the longest continuous colonial occupation, since 1652. The result is a population whose polyglot character, blending the descendants of the original Khoisan inhabitants of the area, Xhosa-speaking Africans from further east, Malay slaves, Indian traders and indentured labourers, Dutch settlers, and French Huguenot refugees, makes a complete nonsense of the regime's racial classification system. This is reflected in the predominance of so-called 'Coloureds' in the Western Cape.

Another important factor is that, with important exceptions such as docks and construction, light industries such as food and beverages, clothing and textiles have prevailed within the area. There is a long tradition of trade unionism in the Western Cape, but the independent unions have yet to make major inroads. The local labour movement is still dominated by the established unions affiliated to TUCSA: these unions are as conservative there as in the rest of the country, though in the Western Cape they reflect the interests of mainly Coloured artisans rather than white workers. Although there have been a number of significant strikes in the area, the main challenge to the regime has come in recent years from Coloured and African school students. There were major risings led by students in 1976, 1980, and again in 1985.[134]

The Unity Movement has been the main left organisation in the Western Cape for over a generation. It was formed in 1943 as the Non-European Unity Movement (NEUM). The main issue which gave rise to it was that of non-collaboration with the regime, which in the late 1930s and early 1940s set up various stooge bodies, the Native Representative Council and the Coloured Affairs Council.

The NEUM emerged out of a campaign against the Coloured Affairs Council which won mass support among Coloured schoolteachers. The participation of the ANC and the Communist Party in the Native Representative Council created an immediate point of differentiation, as did the Communist Party's support for the Smuts government during the Second World War, in line with Stalinist policy internationally. This gave an opening to the Trotskyist Fourth International Organisation, which played a leading role in the campaign against the Coloured Affairs Council and in the formation of the NEUM.[135]

Although critical of the Communist Party's stageism and Popular Frontism, the NEUM did not adopt an explicitly socialist programme. Instead it presented itself as a united front, around the 'Ten-Point Programme' adopted in December 1943, which consisted of a set of minimum democratic demands whose implementation would amount to the dismantling of apartheid (although not, explicitly, of capitalism).

Secondly the Non-European Unity Movement, as its name suggests, laid great stress on the unity of all the oppressed, and on overcoming the divisions fostered among them by the regime. Thirdly, it adopted a policy of non-collaboration with the regime, involving a tendency on the part of the NEUM to put forward the tactic of boycotting apartheid institutions on all occasions.

The NEUM's contribution to the struggles of the 1940s and 1950s was by no means negligible. It was never a purely Coloured organisation. Indeed, under the leadership of I B Tabata, himself an African and a talented agitator, the NEUM played an important part in the resistance of peasants in the Reserves, especially the Transkei, to state-imposed Rural Rehabilitation Schemes and the tribal quisling institutions which formed the kernel of the Bantustans. The NEUM also played some part in the great peasant revolt in Pondoland at the end of the 1950s.[136]

The NEUM nevertheless suffered from two crippling

weaknesses. One was a characteristic Trotskyist failing, namely a tendency to propagandism. This took the form of, in every movement, simply counterposing the Ten-Point Programme to the policies of the ANC rather than focusing on concrete issues of struggle. Secondly, the NEUM generalised from its experience of peasant struggles. Tabata wrote of the 1940s:

> it was of paramount importance, to begin with, to concentrate on winning the support of the peasantry. This was not only because the landless peasants comprise by far the greatest majority, but because they are the most exploited and oppressed and therefore constitute the greatest revolutionary potential. In addition to this there is the all-important factor of migrant labour—that peculiar situation in South Africa where not only the mines and the white farms but also heavy industry are run on peasant labour. Thus no serious struggle could take place in South Africa without the participation and co-operation of the peasantry.[137]

This position amounted to denying the existence of a black proletariat in South Africa, since, on Tabata's analysis, African wage-labourers were primarily peasants. This argument was mistaken even in the 1940s: despite the undoubted importance of rural struggles in that period, the process of proletarianisation was already well-advanced, a situation reflected in the fact that, according to one estimate, no less than 40 per cent of Africans in commerce and private industry were at least intermittently unionised in 1945.[138]

Today, when the destruction of the peasantry and the dependence of the mass of the population on wage-labour have developed much further, the claim has become a dogmatic fantasy. Even in industries such as metals, where migrant labour still predominates, a long-term workforce based in the cities has developed.[139] Yet Tabata was still denying the existence of a stable black working class in discussions with Chris Harman, John Rogers and myself shortly after the Soweto uprising in June 1976.

After the defeats of the early 1960s, the Unity Movement of South Africa (as the NEUM was renamed) was driven into exile along with the ANC and the PAC. There it languished, complaining about the failure of the Organisation of African Unity to provide it with subsidies comparable to those of the other movements. There were various splits, beginning with an important one within South Africa itself in the late 1950s.

Despite these difficulties, the Unity Movement continued to receive considerable support, especially from Coloured and Indian school-teachers in the Western Cape. With the upsurge of the mid-1980s, this tradition resurfaced publicly. The New Unity Movement was launched in Cape Town in April 1985.

To what extent did the New Unity Movement represent a development of earlier policies? On the basic question of the peasantry its president, R O Dudley, told one interviewer: 'I don't think there has been any substantial shift in the Unity Movement position regarding organisation of rural and urban people.'[140] He continued to play down the extent of proletarianisation, arguing that 'South Africa has undergone so many distortions in its development that the traditional classification of classes has to be revised . . . It is a mistake to regard the wage as a deciding factor.'[141]

Dudley did concede that there had been some changes. He acknowledged the central role of the proletariat, though the emphasis was still on the countryside: 'The working class, rural and urban, must give direction to the struggle.'[142] He also admitted that 'a greater emphasis will be placed on the developing trade union movement within the national movement itself.'[143]

However the New Unity Movement did not seem to have any strategy for the unions, beyond attacks on economism which could have come equally from the UDF:

> it is the unwavering aim of the ruling class to neutralise the political power of the workers in political struggle by confining them to 'the business of trade unionism'. The trade unions must find their way to the broad liberatory movement. There can be no separate solution for workers organised in trade unions.[144]

The 'broad liberatory movement' was itself conceived on entirely traditional Unity Movement lines, with stress laid on 'building national unity of all democrats . . . on the basis of a *programme of minimum demands for full and equal citizenship*'.[145] Although the New Unity Movement denounced the UDF's populism, it seemed to offer in reality a left-wing version of traditional ANC/SACP stageism, in which all turns on implementing the minimum programme.

Only an orientation on the working class and its daily struggles with capital could open up a genuine perspective of permanent revolution. Yet when asked of the movement's 'immediate practical projects', Dudley replied: 'Mainly propaganda work, circulating our documents.'[146] The New Unity Movement was stuck in the old propagandist groove.

The Unity Movement remains the largest organisation to the left of the Communist Party. Yet its political weaknesses makes it incapable of providing a credible alternative to the dominant populist ideologies. Many of its supporters are reported to have joined the UDF. Creative initiatives came from elsewhere, on the trade union left and in the Cape Action League.

The political left:
3: The Cape Action League

As its name suggests, the Cape Action League (CAL) is, like the Unity Movement, based mainly in the Western Cape, although it has sympathisers in other parts of the country. CAL originated in opposition to the Koornhof Bills, which led to the formation in August 1982 of the Disorderly Bill Action Committee, representing over 60 unions, civics, and other community organisations in the Cape Town area. This committee soon polarised between ANC supporters and opponents. One issue was the involvement of white liberal organisations such as the student union NUSAS and Black Sash. Black Consciousness supporters opposed their participation on the grounds that they were white.

However the left within the committee went further, objecting to all organisations representing the interests of the liberal bourgeoisie: these included not just NUSAS and Black Sash but black middle-class groups such as the Western Cape Traders Organisation. The unions withdrew in order to avoid these arguments, and then in April 1983 the ANC elements pulled out and launched the Western Cape UDF. The organisations remaining in the committee renamed it the Cape Action League.

CAL took a vigorous part in agitation against the new Constitution—an important issue in the Western Cape since Coloureds were supposedly among its chief beneficiaries. CAL also played, as we have seen, a leading role in the formation of the National Forum and in its adoption of the explicitly socialist Azanian Manifesto.

CAL is a federal organisation, with some 40 affiliates, including eleven or twelve civics, and the Socialists of Young Azania. It is a multi-tendency organisation: among its affiliates are organisations sympathetic to the Unity Movement, for example the Southern Province Educational Fellowship, as well as the Western Cape Youth League, which is strongly critical of the CAL leadership from the left. However, CAL is not merely a united front around immediate demands. According to its media officer, 'what binds CAL together is a full commitment to the leadership of the working class, and the idea that only socialist solutions can bring about radical change in South Africa/Azania.'[147]

The core of CAL is provided by a groups of mainly Coloured and Indian political activists, many of them very experienced, veterans of the Unity Movement, who share a common theoretical understanding. The key figure is one of the most gifted Marxist intellectuals South Africa has yet produced, Neville Alexander. Alexander joined the NEUM while studying at the University of Cape Town in 1953. While studying in Germany in the late 1950s he became active in the SDS and made contact with European Trotskyists, most of who then believed, under the influence of Michael Pablo, that the colonial struggle had become the focus of the struggle for socialism.

Under the influence of the Chinese and Algerian examples, Alexander opted for a guerrilla strategy, an orientation which led to his suspension from the NEUM on his return to South Africa in 1961. He helped form the Yi Chi Chan Club, one of the constituents of the National Committee for Liberation, a united front of radical liberals and leftists which sought—like the ANC—to launch a sabotage campaign in the early 1960s and was also rapidly destroyed by the security police. (Other Trotskyists surrendered to guerrillaism at this time—for example Baruch Hirson, later the historian of the Soweto revolt).

Alexander was arrested in late 1963 and sentenced to ten years on Robben Island. Banned from political activity after his release until 1979, he has since emerged as one of the main leaders of the South African left.

Alexander's main theoretical contribution has been on the national question. In a book begun in prison and published under a pseudonym in 1979, he powerfully exposed the confused thinking on the national question among both the ANC/SACP and the non-Stalinist left, showing that all tended to accept the existence of a number of distinct racial or ethnic groups in South Africa.

Alexander argued that, in the first place, this view was

scientifically untenable, since there are no genetically based racial differences, while the notion of 'ethnicity' is equally metaphysical, involving little more than a cultural euphemism for the old, now disreputable vocabulary of biologically distinct races. Secondly, viewing South Africa as racially or ethnically divided had disastrous political consequences, since it gave credence to the regime's claim that South Africa consists of a 'plurality' of different groups, each with their own right to self-determination, thereby justifying the rejection of majority rule and the establishment of 'independent' tribal regimes in the Bantustans.

Alexander argued that the South African nation will be created in the course of the struggle to overthrow white rule on the basis of the unity of all the oppressed. Hence the title of his book: **One Azania, One Nation.**[153]

More recently Alexander has sought to clarify and develop his views. In the first place, he has drawn on the writings of various Western Marxists (for example Goran Therborn and Benedict Anderson) to argue that nations are historical constructs, contingent products of the class struggle, not natural pre-given entities. Therefore,

> while the nation may mean more or less the same thing at certain times to most of those who constitute it, it usually does not. Or, to put it differently, because the nation has to be constructed ideologically and politically on the basis of the developing, ie also changing, capitalist forces and relations of production, each of the antagonistic classes in the social formation, generally speaking, conceives of the nation differently in accordance with its class ideology.[154]

Secondly, different conceptions of the South African nation carry a particularly important political charge. It is essential to reject not just the regime's view of South Africa as ten or twelve nations, but also the conceptions prevalent within the resistance itself, where either a 'four-nation' (white, Coloured, Indian and African) or a 'two-nation' (white, black) theory is accepted (the latter based on the bankrupt theory of internal colonialism).

Alexander is emphatic:

> 'ethnic' or 'national group' approaches are the thin end of the wedge for separatist movements and civil wars fanned by great-power interests and suppliers of arms to opportunistic 'ethnic leaders'. Does not Inkatha in some ways represent a warning to us all?[155]

Thirdly, the notion of one South African or Azanian nation, transcending colour, language, religion and tribe, has a specific class content:

> Because of the peculiarities of capitalist development in South Africa, the only way in which racial discrimination and racial equality, ie national oppression, can be abolished is through the abolition of the capitalist structures themselves. The only class, however, which can bring into being such a (socialist) system is the black working class. On it, by virtue of its unique historical position, devolves the task of mobilising *all* the oppressed and exploited classes for the abolition of racial capitalism. In doing so, it *has to* unite the workers and their allies by undermining the divisive factors which have as a matter of policy been retained and invented by different ruling-class governments in order to disorganise the South African proletariat. Beyond that, the working class has to devise counter-hegemonic strategies and practices which prepare the ground, in fact will constitute the ground, upon which the Azanian nation will stand.[156]

Alexander's writings represent the richest and most suggestive discussion of the national question in South Africa. He is undoubtedly right to insist that there *is* such a question, that the exclusion of the mass of the population from the rights of citizenship creates a condition of national oppression. He is also right in stressing the importance of overcoming state-promoted 'ethnic' differences: in the light of the recent *pogroms* of 'tribal' outsiders organised by the KwaZulu and KwaNdebele Bantustan regimes, Alexander's warning of the danger of 'separatist movements and civil wars' may well prove to be prophetic.

However, there are some problems with Alexander's approach which could have major practical implications. Starting from the insight that nations are politico-ideological constructs, he has devoted some attention to the Althusserian and post-structuralist theories which stress the active role of language in the formulation and inculcation of ideologies. He concludes:

> it is necessary for the organic intellectuals of the working class to undertake the deconstruction of existing ideological discourses to which the black workers are subject . . . [and take on the task of] creating a new discourse.[153]

Alexander makes it clear that he is aware of the idealist tendencies of the theories he draws on, of the dangers, in other words, of seeing reality itself as something which is constructed within discourse. There is, however, a more specific problem, which is that of treating the development of revolutionary consciousness as essentially a process of ideological struggle through which 'organic intellectuals' create 'a new discourse' and inculcate it into the masses. There is some evidence of such a propagandist orientation on the part of the Cape Action League. Alexander himself is Cape Town director of the South African Council for Higher Education, which is involved in a variety of adult education programmes.

This implicit 'ideologism' on Alexander's part may also have consequences for how one attempts to connect the national and class struggles. The importance Alexander attached to building one nation and his stress on ideological struggle may have predisposed him in favour of Black Consciousness. Certainly his discussion of Black Consciousness in **One Azania, One Nation** was, while critical of its errors and confusions, sympathetic, detecting the gradual emergence of a class analysis of black collaborators. He argued: 'With such a class approach, all vestiges of a two-nation theory will be swept away, and replaced by that of a single nation in a non-racial socialist democracy.'[154]

This appraisal of Black Consciousness may help to explain CAL's alliance with AZAPO within the National Forum. CAL leaders have been eager to detect socialist tendencies within Black Consciousness; thus 'AZAPO's anti- collaborationist stance, its mass base, and its anti-imperialist stance . . . indicates [sic] its commitment to anti-liberalism', in other words 'anti-capitalism'.[155] This has sometimes led to bizarre political misjudgements—for example describing AZACTU as forming the left of the trade union movement![156]

This rather tolerant attitude towards AZAPO is the obverse of the league's hostility to the UDF. In part this reflects the particular circumstances in which the UDF was established in the Western Cape, as a breakaway from the original Disorderly Bill Action Committee. But it is also connected to a rather odd conception of the united front.

Alexander distinguishes between three sorts of unity. The first is 'tactical unity', two different organisations adopting the same tactic. The second is 'strategic unity', 'when two or more organisations with different principles and conceptions of struggle define their political goals during a given phase of the struggle in the same terms.' The united front is one example, but the popular front is not, since the latter is 'a bloc of classes [which] includes one or other section of the capitalist class, usually the liberal bourgeoisie.' Thirdly there is 'principled unity', when 'the different organisations come together to accept the same programme of principles and for all practical purposes behave as one party.'[157]

This approach is thoroughly unsatisfactory. In the first place, the distinction between the three levels of unity is not well drawn. 'Tactical unity' is no form of unity at all, since, to judge by the example Alexander gives, that of AZAPO and Inkatha both boycotting a community council election, it need not involve any practical collaboration at all. The united front is, furthermore, conceived by Alexander as having a much stronger and more enduring basis than Lenin or Trotsky ever thought, as is clear from the remark that:

> often the successful united front leads to a converging and even a merging of parties that were previously opposed to or in competition with one another. The prevailing spirit in a united front is one of tolerance for the other parties' point of view within the framework of the common strategic goal.[158]

Strategic unity is thus seen as leading naturally to principled unity. This does not correspond to the theory and practice of the Bolsheviks and the early Comintern. Here the united front involved practical collaboration around immediate questions of struggle between organisations otherwise bitterly opposed to each other— for example the united front between Kerensky and the Bolsheviks against Kornilov. Moreover, as this example suggests, the united front does not end the struggle between the collaborating parties— on the contrary, Lenin, Trotsky and Gramsci all argued that it was an intensification of that struggle, revolutionaries using the tactic to show in practice their greater consistency than the non-revolutionary leaders and thereby to win away the latter's rank and file.

Secondly, is it always wrong to collaborate with organisations which represent the interests of the bourgeoisie? Absolutely not. The united front was developed by the early Comintern precisely to allow the Communist Parties to relate to the supporters of the social-democratic parties—what Lenin called bourgeois workers' parties. One might say that these parties are not the open instruments of big capital, but then neither is the ANC, yet.

CAL invokes Lenin's critique of Menshevism.[159] But Lenin attacked the Mensheviks for giving the liberal bourgeoisie the leading role in the revolution, not for ever forming united fronts with them. At the Second Comintern Congress in 1920 he argued that the Communist Parties should co-operate with 'revolutionary-democratic' movements of the colonial bourgeoisie.

The Marxist critique of Popular Frontism has been aimed at the idea of strategic alliances with a section of the bourgeoisie in which the proletariat's interests are subordinated to those of 'democratic' capital, and does not imply that it is always wrong to have a united front (in the classical sense, not Alexander's) with bourgeois organisations.

The effect of CAL's muddled conception of unity, and their remarkably tolerant attitude towards Black Consciousness, is to commit them to a long-term alliance with AZAPO (culminating in a single organisation?) and to rule out serious united-front work with the UDF. Given the political and ideological hold which Congress has on the black masses, this is a very serious weakness.

These criticisms should not be taken as dismissing lightly the obstacles to joint work with UDF supporters. The undemocratic, often Stalinist and sometimes murderous treatment of dissenters by the ANC/SACP leadership makes united activity often very difficult. But there is one real forum where such activity can take place, namely the independent unions.

Unfortunately the unions do not figure significantly in CAL's strategy. This is not simply a consequence of the weakness and conservatism of the Western Cape labour movement. CAL is rightly critical of the economism of the FOSATU left. However, its own orientation is firmly on the community. CAL itself is a federation of civics and other community organisations. Its youth affiliate, Socialists of Young Azania, was very active in the high-school struggle in 1985, for example building the Western Cape Students Action Committee as a broad united organisation (embracing, incidentally, UDF and Black Consciousness supporters).

It is absolutely essential for revolutionaries to be involved in such struggles, but it seems as if CAL's strategic orientation is on the community. The argument seems to be that workers exist in the townships as well as in the factories, and that community organisations involve broader issues than those of the trade union struggle.

Both propositions are true enough, but they slide over the question of power. It is only in the mines and factories that workers can develop the collective strength to overthrow the state. Community struggles have again and again exploded to shake the state, but, as we have seen, have always been contained and eventually crushed. The key question is how to use the industrial muscle black workers are developing for political ends.

The Cape Action League does not address this question. It is an organisation possessing an impressive cadre of experienced activists and young agitators. It is theoretically creative and has had a real impact on resistance politics during its brief existence. Yet on the evidence I have given it has yet fully to break with the propagandism of the Unity Movement. It is therefore liable to the danger of degenerating into a form of left populism.

Party and class in South Africa

The trade union and political left in South Africa mirror each other's strengths and weaknesses. The trade union left recognise the decisive importance of organising the black working class. However they have no conception of how to build the political alternative essential if COSATU is not to become an appendage of the ANC/UDF. **Inqaba,** the Unity Movement and the Cape Action League are perfectly well aware of the unions' political weaknesses, but tend simply to counterpose the economic class struggle to political organisation, which always takes place outside the workplaces, whether that be the UDF or the Unity Movement or CAL themselves, all, in any case, township-based movements.

Remedying these faults depends on the left understanding and applying two of the central concepts of classical Marxism—the mass strike and the revolutionary party.

Rosa Luxemburg's great text **The Mass Strike** is often quoted in Marxist writing on South Africa, but its significance is not usually understood. The mass strike is the great absence in the struggle in South Africa. Stay-aways are *not* mass strikes in Luxemburg's sense. They are an extension of township-based action, do not arise from workers' own initiative, and are not based on workplace organisation. These criticisms were made twenty-five years ago, but they are obviously relevant to recent stay-aways, which were initiated and, certainly in the case of the Port Elizabeth strike, enforced by community organisations.[160]

The importance of genuine mass strikes for Luxemburg is that they arise from workers' own activity, draw into struggle and are often initiated by 'backward' and unorganised layers of the class, tend to unite the whole of the proletariat across sectional divisions, and transcend the barrier between politics and economics, posing the question of state power. The interaction of economic and political struggles which they typically involve means that strikes for higher wages, for example, will strengthen the broader political movement by raising workers' confidence, organisation and consciousness.

The history of mass strikes stretches from Russia in 1905, the occasion of Luxemburg's original analysis, to Poland in 1980-81. They provide the soil from which *soviets* emerge, uniting workers around the question of state power.

The struggle in South Africa today is characterised by a contradiction, since the township struggles have tended to radicalise into bitter confrontations with the state, while the workers' movement remains confined to the trade union struggle. This contradiction will be resolved in one of three ways: the temporary collapse of the township risings (as in 1976 and 1980); negotiations between the regime and the ANC (unlikely at the present stage); or a mass strike movement which creates a genuinely revolutionary situation.

One cannot predict *when* such revolutionary mass strikes will develop, but *that* they will develop seems certain. The concrete circumstances of South African capitalism—its structural crisis, the serious obstacles facing any bourgeois solution, the existence of a powerful and oppressed working class—all create a climate in which explosive political struggles by the black proletariat are likely to develop at some time in the future.

The mass strike poses the question of power, but does not solve it. The experience of *Solidarnosc* in Poland, much studied by the South African left, confirms this. Without a revolutionary party which fights within all the mass organisations of the working class to win a majority for the seizure of power, and which takes on the tasks required for a successful insurrection—above all, exploiting the contradictions within the ruling-class camp to win over sections of the armed forces (more than 20 per cent of operationally deployed troops and nearly 50 per cent of the regular South African Police are black)[161] and arm the masses—even the greatest workers' movement will be defeated.

There are two particular misconceptions among South African socialists concerning the relation between party and class. One is to the effect that the classical argument for a revolutionary party does not apply to South Africa—because it presupposes the existence of a trade union movement dominated by a reformist bureaucracy. But, it is claimed, to believe that trade unions in South Africa will conform to this pattern is to succumb to a 'Eurocentric' way of thinking.

Now it is certainly true that there are different sorts of trade unionism. Tony Cliff and Donny Gluckstein contrast the classic trade union bureaucracy which developed in Britain in conditions of imperialist expansion with the revolutionary unions in Russia, which emerged in 1917 in conditions where the barrier between economics and politics had broken down and *soviets* and a mass revolutionary party already existed.[162] Trade unions in South Africa have developed, however, in conditions which correspond to neither of these situations. South African capitalism suffers from deep structural conditions which doom it to protracted crises and force it into continued dependence on ultra-cheap labour. But neither does there exist in South Africa today a revolutionary situation.

The trade union bureaucracy is, in any case, not a phenomenon unique to the advanced capitalist countries, nor does it arise, as Lenin mistakenly argued, from a labour aristocracy which lives off the super-profits of imperialism.[163] A tendency towards bureaucracy is inherent in trade unions. They are mass organisations which workers build in order to defend and improve their conditions within the framework of capitalism. They thus arise from workers accepting a self-denying ordinance, from their not recognising, or not feeling confident enough to confront the necessity of seizing state power.

As long as workers so limit themselves, their struggles must inevitably end in compromise with capital. This creates the need for a layer of officials to negotiate the terms of this compromise, and with it the terms on which workers are exploited. It is this process which gives rise to the trade union bureaucracy.

No honest observer of the independent unions in South Africa can deny the existence of bureaucratic tendencies within them. This is not simply true of those unions which have been used by black middle-class elements in the leadership as a means of self-aggrandisement (there is unfortunately a long history of this in South Africa), but even of unions such as MAWU which are seen, and rightly so, as on the left of the movement because of their militancy and stress on rank-and-file control. Eddie Webster writes of MAWU:

> There is evidence that decisions that go beyond the immediate concerns of the shop floor are made at leadership level with limited participation outside this group. The clearest illustration of this is the nature of decision-making over registation. This issue was first discussed in the NEC [National Executive Committee], and the national organiser led the discussion on the pros and cons of registration. It was then referred to the BECs [Branch Executive Committees] and some delegates discussed it with the shop stewards. The final decision was made at the NEC where consensus was established to register conditionally. Although a discussion took place at the 1979 AGM, no decision was made there. Only 200 people attended. This tendency to concentrate participation on certain issues in the hands of a small number of people was increased further once the decision to register was made.[164]

The increased involvement of the independent unions in state-promoted forms of collective bargaining is likely to intensify these tendencies. MAWU's decision to join the Industrial Council for the metal industry in 1983, perhaps justified on tactical grounds, undoubtedly carried the risk of further distancing the union leadership from the shop floor. All this is more true of a union like the NUM, built much less methodically from below than MAWU and carefully avoiding confrontation with the Chamber of Mines. The tendency of the unions to invoke state institutions such as the Industrial Court in order to counterbalance the bosses' strength again is likely to increase bureaucratisation.[165]

There are, of course, important counter-tendencies. One is the widespread development of strong rank-and-file workplace organisation. An important feature has been the emergence of forms of organisation embracing workers across different plants—the shop stewards' councils formed in various areas by MAWU stewards and the FOSATU locals, twenty-two of which had been formed by the end of 1984, bringing together stewards from different industries. These locals are to be continued and developed by COSATU, and could form an important means of co-ordinating class-wide action from below.

More fundamental, however, is the position of South African capitalism. The continual denial of citizenship rights to the black majority, and the dependence of major industries on migrant labour mean that no stable separation of politics and economics, of the sort crucial to Western reformism, can develop. The unions will therefore constantly be forced to involve themselves in politics: indeed every strike still involves, to some degree, a confrontation with the state. These circumstances make it difficult for a consolidated labour bureaucracy to entrench itself.

These counter-tendencies do not however remove the dangers inherent in trade unionism of a bureaucracy developing. The example of *Solidarnosc* shows how even a weak and embryonic reformist layer can disastrously hold back a mass movement. It is vital to draw the necessary conclusion: a workers' party must be built.

This brings me to a second misconception, which concerns how such a party should be built. The British Labour left group Socialist Organiser argues that 'the best way forward would be a workers' party based on the trade unions. In form it could be similar to the British Labour Party.'[166] One might be tempted to dismiss this as just an extension of specifically British misconceptions to South Africa: Socialist Organiser want a South African Labour Party in order to have something to enter, while Inqaba think the ANC *is* the Labour Party, even though they aren't allowed to enter it.

However, the idea of such a trade union-based party has a resonance in South Africa. Metalworkers' leader Moses Mayekiso, who supports the idea, said in August 1985: 'Yes, it will be formed . . . next year. It's a possibility. People are discussing it heavily at the present moment.'[167] Mayekiso was undoubtedly too sanguine: given the setbacks suffered by the trade union left, reflected in the terms on which COSATU was established, it seems very unlikely that the unions, or even one wing of them, will establish a labour party.

Were such a party nonetheless to emerge it would be an important development, and one to which socialists would have to relate very seriously indeed. But it does not follow that, as one of the defenders of a labour party puts it, its formation is 'the vital next step in the development of the workers' movement in South Africa.'[168] The reason quite simply is that a labour party would not overcome the contradictory consciousness of black workers, the amalgam of workerism and populism which even most of the best militants accept.

A labour party would reflect all the unevenness of the black proletariat, a class whose consciousness stretches from tribalism to revolutionary socialism. Even the proponents of a labour party themselves implicitly concede this point. Socialist Organiser admits that 'many of the younger shop stewards are active supporters of the UDF or the . . . National Forum.'[169]

This immediately raises a crucial problem for this political perspective. How could a labour party embracing such a broad political spectrum present an alternative to the populist ideologies that currently predominate in the black working class? Embracing the backward as well as the advanced layers of the class, it would in all probability reproduce the vacillations of the emerging trade union bureaucracy.

The workers' party which South Africa needs cannot therefore be based on the trade unions. The unions are, however, crucial to the development of the socialist left in South Africa. It is through the daily battle with capital, developing into mass strikes, that black workers will develop the organisation, confidence and consciousness required to make a revolution. The central arena of activity by revolutionary socialists in South Africa is the independent unions. As we have seen, it is a principal failing of such groups as the Cape Action League that they have not grasped and acted on this proposition.

However the revolutionary socialist party of the future cannot, as we have seen, start as a mass party based on the unions. It can only begin with the initially tiny minority of socialists who accept the need for the revolutionary overthrow of capital by the black working class. Experience shows that this minority can, in periods of mass struggle, grow and win the support of ever wider layers of the proletariat. But the minority has first to be organised so that it can relate in a systematic way to workers' struggles, involving itself in the strike movements where class consciousness can develop by leaps and bounds.

It follows that the main task in South Africa today is what Trotsky called the primitive accumulation of cadres. Socialists, wherever they find themselves—in the unions, the community organisations, the established left groups, or academic isolation—

need to gather together to hammer out a common basis for activity.

This necessarily involves a process of political clarification. Effective common activity by socialists presupposes a shared theoretical understanding. This means reaching agreement on the burning questions discussed in this book—the nature of South African capitalism, the existence of national oppression, the necessity of socialist revolution, the central role of the black working class, the essential need for a revolutionary party.

But there are other, apparently more remote questions which would require clarification. The South African left has tended, for example, to ignore the issue of the 'socialist' countries, beyond a principled anti-Stalinism and support for workers' struggles in countries such as Poland. Even as sophisticated an organisation as the Cape Action League is agnostic on the class nature of the Soviet Union. But this is a question with vital political implications: to describe the Eastern bloc as socialist or 'post-capitalist' because of the existence there of state ownership is to break the identification of socialism with workers' power generally made on the South African left. The necessary process of political clarification could not, therefore, confine itself to purely South African issues.

Discussion cannot, however, go on without end. It would have to terminate in agreement on practical activity.

Above all, the sort of exchange and development of views I am advocating would be fruitless unless it led to the formation of a socialist organisation. Without such an organisation, however small, to lay the basis of a revolutionary workers' party, the enormous potential revealed by the black proletariat in South Africa will go to waste, and the inspiring revolts of the past decade will end in defeat and betrayal.

South Africa has a rich history of struggle, and a lively and creative left. The emergence of the independent workers' movement since the early 1970s has created a historic opportunity—to sweep away the horrors of apartheid and with it the capitalist system which has battened off the system of racial domination. For this opportunity to be realised the left must now take a step forward and begin to build a workers' party. Socialists elsewhere cannot do the job for their South African comrades. But they can and should contribute to the process of political clarification essential to creating a revolutionary organisation. Such has been the aim of this chapter.

Chapter five:
State of Siege: South Africa under emergency rule
(July 1988)

ON 12 JUNE 1986 P W Botha, the South African State President, announced that he had declared a nation-wide state of emergency. His proclamation came after nearly two years of the greatest popular insurgency against white rule in South African history. An earlier state of emergency, declared in thirty-six magisterial districts on 21 July 1985 and extended to the Western Cape on 25 October, had failed to stem the tide of mass rebellion in the black townships. It was lifted in March 1986.

Many opponents of apartheid were tempted to dismiss the new emergency as a similarly ineffective measure. Even on the left, the Marxist Workers' Tendency chose to assert in November 1986 that the period since the township risings began in September 1984 represented 'the opening phase of the South African revolution.'[1] Such expectations proved to be based on illusion. The state of emergency marked a shift to a qualitatively more intense level of repression:

> By June 1987, over 26,000 people had been detained. In eight months of this emergency, security police detained as many people as the total held under previous emergencies and security legislation for the past 26 years. Internationally, South Africa is now second to none on an index of repression.[2]

A year after the emergency was imposed, Patrick Laurence, writing in the anti-apartheid Johannesburg **Weekly Mail**, sought to measure the scale of the defeat inflicted on the popular resistance:

> The success of the emergency in slowing and, in places, halting revolutionary violence—though not, of course, state violence—is

manifest in official figures. There has been an 80 per cent decrease in violent acts of rebellion since 12 June, according to Deputy Law and Order Minister Roelf Meyer.

These figures may not reflect counter-revolutionary violence by vigilantes and the security forces. But they cannot be dismissed as mere manipulation of facts, behind a screen of press restrictions, by the Bureau for Information and the Police Division of Public Relations. There are independent pointers of the scale of counter-revolution.

Townships which were strongholds of the 'comrades' in late 1985 and early 1986 are today largely under the control of pro-government forces.

To cite three examples: Alexandra, on the outskirts of Johannesburg, is now ruled by a white administrator and earmarked for upgrading by a counter-revolutionary Joint Management Centre; in KwaNobuhle, in the Eastern Cape, vigilantes have gained the upper hand; and at Crossroads, near Cape Town, Johnson Ngxobongwana rules supreme after the *witdoeke* vigilantes routed anti-apartheid activists, allegedly with police help.[3]

At the end of 1987 the **Weekly Mail** reported on the situation in the Eastern Cape, during 1984-86 the area where mass resistance to the state reached its highest level:

The Eastern Cape was the frontier of resistance last year but all that crumbled in 1987.

Over the past twelve months, resistance in the townships moved from the barricades in the streets into the courts. Small legal victories have been the only weapon against repression...

The state's new strategy has succeeded in dividing and confusing people, says Andile Sindelo, general secretary of the Eastern Cape Youth Congress [Ecayco], a branch of the South African Youth Congress.

This year's detentions, harassment and intimidation have crushed the youth movement, he said. The majority of Ecayco's regional executive was detained this year, including the president, Monde Mtanga, two weeks ago. Of the 57 youth congresses in the Eastern Cape, few are operating. An attempt has been made to revive these organisations but 'people can't work effectively under the state of emergency', Sindelo said...

Alternative government structures like street and area committees have suffered the same fate... In Uitenhage the committees are a thing of the past as the emergency has made it impossible for people to meet. Vigilante action and municipal police harassment has divided the community.

At the beginning of 1986 only 18 of the 45 [African] town councils under the then East Cape Development Board were still functioning. In all, 173 councillors quit in the wake of widespread and often violent opposition to participation in structures established under the Black Local Authorities Act.

But, up until November this year, only five councils in the region were still not functioning.'

An even grimmer indication of the degree to which the anti-apartheid resistance had been driven on the defensive was provided by events in Natal. There, in the African townships around the provincial capital of Pietermaritzburg, activists of the United Democratic Front (UDF) and the Congress of South African Trade Unions (COSATU) found themselves engaged in savage fighting with supporters of Inkatha yeSizwe, the tribal mass movement headed by Mangosuthu Gatsha Buthelezi, chief minister of the KwaZulu Bantustan. While Botha's troops and police stood by, the slaughter claimed hundreds of lives.

The régime's confidence was underlined on 24 February 1988, when it effectively banned seventeen anti-apartheid organisations, including the UDF and the black-consciousness Azanian People's Organisation (AZAPO). When the Anglican Archbishop of Cape Town, Desmond Tutu, led a march on parliament to protest against the bannings, the police waded in with mass arrests and turned their water-cannon onto clergymen who sat down in the streets. In New York, South Africa's representative to the United Nations defiantly challenged the world to 'do your damnedest'.

There can be no doubt, then, of the scale of the defeat suffered by the resistence to white rule since June 1986. But how was it that a mass movement which for nearly two years shook South Africa from top to bottom was crushed with such comparative ease? How serious a setback has it suffered? What now is the strategy of the régime and how secure is its own social base? And what is the way forward for the forces fighting apartheid? These are some of the questions I shall try to answer in this concluding chapter.

The limits of the 1984-86 upsurge

The upswing of mass struggles which began in the townships

of the Vaal Triangle south of Johannesburg in September 1984 had two main elements.⁵ First, the black townships were the centres of popular rebellions directed at the state itself and those aligned to it—African town-councillors, policemen, informers and the like. At its highest level township resistance gave birth to political structures intended both to co-ordinate mass resistance and to lay the basis for an alternative, popular form of state power—thus, in the Eastern Cape and elsewhere, networks of street and area committees and people's courts were formed. Perhaps the most important social force in sustaining the township risings were school-students, whose capacity to organise is enhanced by being the only group concentrated daily in large numbers within the black areas themselves. Politically, the UDF was hegemonic within the townships, with the youth especially becoming increasingly open in their allegiance to the exiled ANC and even to the South African Communist Party.

The second main driving force in the resistance was provided by the independent unions. Black workers, whose major industrial unions were united in COSATU in December 1985, began, from the November 1984 stay-away in the Transvaal onwards, to throw themselves into the political struggle. From the new 'super-federation's' inception, the COSATU leadership increasingly openly allied themselves to the UDF, and advocated the use of black workers' industrial power for political ends.

The measures of the first state of emergency made no appreciable impact on the resistance. Indeed perhaps the highpoint of township insurgency came at the end of February 1986. Militant black youth—known universally as the 'comrades'—went on the rampage in Alexandra township, in northern Johannesburg, after a local AZAPO leader had been murdered. They set fire to several factories adjoining the township, then ambushed a Hippo armoured personnel carrier. The Hippo swerved to avoid a specially dug giant trench and tipped over. Its six police occupants were killed and their weapons turned against the security forces. It took mass shootings, the encirclement of Alexandra by the South African Defence Force, and the intervention of Tutu and other UDF leaders appealing for calm for the state to regain control of the township—which is near Johannesburg's fabulously rich white northern suburbs, such as Sandton.⁶ Two months later the militancy of the black workers' movement was demonstrated when one and a half million workers went on strike on May Day in support of the independent unions' demand that 1 May should be made a public holiday.

Formidable though mass resistance was to the first emergency, it was subject to severe limitations. The struggles from September 1984 onwards posed the question of political power. Underlying the popular rebellions was the demand that state power be transferred from the National Party régime to the black majority. But although the struggle *posed* the question of power it did not provide the means of resolving it in the masses' favour.

Thus many ANC/UDF supporters argued that the street committees and people's courts formed in many townships represented a form of 'dual power' in Lenin's sense, in other words the beginnings of a new state rivalling the existing white-dominated state. Even the orthodox Trotskyist MWT talked of 'the existing embryonic "soviets" '.' But workers' councils or *soviets*, such as those thrown up by the Russian revolutions of 1905 and 1917, reflected the development of a powerful workers' movement based in industry and involving the formation of workplace bodies such as factory committees. The *soviets* were based on the assertion of working-class power in the workplaces and its *extension* beyond them to the broader political arena.' The street committees, by contrast, were community-based bodies, based on an alliance of various social layers in which middle-class UDF leaders and school-students, rather than workers, were likely to predominate. The usual absence of the kind of delegate-based democracy characteristic of the independent unions was, indeed, one of the main criticisms raised against township organisations by the left,' although in some cases—Alexandra and Cradock, for example—the street committees were based on delegate structures.

This points to a more general feature of the situation—the fact that township resistance was relatively more politicised and more in direct confrontation with the state than the workers' movement. This was partly a consequence of the fact that, given the detailed state control over African urban life, any political activity is likely to run immediately into conflict with one or other agency of Pretoria. But it also reflected the fact that the black working class had emerged as an organised force by fighting around economic issues such as wages and conditions rather than by directly challenging the government.

The period after 1984 did see the unions increasingly participate in 'stay aways', or political general strikes—four in 1984, twenty-two in 1985, twenty-five in 1986. While these actions assumed an increasingly massive character, accounting for 3.5 million strike-days in 1986, 77.8 per cent of the working days 'lost' that year, they remained more demonstrative protests than direct challenges to the power of the state.[10] In that sense, South Africa in 1984-6 did not see anything on the scale of the mass strikes and factory occupations through which, in the summer of 1980, the Polish working class confronted the Gierek régime.

If the full strength of the working class had yet to be mobilised against the South African state, the balance of military power remained overwhelmingly in the régime's favour. State power ultimately depends on the control of the means of coercion; these remained overwhelmingly in white hands. The South African Defence Force (SADF) is fundamentally a white citizen army composed of

> two distinctive bodies. One includes the 'full-time' forces, consisting of the Permanent Force of professionals or careerists and the national servicemen who are called up for two years. The latter are mostly white males doing compulsory service, but there are a number of Coloured and Asian volunteers. The second component of the SADF is the 'part-time' reserve, composed of several hundred thousand Citizen Force and Commando Force members.[11]

Every white male resident, after two years' full-time national service, joins the Citizen Force, and must serve a further 720 days spread over fourteen years. He is then transferred to the Active Citizen Force Reserve, where he serves twelve days annually for another five years, and thereafter joins the Commandos, serving twelve days a year till he reaches the age of 55. The effect is to provide the régime with a large pool of trained white manpower that forms the main line of defence of the existing order in South Africa.

The popular resistance was not remotely able during 1984-86 to begin to match the military power of the state. While the February 1986 insurrection in Alexandra was one of a number of episodes in which the comrades were able to gain access to weapons, in every case the security forces were able to re-impose control.

Nor were the guerillas of Umkhonto we Sizwe (MK), the ANC's military wing, able to fill the gap. Summing up the two years following the ANC's consultative conference in June 1985, one sympathetic witness, the historian Tom Lodge, observed:

The state has yet to be confronted with a military threat which seriously stretches its resources... Umkhonto's campaign falls well short of representing a major threat to the physical security of apartheid's beneficiaries, to the operation of government outside the townships or [to] the day-to-day functioning of the economy. It is directly responsible for only a minor proportion of the political violence since September 1984. For every weapon deployed by the Umkhonto cadres, the police claim to have discovered another four in arms caches...

Trials indicate considerable police success in locating even experienced Umkhonto units. Such evidence also suggests that a large number of major incidents are the work of a fairly small body of men and women. With an estimated 400 or so trained combatants at any one time, Umkhonto's strength and capacity is comparable with that of, say, the Zimbabwean African National Liberation Army in the first half of the 1970s. But Umkhonto confronts a much more formidable opponent than the Zimbabweans faced...

In contrast with the sense of impending triumph in public statements issued early in the year, the ANC's assessment of its achievements in a document circulated to national command centres in October 1986 was soberly critical.

'Despite our efforts,' it argued, 'we have not come anywhere near the achievement of the objectives we set ourselves'. ANC underground structures remained weak and unable to supply reliable support for Umkhonto cadres. Umkhonto units still operated largely in isolation from 'mass combat groups'. The document expressed concern about attacks on shops as well as the casualties inflicted by landmines. These it called 'political setbacks'

Internal organisational shortcomings had hindered the ANC from exploiting the 'revolutionary preparedness' in certain communities.[12]

ANC strategy: Towards negotiations

Despite this very unfavourable balance of military forces, the ANC continued to use language implying that a final settling of accounts with the South African state was not far off. For example, the ANC national executive proclaimed 1986 'The Year of Umkhonto we Sizwe', in which MK together with 'mass combat units' would create 'insurrectionary zones' covering the country 'in its entirety' and compelling the regime to effect 'a strategic retreat'.[13] Such pseudo-revolutionary rhetoric could only create expectations of imminent armed insurrection which the ANC was incapable of fulfilling.

In fact, the ANC leadership remained firmly oriented on compelling the regime to negotiate. Armed struggle, stay-aways, township revolts, and international boycotts were simply different forms of pressure intended to force Botha to the conference table. And, indeed, for a period it seemed as if the ANC's hopes of talks would be realised. The turmoil inside South Africa both compelled Western governments to take seriously a movement which they had previously ignored and encouraged a succession of visits to the ANC headquarters in Lusaka, Zambia, by nervous members of the white South African establishment.

The most important of these meetings took place on 13 September 1985, when a delegation of white businessmen headed by the head of Anglo-American, Gavin Relly, met Oliver Tambo and other ANC leaders. Naturally the issue about which Relly and company expressed most concern was the clause in the Freedom Charter providing for nationalisation of 'monopoly industry'.[14] Tambo did his best to reassure them, along lines most clearly stated in response to a question from Tory MP Norman St John Stevas when he gave evidence the following month to the British House of Commons Select Committee on Foreign Affairs:

> Is it your intention to destroy the capitalist system as such, or to reform it?
>
> (*Mr Tambo*) No, we do not want to destroy it. The Freedom Charter does not even purport to want to destroy the capitalist system. All that the Freedom Charter does is to envisage a mixed economy in which part of the economy, some of the industries, would be controlled, owned by the state (as happens in many countries), and the rest by private ownership—a mixed economy.[15]

Nelson Mandela, the ANC's jailed president, took the same stance even more emphatically when he met the Commonwealth Eminent Persons Group shortly before the second emergency was declared. He told them that 'he was a nationalist, not a communist,' and that 'the Freedom Charter was not a document designed to establish even socialism in South Africa.'[16]

The clearest statement, however, of the ANC's willingness to arrive at an accommodation with big capital came in a speech made by Winnie Mandela to the congress of the South African National Union of Mineworkers (NUM) in February 1987, well after the imposition of the second emergency. She claimed that 'the transfer of ownership, control and direction of the economy as a whole' would take place

> hand in hand with true business patriots of this land... it is in this area that the importance of NUM, of COSATU, of all relevant labour movements in joint consultation with the business sector cannot be over-emphasised... The government has gone out of its way to discourage business and labour solidarity as seen in its hysterical reaction to big business's attempt to communicate with Lusaka. The government fears the democratisation of capital as this would logically lead to organised labour having a say in decisions which are likely to affect their lives.[17]

This plea for class collaboration was all the more striking in being made to a union about to go into a major test of strength with the Chamber of Mines, composed of such 'business patriots' as Gavin Relly! No wonder that Dr Sam Motsuenyane returned from a two-day meeting in Lusaka saying that the ANC agreed 'to an astonishing degree' with the policies of the National African Federated Chambers of Commerce, which he headed.[18]

The period before the second emergency saw the ANC's expectations grow that forces were building up to compel Botha to the negotiating table. When on 7 February 1986 Frederick Van Zyl Slabbert, leader of the Progressive Federal Party, whose main backer is English-speaking big business, resigned in disgust at the white parliamentary farce, ANC secretary-general Alfred Nzo declared: 'An act of vision has made this February day a moment of pride for all the people in South Africa.'[19]

The most serious attempt to bring Pretoria and the ANC together was made by the absurdly named Commonwealth Eminent Persons Group (EPG), which was appointed in order to get the Commonwealth leaders off the hook after their conference at Nassau in October 1985 reached an impasse over Margaret Thatcher's refusal to countenance serious sanctions against South Africa. In March 1986 the EPG put a 'possible negotiating concept' to the South African government. This envisaged the ANC 'entering negotiations and suspending violence' in exchange for the withdrawal of the SADF from the townships, the release of Mandela and other political prisoners, and the unbanning of the ANC and the Pan-Africanist Congress. The EPG described the ANC leadership's response to these proposals as 'encouraging'.[20] Unfortunately it takes two to tango. As we shall see, P W Botha decided to sit out the dance.

The regime takes to the offensive

The mass upsurge of 1984-86 had put the transfer of political power to the black majority on to the agenda. The main resistance organisation, however, the ANC, lacked the military means to overturn the white state—and in any case expected to achieve power through negotiations with the ruling class. The workers' movement, despite the enormous advances made since the early 1970s, as yet lacked the collective strength or the political leadership to offer an alternative strategy to the black masses.

In these circumstances, it was likely that a mood of demoralisation and retreat would set in inside the townships as the youth found that their battles with the security forces did not bring tangible victories. Previous waves of youth revolt—in 1976-77 and 1980—had eventually burned themselves out. What I wrote in the previous chapter, first published in April 1986, proved to be true: 'While the present upsurge has had a greater duration and intensity, it too will in all likelihood run aground on the rocks of state violence and popular exhaustion.'[21]

The scale of the mass insurgency of 1984-86 was, however, quite unparalleled, and so required a determined and systematic response by the regime. In the months before the second emergency, the government's behaviour was erratic and uncertain. P W Botha first imposed an ineffectual emergency in July 1985, then followed it with his disastrous 'Rubicon' speech to the Natal congress of the National Party on 15 August. Sold in advance as offering a package of reforms, the speech proved to be a bellicose rant. Botha's finger-wagging warning to the world— 'Don't push us too far!'—helped to send the rand into free fall and forced Pretoria to impose a moratorium on its debt repayments to the Western banks.

In a speech to parliament on 31 January 1986—'Rubicon II'— Botha was, however, far more conciliatory, referring to 'the outdated concept of apartheid', and promising to scrap the pass laws and give 'all South Africans' the right to 'participate in government through their elected representatives'. In March the state of emergency was dropped, though only to be imposed again with far greater vigour on 12 June.

To a significant degree these vacillations reflected the objective contradictions in which the regime found itself.

One major pressure on Botha, to refuse to make any significant concessions to the black resistance, came from the swelling white backlash which was sweeping the small rural towns of the Afrikaner *platteland* in the Transvaal and the Orange Free State. On 22 May the fascist AWB succeeded in preventing foreign minister Pik Botha, one of the cabinet's leading advocates of reform, from addressing a meeting in the small Northern Transvaal town of Pietersburg. The growth of the AWB under the leadership of the demagogue Eugene Terr'Blanche was one symptom of the increasing disaffection of sections of the white population. Not the least alarming thing about Pietersburg for the government was the failure of the police to intervene to break up the AWB demonstration

The catalyst for the clampdown may, however, have been provided by the EPG. The regime's initial response to the group's 'negotiating concept' was favourable. Pik Botha wrote to them accepting the idea of reciprocal moves by the ANC and Pretoria— the one to 'suspend violence', the other to release Mandela and reduce the level of repression. The EPG flew to South Africa, only to hear a belligerent speech by Botha to the President's Council on 15 May demanding that the ANC unilaterally 'renounce violence'. Returning to South Africa after visiting the ANC in Lusaka, the group learned, on the very day that they were due to meet the cabinet's constitutional committee, that the SADF had attacked the capitals of three neighbouring black-ruled states, including Lusaka. Pretoria had slammed the door shut.

What caused this abrupt reversal?

The regime has often made evident its desire to free Mandela rather than let him die on its hands. Nevertheless, the terms proposed by the EPG may have conjured up the vision of a process of negotiation which escaped Pretoria's control. Mandela's very release, especially if the SADF had indeed been withdrawn from the townships, might have provoked a new and even greater surge of popular militancy. The regime might have found itself on an escalator leading relentlessly to black majority rule. The way in which the settler state in Zimbabwe suddenly fell apart in 1979-80, its leaders trapped into offering increasingly major concessions to black demands, may not have been far from the minds of Botha and his advisers. So the Commonwealth initiative, which brought Pretoria and the ANC closer to the negotiating table than they had ever been, was ditched.

It was one thing to send the EPG packing, quite another to break the mass resistance in the townships. A testing ground for the methods used nationally once the second emergency was imposed was provided by the squatter camps at Crossroads, near Cape Town.[23] Ever since Crossroads had been established in 1975 it had been a focus of opposition to the regime's policy of forced removal of 'illegal' Africans to the Bantustans. The struggles to prevent the destruction of Crossroads indeed provided a major stimulus to Pretoria's adoption of a policy of 'orderly urbanisation', which involved tolerating African migration to the metropolitan areas provided it occurred on the government's terms.

As the camp acquired a relatively secure status, and its leaders became involved in negotiations with government representatives, a process of class differentiation occurred within Crossroads, with the emergence of a politically dominant group headed by Johnson Ngxobongwana, who were able to accumulate capital through the imposition of 'taxes' on residents. Ngxobongwana was able politically to marginalise the militant women who had led the early struggles against the state's attempts to destroy Crossroads. His supporters increasingly resorted to force in order to crush his opponents, and by April 1983 'Ngxobongwana's army' had emerged. They became known as the *witdoeke*, after the pieces of white cloth they wore to identify themselves during the regular bouts of fighting in the camp.

This did not prevent Ngxobongwana becoming one of the leading figures of the UDF in the Western Cape and chair of one of its main affiliates, the Western Cape Civic Association. Josette Cole comments in her important history of Crossroads:

> Those who were less trusting of Ngxobongwana, or had been targets of his economic exploitation and repression inside the community, watched from the sidelines with a certain amount of cynicism. But in 1983, Ngxobongwana was a 'popular leader' in the eyes of the leaders of most of the UDF affiliates. History would show that they had backed the wrong horse.[24]

The drastic escalation of popular struggle and state repression experienced by the Western Cape generally in 1985 undermined Ngxobongwana's alliance with the UDF. In Crossroads the crisis was rendered more acute by the government announcement of plans to resettle all African squatters in the new 'high-density' township of Khayelitsha. More militant forms of resistance—rent and consumer boycotts, for example—developed at Crossroads. Above all there emerged, as elsewhere, the *maqabane* or comrades, young activists following the lead of the UDF-affiliated Cape Youth Congress (CAYCO).

The rise of the comrades posed a direct challenge to Ngxobongwana's control over Crossroads. He broke with the UDF and began to court the regime, in the hope of state funds and support which might allow him to control portions of the camps which would be 'upgraded' into a permanent residential area. The price for this would be his cooperation with the state's efforts to destroy the rest of Crossroads and drive its inhabitants into Khayelitsha.

The resulting alliance between Ngxobongwana and the security forces was aided by the tactics of some of the *maqabane*:

> The intimidatory methods used by militant youths in enforcing a consumer boycott and Black Christmas [in other words no celebrations] during the last months of 1985 had...created the potential for mobilising reactionary forces against comrades and residents in some way aligned with these campaigns. During these campaigns, organised in the last half of 1985 by a variety of UDF affiliates, militant youths from the black townships often ruthlessly dealt with residents suspected of not supporting the campaigns. There were, for example numerous reports of militant youths forcing residents to drink fish oil, or swallow washing powder, as punishment for not following the 'correct line'. The actions of these 'comrades' alienated a large percentage of residents from the townships and surrounding squatter camps.[25]

Isolated by their own tactics, the *maqabane* were vulnerable to the offensive launched by Ngxobongwana and the state in the run-up to the second emergency. Between 17 May and 12 June 1986 hundreds of armed *witdoeke*, with the support of the police, attacked and destroyed four of the squatter camps at Crossroads. These operations, 'carefully planned and executed with military precision', resulted in a hundred deaths and the forced removal from their homes of 70,000 squatters.[26] The battle of Crossroads represented a major victory for the regime: its alliance with a former UDF leader had achieved far more than ten years of efforts by white officials.

Socialist Worker argued at the time that the *witdoeke*-police assault on Crossroads represented a major watershed:

> Attacks by the security forces have tended to unite communities and encourage them to fight back. The vigilantes, on the other hand, spring from the latent, often class-based divisions within the communities. Their attacks *widen* those divisions and make any fightback more difficult. And these attacks are much more directed at militants and activists than the army's blanket raids.
>
> The reason why the vigilantes have started to appear now lies in the scale of the township revolt and, in some cases, the way in which it has been organised. In many areas the consumer boycott, which has been very successful, has been implemented through well-organised democratic bodies such as action committees. Because the majority of the township are involved in the discussion about the action, the reactionaries have been isolated. But in other areas this organisation has been missing and the boycott has instead been imposed by groups of youths physically stopping people from breaking the boycott.
>
> Under these circumstances the divisions which have long existed become real ones...
>
> The struggle is screaming out for a clear direction, a clear leadership, a clear sign of the power that can bring the system down... Many people in South Africa recognise the crying need for mass activity in the factories to transform the situation. Many have insisted that this month's action [commemorating the tenth anniversary of the Soweto rising] should be a general strike, not a stay-away: a factory rather than a community-based struggle...
>
> Nothing stands still in South Africa. If the movement doesn't throw up forms of struggle to take it forward, then it can stagnate and ultimately suffer a massive reversal.[27]

This analysis proved all too accurate. The pattern revealed at Crossroads—an alliance between the white state and conservative black forces—proved capable of wider application, as the second emergency was to show. The repression mounted after 12 June 1986 involved an intensification of methods used previously.[28] Directed above all at the UDF and its affiliates, this took a number of forms.

In the first place detention without trial was used on an unprecedented scale. Ten thousand of the detainees were aged eighteen or under—40 per cent of the total. The mass detention of children, some as young as eleven or twelve, reflected the regime's determination to destroy resistance in the schools, the chief focus of organised militancy within the townships.[29]

A second, much less widespread but nevertheless important feature of the repression was the use of treason trials to take leading political activists out of circulation. The most important of these was the long-running trial at Delmas, where nineteen UDF activists, including such leading figures as Popo Molefe, Terror Lekota and Moss Chikane, faced charges of conspiring with the ANC and the SACP to establish the UDF. A significant shift during the second emergency was the laying of treason charges against township militants for their involvement in day-to-day anti-government activities. The metalworkers' leader Moses Mayekiso and four other alleged leaders of the Alexandra Action Committee were accused of setting up people's courts and street committees. The aim appeared to be to cast a much wider net over grassroots political activity.[30]

There were other, more direct ways of getting rid of troublesome activists. Even before the first emergency Matthew Goniwe and three other leaders of the Cradock Residents Association, one of the most militant affiliates of the UDF in the Eastern Cape, had been assassinated by unknown assailants. In 1986-87 the increasing use of death squads to eliminate UDF activists was simply one of the proliferating forms of 'informal repression' resorted to by the regime.[31]

The most important development was the emergence of groups of armed African vigilantes. Already during the first emergency, squads recruited from the more backward sections of the urban black population—generally unemployed or migrant workers—and led by notables with a material stake in the existing order, began to launch a reign of terror in parts of the country.[32] Known by various names—the *imbokotho* in the KwaNdebele Bantustan, the 'A-team' in many townships—the vigilantes made local UDF activists and especially the 'comrades' of the youth congresses their particular targets. The victory of the *witdoeke* at Crossroads proved to be the beginning of a more general offensive. Backed by the armed might of the SADF and SAP, the vigilantes took advantage of the weakening of township organisations by the mass detentions of June 1986 and launched vicious assaults in many townships.

Their role was formalised when many of them were recruited and armed by the state as municipal policemen. Given three weeks' training, these *kitskonstabels* or 'instant cops', as they came to be known, were then sent out on to the streets to maintain order. It is little wonder that mass resistance organisation even in the militant Eastern Cape wilted under the weight of this offensive.

In Natal the regime enjoyed the advantage of an alliance with a mass right-wing African force, Buthelezi's Inkatha movement. Buthelezi is a key figure in South African politics.[33] As chief minister of the KwaZulu Bantustan, he claims the loyalties of Zulu-speakers, according to the state's ethnic classification the largest African group, whose traditions involve the memory, carefully cultivated by Buthelezi, of the great Zulu kingdom, the most powerful state in early nineteenth-century south-east Africa. Through the KwaZulu 'state' Buthelezi controls his own police force and administers most of the African townships serving the Durban-Pinetown area, South Africa's second greatest conurbation.

The key to Buthelezi's broader influence lies, however, in Inkatha. First formed in 1928 as a Zulu cultural movement by King Solomon Dinuzulu, Buthelezi's uncle, it was revived in 1975. Buthelezi presented the revived Inkatha as a national movement, in the traditions (and indeed using the colours) of the ANC. He often harked back to the fact that he had been a member of the ANC Youth League while a student at Fort Hare College in 1948-50. His contacts with the ANC were, indeed, to continue for another 30 years at least. Oliver Tambo told the British House of Commons Foreign Affairs Committee: 'We proposed the formation of Inkatha to Chief Gatsha Buthelezi and he acted on our advice.'[34]

The ANC executive explained to their 1985 consultative conference that they had hoped to 'use the legal opportunities provided by the Bantustan programme to participate in the mass mobilisation of our people.'[35] They soon found that they had bitten off more than they could chew. As late as October 1979, however, Buthelezi, accompanied by seventeen members of his cabinet, met the ANC executive in London. The two sides 'accepted each other's legitimacy and role in the struggle.'[36] But formal relations were broken off after Buthelezi publicised the meeting, and his attacks on the ANC 'Mission-in-Exile' became increasingly vehement. Nevertheless, as the ANC executive acknowledged, 'in a way he is our fault.'[37]

By 1985 Inkatha claimed a million members, almost all Zulu-speakers. Its structures and those of the KwaZulu Bantustan were inextricably interwoven. At its core is an alliance between Bantustan chiefs and entrepreneurs, intent on using the KwaZulu 'state' to acquire capital, and South African big business. This alliance operates at several levels. Through various agencies— the KwaZulu Finance and Investment Corporation and Inkatha's Khulani Holdings—various joint investment projects have been organised with some of the biggest corporations in South Africa.[38] At the political level, Buthelezi offered the white ruling class the prospect of 'power-sharing' with a powerful black leader strongly committed to maintaining capitalism in South Africa.

Within Natal itself, Buthelezi was involved in a succession of initiatives culminating in the Indaba proposals unveiled in November 1986. These envisaged the establishment of a 'KwaNatal' regime based on a multiracial parliament hedged with safeguards designed to protect white privileges. The proposals, which would have made Buthelezi the dominant figure in Natal, were rejected by the government, but won the support of the English-speaking opposition parties, traditionally the key force in white provincial politics, and of big capital.[39]

Of more immediate importance was Inkatha's role in Natal's African townships, many of which are actually controlled by the KwaZulu administration. The upsurge of mass resistance after September 1984 inevitably challenged Buthelezi's dominance at a time when it had become increasingly important that he should show the white establishment that he could deliver black acquiescence to the 'KwaNatal' option. Moreover the formation of COSATU, openly aligned to the UDF, brought the independent unions, some of which in their early days after the 1973 Durban strikes had received some encouragement from the KwaZulu authorities, into conflict with Inkatha. On May Day 1986 Buthelezi launched his own trade union front, the United Workers Union of South Africa, in order to counter the threat from COSATU.[40]

As popular insurgency and working-class militancy began to affect Natal's black townships, the scene was set for bloody conflict.

In many cases the emergence of the UDF and COSATU gave political expression to older conflicts. Black communities in Pietermaritzburg, for example, had a long tradition of independence, based in part on the freehold rights still enjoyed by African landowners in Edendale township, and they resisted incorporation into KwaZulu. In 1984-85 youth organisations sprang up and enforced a consumer boycott. This led to clashes with Inkatha, which was able to 'win support from older residents alienated by the extremist measures youths employed to police the boycott—forcing boycott-busters to drink cooking oil.'[41] COSATU was drawn in, not only because of its alliance with the UDF but also because of the tensions arising from the long drawn-out and bitter dispute at BTR Sarmcol's Pietermaritzburg plant, in which Buthelezi backed the management.

However it was Inkatha which savagely raised the political stakes. Its supporters went on the rampage in Durban's townships after school students mounted a boycott in protest at the murder of local UDF leader Victoria Mxenge on 1 August 1985. Seventy-five people were killed, and a thousand Indians, the particular targets of Inkatha violence, driven from the squatter town of Inanda.[42] Thereafter Inkatha vigilante squads, known as *amabutho*, were involved in increasingly frequent attacks on UDF and COSATU activists. The violence reached its crescendo in Pietermaritzburg after Inkatha launched an aggressive membership drive in August 1987. By the end of the following March some 622 people had died in political violence in the Pietermaritzburg townships since the beginning of 1987.[43]

The dilemmas of white power

The second emergency therefore saw a qualitative increase in the level of violence combined with the successful mobilisation by the regime of conservative African forces. As a result the mass resistance, especially in the townships, was left struggling to survive. But how did this offensive relate to the Botha government's reform policies?

Many observers argued that June 1986 marked a radical break. The well-informed Centro de Estudos Africanos, attached to Eduardo Mondlane University in Mozambique, for example, claimed that the regime ' is now firmly set on a course of attempting to cling to power through naked terror regardless of the effect on the country as a whole or the international consequences.'[44] Assertions of this kind are often (though not in this case) linked to the idea that South Africa under Botha has become, or is in the process of becoming, a military dictatorship unaccountable even to the white electorate.

To address these issues requires an analysis of the nature of the South African state.[45] The common tendency of the apartheid regime's opponents to label it as fascist reflects primarily the desire to condemn its racist and oppressive character rather than any serious examination of its political structures and social base.[46]

I have already cited in chapter two David Kaplan's characterisation of the South African state as 'a racially exclusive bourgeois democracy'. This form of state presupposes a racially divided working class. White workers were incorporated into the parliamentary regime through their political enfranchisement and material privileges. The increasingly proletarianised African population, while denied the rights of citizenship, were permitted limited, racially based forms of political representation even during the apogee of apartheid in the 1960s and 1970s through the Bantustans and municipal bodies in the townships.[47]

The survival of a particular, albeit very limited, form of bourgeois democracy even under National Party rule after 1948 was reflected in the willingness of the courts on occasion to overrule government actions.[48] The judiciary is, of course, no more 'neutral' than any other state apparatus, but the degree of independence from the executive displayed by some judges helped to create a space within the state which resistance forces such as the UDF and the independent unions proved willing to exploit. This had obvious advantages in hampering or delaying particular attacks by the security forces, but it could also act as a means of incorporation, especially in the case of the unions, which became increasingly active in bringing cases before the Industrial Court to enforce their legal rights on employers.[49]

The National Party was based on an alliance of the Afrikaner bourgeoisie and petty bourgeoisie, which came to power in 1948 by winning mass support, especially among the white farmers and workers of the Transvaal.[50] One of the characteristics of National Party rule was the degree of cohesion it secured among the mass of the white population for almost a generation.[51] By the late 1970s, however, the old Nationalist coalition was breaking up under the pressure of social and economic changes—above all the increasing domination of the party itself by Afrikaner big capital and the emergence of a militant and politicised African working class. P W Botha's election as party leader in September 1978, and his adoption of policies designed to incorporate sections of the black population, brought the tensions within the party to the surface.

The class antagonisms dividing Afrikanerdom were dramatised in February 1982, when twenty-three Nationalist MPs broke away to form the Konserwatiewe Party (Conservative Party, KP) under the leadership of Andries Treurnicht. The main plank of the KP's policy was opposition to Botha's new constitution, which embodied the principle of limited 'power-sharing' with Coloured and Indian leaders. The bulk of Afrikaner capital swung behind Botha—above all the great SANLAM empire—as did the big farmers of the Cape, Natal and the southern Orange Free State. The appeal of the KP and the other party of the far right, the HNP, was mainly to white workers and to the smaller Afrikaner maize farmers of the Transvaal, the northern Orange Free State and the north-eastern Cape.[52]

This process of class realignment among Afrikaans-speaking whites was closely connected to other changes. One was the centralisation of power in the hands of an increasingly militarised executive.[53] We have already seen that Botha's elevation to the premiership was accompanied by the growing involvement of the SADF in decision-making. Botha replaced the rather chaotic and *ad hoc* procedures used by his predecessor, John Vorster, with a highly formalised system of committees at the apex of which were four cabinet committees: for economic affairs, social affairs, constitutional affairs and the State Security Council (SSC).

The SSC emerged as the main government decision-making body. Presided over by Botha and including the most important cabinet ministers and such key state officials as the heads of the SADF and the SAP, it met fortnightly before the cabinet, which increasingly acted as a rubber stamp.

The political influence of the military was increased by the involvement of SADF officers in the large secretariat which services the SSC and its working committees, and in the network of regional Joint Management Centres and local Joint Management Committees whose role it is to implement the regime's 'total strategy'. The unfolding crisis after September 1984 further enhanced the importance of this highly secretive and unaccountable National Security Management System by bringing the SADF into the townships.[54] These trends were also reinforced by the 1983 Constitution, which created an executive state presidency largely insulated from parliamentary pressures, and whose first occupant was the military's patron, P W Botha.

The new constitution was of course a key element in Botha's strategy. As formulated at the end of the 1970s this strategy had three main elements (which have already been examined in detail in chapter 2): first the concession of certain economic rights—for example to form trade unions and to own land—to those Africans with the right to reside in urban areas (the so-called 'section tenners'), who were now recognised as a fixture in legally 'white' South Africa; secondly the replacement, as far as possible, of legal racial discrimination with internationally more defensible socio-economic inequalities, which would, it was hoped, increasingly cut across the black-white divide, replacing race with class as the main antagonism; and thirdly the political incorporation, within the framework of continuing white domination, of privileged sections of the black population.

The tricameral parliament created by the 1983 Constitution, with its Coloured and Indian Chambers effectively subordinate to the white House of Assembly, was an attempt to achieve this objective. Henry Kissinger cynically described the constitution as an example of 'how a dominant minority intent on maintaining control could manipulate patronage by co-opting clients to assist it.'[55]

Botha's strategy ran aground on the rocks of mass resistance—first the emergence of a militant black workers' movement, then opposition to the new constitution among Coloureds and Indians, and finally the mass insurgency of 1984-86, powered by the revolt of the African majority, who were excluded from the new dispensation. The regime's response was, as we have seen, to resort to ruthless repression after an initial period of hesitation.

This increased reliance on violence did not, however, mean the abandonment of reform. Thus Botha's 'Rubicon II' speech in January 1986 offered a number of concessions. One—a National Statutory Council incorporating African representatives—was effectively still-born thanks to Buthelezi's refusal to participate unless Mandela was released and the ANC unbanned. But Botha's promise to scrap the pass laws was implemented by the Abolition of Influx Control Act, although Africans linked to the four 'independent' Bantustans—the Transkei, Bophuthatswana, Ciskei and Venda—were still liable to be discriminated against as 'aliens'. The regime's response to the township risings was what Laurine Platzky called a 'combination of restructuring and repression' rather than mere 'naked terror'.[56]

One reason for this was that the regime was in any case beginning to shift away from aspects of the strategy first formulated in the late 1970s.[57] One important element in this strategy, embodied in the 1979 Riekert report, was the attempt to reinforce the division between those Africans with section ten rights, allowing them to reside in the 'white' urban areas, and the majority tied to one or other of the Bantustans and allowed into the 'white' areas only as migrant workers. Roughly speaking, the idea was to grant certain privileges to the former, and to intensify apartheid controls on the latter. This policy of dividing urban 'insiders' from rural 'outsiders' has proved a complete failure.

One reason for this is that the elaborate system of labour controls perfected after 1948 has in recent years been unable to prevent an increasing influx into the cities of rural Africans fleeing drought and impoverishment in the Bantustans. Stanley Greenberg argues in an important recent study which undermines the image of a monolithic and omnipotent apartheid state:

> A close examination of the labour control framework in the post-1976 period reveals a widening gulf between the legal order—its completeness and rationality—and the control order in practice. The system of administration, increasingly unwieldy and confronting increasingly complex markets and growing labour surpluses, has lost control of the bureaucracy on the ground: central policy directives are frequently ignored or reversed, despite strenuous efforts by upper-level officials to achieve uniformity. The bureaucracy is understaffed and underfinanced, unable to implement policy or police the system effectively.
>
> Indeed, in large areas of urban South Africa the system of control has become intermittent, incapable of coping with the tremendous growth of illegal squatting and illegal employment. In the rural areas the tribal labour bureaucracy has broken down, abandoning large portions of the Bantustans. The system of administration has given way to corruption, withering markets, and illegal flight to the cities.

With the system weakly controlled from the top, local interests—farmers and industrial employers in particular—have been able to demand access to 'illegal' labour supplies. In the process, they have reinforced the unevenness of the system and encouraged Africans to circumvent the order of control."

The erosion of influx control may help explain the regime's decision to scrap the pass laws.

One respect, however, in which state policy has been successful has been in encouraging commuting. A significant section of the African workforce resides in one of the Bantustans and travels daily to work in a 'white area'. This may involve long and gruelling travel from one of the vast resettlement camps, such as Winterveld near Pretoria; sometimes existing townships, such as the majority of those in the Durban-Pinetown area, are reclassified as part of a Bantustan.

The crucial consequence of these structural changes is the massive increase in the size of the cross-border commuter labour force and the relative decline of long-distance labour migration. Despite their formal legal status, commuter populations have become effectively indistinguishable from urban insiders, even though they are located on the peripheries of the metropoles. Recent legislation has recognised this by allowing commuters to retain section ten rights.

What these processes amount to is the occupational and residential stabilisation of the African working class in and around the metropolitan areas—the formation of...new regional proletariats in South Africa."

The development of these regional economies, which cut across the division—central to traditional apartheid—between 'white' urban areas and black 'Homelands', underlies what William Cobbett, Daryl Glaser, Doug Hindson and Mark Swilling call 'an emerging strategy which has been pursued with increasing determination by reformers within the commanding heights of the state since late in 1984.'⁶⁰

This strategy involves the development of a three-tier 'regional-federal' system of government. At the first and lowest tier, local authorities elected on a racial basis will administer the 'own affairs' of their respective communities. 'General affairs' affecting all races within a metropolitan region will be managed by a Regional Services Council representing all the local authorities in the area, but with white councils having the preponderant say. At the second tier, the four elected white provincial councils have been abolished and replaced by appointed executive committees. The key units at this level are the government's eight development regions, which cover both Bantustans and 'white' areas. The Indaba proposals for 'KwaNatal' are an indication of how multiracial 'power-sharing' could develop in the second tier." As a step in this direction, an inter-racial Joint Executive Authority was established in November 1987, representing both the white provincial council and the KwaZulu Bantustan government.

One consequence of 'regionalisation' is, paradoxically, a further concentration of power in the hands of the central government, the third tier. While the old Department of Bantu Administration and Development, in recent years renamed Cooperation and Development, which used to have comprehensive power over Africans' lives, has largely been dismantled, responsibility for the first and second tiers of government lies with the Department of Constitutional Development and Planning, headed by Chris Heunis, one of the architects of reform.

An advantage, however, of the devolution of authority to the first and second tiers is that it would be these bodies which would have to carry the can for the wretched public services provided for urban blacks, and for measures designed to transfer resources from affluent white suburbs to African townships.

'Regionalisation' in this respect converges with another main theme in the regime's policies, namely a reduction in the economic role of the state and the promotion of private enterprise. Botha made a significant step towards translating what had largely been monetarist rhetoric into at least some reality when he opened parliament on 5 February 1988, announcing that the government intended to privatise such key state companies as the Electricity Supply Commission, the Iron and Steel Corporation (ISCOR) and the South African Transport Services.

The logic behind such policies is to distance the white-dominated central government from the kind of social and economic grievances which lie behind much popular militancy. Daryl Glaser explains:

> Through these measures, reformers hope to deflect pressure away from the central state, both by 'regionalising' conflict over allocation outcomes and by transforming intermediate and lower levels of the state into more attractive political prizes. By further delegating

responsibility for certain kinds of social goods to the private sector, reformers hope to 'depoliticise' certain kinds of allocation outcomes, presenting them as the product of impersonal market forces.[62]

The success of the strategy depends, above all, on the recruitment of black collaborators. The regime's intention is to involve Africans at every level of government, although representation will still be on a racial or even ethnic basis. Various economic incentives have been offered to the black middle class. Blacks may now trade in the central business districts. They may not, however, live in the city centres (though in parts of inner-city Johannesburg such as Hillbrow, 'grey areas' have emerged where the Group Areas Act is no longer enforced). The Small Business Development Corporation spent R440 million in 1983-88 on loans to 18,657 mainly black entrepreneurs and R150 million on property developments in African townships. Government and big business bodies such as the Urban Foundation are spending R1.2 billion on building low-cost homes for Africans.[63]

Building societies have moved in to provide mortgages for Africans who have had the right to own their own homes in urban areas restored to them, and private developers have moved in to build the houses—though one Urban Foundation official estimated that the developers could meet the demand of between 5 and 8 per cent of the population in the Pretoria- Witwatersrand-Vereeniging region (PWV), where there is a shortfall of at least 320,000 housing units.[64]

Improving the material situation of at least some blacks does not represent any weakening of the regime's intention to hang on to power. The showcase of Pretoria's policy of 'urban renewal' is Alexandra township, scene of the February 1986 insurrection: R95 million were allocated as the first instalment of a comprehensive upgrading of the township involving road-building and repair, the construction of a modern sewerage system and water drainage system, and a house-building programme. But the township, sealed off by the SADF from neighbouring factories and white suburbs at the beginning of the second emergency, remained under military occupation and was administered by a Joint Management Centre chaired by a police colonel and answerable to the State Security Council, while Moses Mayekiso and other leaders of the Alexandra Action Committee stood trial for treason.

Alexandra is only one of thirty-four 'oilspots'—militant

townships—selected for 'upgrading', on which R3.2 billion was spent in 1987-88 alone as part of an intensive programme directed by the State Security Council to remove the causes of unrest through a combination of repression, material improvements, infiltration and co-option.[65]

Nevertheless, even this highly authoritarian reform process needs some means of incorporating urban Africans at the national as well as the local and regional levels. Various devices have been proposed. Stoffel van der Merwe, a minister close to Botha, suggested in 1985 that an assembly responsible for African 'own affairs' outside the Bantustans could be established, which would send representatives along with the tricameral parliament and the Bantustan leaders to a broad coordinating body.[66] In April 1988 Botha revamped his own proposal, first made in January 1986, for a national Statutory Council, now renamed the 'Great Indaba', on which both urban African and Bantustan leaders would sit. He also flew several other kites: elected regional bodies for African 'own affairs', and the inclusion of Africans in the President's Council and in the electoral college which chooses the state president.

Underlying the increasingly baroque political structures created or envisaged by the regime is one objective: to preserve the substance of white domination. Federalism—variants of which are supported not simply by the National Party leadership but, as we shall see, by big business—is conceived as an alternative to the main demand of the resistance: one person, one vote within a united South Africa. As Cobbett, Glaser, Hindson and Swilling observe:

> Proponents of federalism argue that the only way to prevent a black majoritarian state imposing socialism or a welfare state from above is to establish relatively autonomous local and regional political entities. These would hold sovereign power over limited coercive apparatuses and economic policies, fragmenting a national majority regionally.[67]

Botha's reform strategy, even in its most recent 'regional-federal' form, faces two fundamental contradictions. In the first place, South Africa is suffering from a long-term, deep-seated economic crisis, a reflection of its failure to break out of its place in the global economy as an exporter of raw materials and join other Newly Industrialising Countries which have penetrated world trade in manufactured goods.

The consequence is protracted economic stagnation—a far more fundamental feature of the economy since the early 1970s than short-term economic upswings, such as those at the end of the 1970s and in 1986-88 brought about by temporary surges of the gold price. The real annual growth rate of gross domestic product fell from an average 5.8 per cent in the 1960s, to 3.3 per cent in the 1970s and 1.8 per cent in 1980-87. The resulting squeeze on living standards—real income fell by 11 per cent in 1984-87[69]—helped to produce the mass risings and strikes of the mid-1980s. But the underlying economic crisis also limits the resources available to improve the material situation of black people. A privileged minority may benefit, but only at the price of alienating the excluded black majority.

Economic concessions to Africans have also been accompanied by attacks on the living standards of the mass of whites. Botha's monetarist policies implied an offensive against the 'welfare state for whites' which had been created by successive National Party governments. Job reservation was abolished, fees were introduced in white state schools, subsidies to white maize farmers were slashed, while white unemployment rose from 6000 in 1981 to 32,000 in 1986.[70] Economic grievances, as well as political fears, underlay the growth of the far right.

The February 1988 budget showed Botha ready to press ahead: at the same time as widespread privatisation was announced, a public sector wage freeze was imposed. In an article headed 'Hallo to Big Business. Goodbye to White Workers', the **Weekly Mail** commented:

> State employees [form]...about one in three economically active whites. By freezing civil servants' wages, Botha was effectively saying to those whites that their real incomes would go down. It is precisely on this group of voters that the Conservative Party has been concentrating its efforts.[71]

The rise of the far right—the KP, HNP and AWB—highlighted the second major contradiction facing the reform strategy. This received its classic statement from Alexis de Tocqueville in 1840:

> The most perilous moment for a bad government is when it seeks to mend its ways. Only consummate statecraft can enable a king to save his throne when after a long spell of oppressive rule he sets to improving the lot of his subjects.[72]

Authoritarian reform of the kind pursued by Botha runs two risks. The first is that limited concessions simply encourage the oppressed to demand more. That certainly was the effect of the tricameral constitution. The exclusion of the African majority strengthened the popular demand for a genuine non-racial democracy.

The result is that severe limits are imposed on the regime's ability to incorporate even the more conservative wing of the African middle class. Thus Buthelezi has consistently refused to participate in Botha's various constitutional proposals, including the National Statutory Council, until the ANC is unbanned and Mandela and its other leaders released. Were he to accept lesser terms, Buthelezi would in all likelihood be outflanked from the left by the ANC, and end up as Muzorewa did in Zimbabwe, a wretched black puppet without a popular base of his own.

Secondly, even limited political reforms threaten to undermine the regime's existing popular base. The material privileges of working-class and middle-class whites, and of the smaller white farmers, depend upon the preservation of white political domination. Any move away from the *status quo* is easily interpreted as a threat to their survival, and these fears are intensified by the township risings and the deteriorating economic position of most whites. Hence the rise of the far right, whose clearest electoral expression came in the whites-only general election of 6 May 1987. While the National Party's share of the vote was eroded, the liberal opposition—the Progressive Federal Party (PFP) and the New Republic Party (NRP)—were squeezed, and the KP emerged as the official opposition:

Percentage shares of the vote in the 1987 election
(1981 share in brackets)

PFP	NRP	Inds*	NP	KP	HNP
14.1	1.9	1.3	52.4	26.3	3.1
(19.4)	(7.8)	(-)	(57.0)	(-)	(14.1)

*Three dissident Nationalists, including the former South African ambassador to London, Dennis Worrall, stood as Independents.

Three parliamentary by-elections in the Transvaal in March 1988 indicated that the right-wing surge was continuing. In two rural seats, Standerton and Schweizer-Reinecke, the KP held on with increased majorities. The swing in their favour indicated that they could win every white local election in the Transvaal except Johannesburg, and double their representation in parliament.[73]

The KP went on to hold on to the urban seat of Randfontein with a 9 per cent swing—sufficient in a general election to dislodge a number of ministers and deputy ministers, including F W de Klerk, National Party leader in the Transvaal.[74]

One crucial feature of the rise of the far right has been a tacit alliance between two very different political formations, the KP and the AWB.[75] The KP's character very much reflects its origins as a Nationalist breakaway: a quarter of the National Party's district and branch committees in the Transvaal joined the new party when it was formed in March 1982. While Treurnicht rejects political power-sharing, standing by the old Homelands policy, he is willing to envisage social and economic concessions to Africans, and, unlike the more fundamentalist—and shrinking—HNP, does not demand that Afrikaans become the only official language: a reflection of the KP's desire to win English-speaking voters and more generally of its essentially electoral strategy.

The AWB, by contrast, is a classical fascist movement whose ideology draws on anti-semitism, Mussolini-style corporatism and Christian fundamentalism (its swastika-like emblem is based on three sevens, which supposedly counter the Biblical 'number of the Beast', 666). Its aim is an Afrikaner *volksstaat*, or people's state, based in the territory of the old Boer republics—the Transvaal, the Orange Free State and Northern Natal. The AWB's anti-parliamentarism is reflected in its involvement in two paramilitary formations: its own uniformed corps, the Stormvalke, and a broader white militia, the Brandwag.

The AWB was estimated in 1986 to have 100,000 members. Certainly Terr'Blanche has been highly successful in orchestrating Nazi-style mass rallies. There is evidence that the AWB has sympathisers in the security forces, especially the SAP. In practice however, despite the obvious contrasts between the KP and the AWB, their activities have often proved complementary; AWB mobilisations have helped to rally support for Treurnicht's parliamentary candidates.

Commentators differ over the far right's ability ever to displace the National Party. Steven Friedman argues that the KP cannot hope to win more than a third of the seats in the white House of Assembly since

> its potential base is both regional and confined to a section of white
> society. It has made no real inroads in the Cape and Natal and draws

support from groups—farmers, workers—whose voting power has declined since 1948.[76]

The far right's growth may indeed help the National Party replace some of its lost voters, by scaring relatively liberal English-speaking voters towards Botha, particularly since he offers them the option of controlled change. One cabinet minister told Van Zyl Slabbert, while he was still leader of the PFP: 'Come election time all we do is show Eugene Terr'Blanche giving his Nazi salute on TV and your voters will flock to our tables in the northern suburbs of Johannesburg.'[77] This may indeed explain the squeeze on the liberal opposition in the 1987 election.

Certainly the far right do not offer a coherent strategic alternative capable of taking South African society out of its present crisis. It is hard to imagine circumstances in which an AWB regime would not be regarded by big capital as a major catastrophe. And the KP's nostalgia for a modified version of Verwoerdian apartheid bears little relation to the realities of a changing social formation. The right's own confusion is well-reflected by another of Slabbert's anecdotes. One afternoon in parliament a Conservative MP sat down beside him:

> He shook his finger at the government. 'You see those bastards. We are going to break them. I promise you that!' He paused a while, sneaking a sideways glance to his colleagues, and winked at me. 'But once we have broken them, you fellows had better take over, because our plans are not going to work either!'[78]

Whatever the prospects for the far right (and their electoral growth has defied numerous predictions that it has reached its peak), they can exercise a major influence on government policy without ever taking office themselves. One factor working in their favour is the power of historical analogy. The National Party came to power originally by outflanking, from the right, the United Party formed in 1934 by Jan Smuts and the Nationalists' own first leader, Barry Hertzog, as a means of fusing Afrikaner and English-speaking interests. As the modern National Party comes increasingly to depend on the votes of English-speakers, just as Hertzog and Smuts did, the parallels force themselves onto the various party leaders (Botha himself was a Nationalist organiser in the 1930s). Moreover, the KP advance in the Transvaal threatens the survival of Nationalist ministers and parliamentarians.

The government has often timed repressive measures to

accommodate electoral pressures: the June 1986 emergency followed the AWB's successful assault on Pik Botha's Pietersburg rally; in April 1987, immediately before the general election, the SAP twice stormed COSATU House in Johannesburg; the February 1988 bannings took place shortly before the Transvaal by-elections.

It is, in any case, easy to overestimate the coherence of the regime's strategy. Ever since Botha took charge, it has involved constant hesitations and vacillations. These do not simply reflect pressures on or conflicts within the National Party. There is considerable resistance to reform in the state apparatus itself, among white civil servants, who have a vested interest in maintaining the present system of detailed state regulation of economic and social life as part of the administration of the apartheid laws.

Stanley Greenberg, whose interviews with officials in the influx-control bureaucracy have uncovered the large scale survival among them of traditional apartheid ideology, writes:

> While Afrikaner businessmen and intellectuals have been reconstructing the ideological foundations of the social order, state officialdom has remained, in essential terms, unreconstructed... these officials, whose function and identity rest on the conventional stateist ideology, have held tightly to its core tenets. Above all, they have resisted efforts to relinquish the state's visible control of civil society and to put their faith instead in market processes. Even with the government seemingly ready to abandon the most direct form of control—the pass laws—many of these officials have clung tightly to the mechanisms of control. Politicians and officials have consequently clashed increasingly over how to maintain control, how to come to terms with a growing and assertive Afrikaner bourgeoisie, and how to respond to the spreading expressions of African disaffection."

Greenberg points out that these conflicts within the state itself are indicative of a broader problem facing the regime. The old ideology of apartheid, based on the claim that state intervention was necessary to permit the separate development of the different races, is no longer credible. But the reformers have been unable to come up with a plausible alternative.

Policies such as regionalisation and privatisation are part of what Greenberg calls 'a broad strategy to depoliticise the social order, although the main elements of white privilege have been maintained intact.'" But the ideological rationale for such measures—a mixture of monetarism and academic theories about 'consociational' political systems in which different ethnic groups share power (the Lebanon used to be held up as a model of such an order!)—is hardly likely to grip the mass of lower-income whites, especially since they are materially threatened by *laissez-faire* economic policies. It is little wonder that traditional Afrikaner nationalism, brilliantly dramatised by AWB rallies which exploit the nostalgic myth—first constructed by the National Party—of the old Boer republics, should have such a powerful popular appeal.

One solution for the regime might be simply to cut the Gordian Knot and scrap white parliamentary institutions altogether. Botha's technocratic and authoritarian style, and the high-profile involvement of the military in decision-making, encourage belief that a 'silent coup', as the **Weekly Mail** called it, is taking place. But while it is certainly true that changes under Botha have helped insulate the executive from pressure from the white electorate— and indeed from the oppressed, should black intermediaries become increasingly involved in 'power-sharing'—there are limits to this process.

The core of the coercive institutions of the state remains the predominantly white security forces. The regime's ultimate defence against popular insurrection would be a white *levee en masse*. To disenfranchise the white population while continuing to rely on their firepower would deprive the regime of one of its remaining elements of legitimacy and invite armed resistance from the AWB's paramilitary forces and its sympathisers inside the SAP and the SADF. A civil war among the white population would drastically shift the balance of forces in favour of the black majority. A pro-reform dictatorship would, therefore, be an extremely risky strategy, courting ultimate disaster.

Despite Botha's authoritarian tendencies, he has tailored his policies carefully to win support among the white electorate and has made frequent personal interventions in parliament. As Harold Wolpe observes: 'What has been erected…is a parliamentary regime with great power centralised in a militarised executive.'[81]

Capital versus apartheid?

The Botha regime appeared in the mid-1980s to be in conflict, not merely with its traditional white base, but also with big business. Various developments seemed to support this view.[82] Most visible was the apparent tendency of Western capital to disengage from South Africa, reflected both in the numerous cases of disinvestment by multinationals during and after the 1984-86 crisis, and in the flight of money from the country which forced Pretoria at the beginning of September 1985 effectively to default on its loans from foreign banks.

Shortly afterwards, Anglo-American chief Gavin Relly, the most powerful capitalist in Africa, held a cordial meeting with ANC leaders in Zambia. This was followed by a call in January 1986 by the Federated Chambers of Industry (FCI) for the regime 'to create rapidly and urgently a climate for negotiation and a generally accepted framework within which negotiation can occur.'[83] The FCI went on to condemn the second emergency, only to receive an angry brush-off from Botha.

The regime's most spectacular row with big business came, however, when a special commission of inquiry was appointed to investigate the part played by one of its most outspoken critics, Chris Ball, the managing director of the First National Bank (formerly Barclays South Africa), in financing an advertisement calling for the unbanning of the ANC.

Such incidents seemed to suggest that a break was in sight between capital and the white state. Whatever advantages big business might have derived from apartheid in the past, the argument went, these were now outweighed by the disadvantages.[84] Capital no longer had an interest in the maintenance of white rule in South Africa. Episodes such as the Zambian meeting between business leaders and the ANC represented the opening stages in a process of negotiation which could lead to a settlement similar to the Lancaster House agreement of December 1979, which ended the war of liberation in Zimbabwe and permitted the establishment of black majority rule on terms that proved perfectly compatible with the continued domination of capital. Why should not Oliver Tambo follow where Robert Mugabe had led the way?

Certainly, as we have already seen, there is nothing about the ANC's politics which would prevent such an outcome—indeed Congress leaders have clearly welcomed the prospect of such negotiations. Moreover, some Marxist analyses do proceed along lines which assume a crude functional fit between apartheid and capitalism, such that once the relationship between the two is established it can never, in principle, be altered or abolished. It is extremely unwise to assume that there is a necessary relationship between the capitalist mode of production and a particular form of state, as those revolutionaries discovered who argued that the fascist regimes of southern Europe and the military dictatorships of Latin America could only be removed by the overthrow of capital.

From this point of view, the following remarks by Harold Wolpe provide, despite his overall commitment to ANC/SACP orthodoxy, a useful theoretical framework for discussing the current position of big business in South Africa:

> The relationship between capitalism and white domination must be seen as an historically contingent, not a necessary one. Moreover, that relationship will be both functional and contradictory at the same time—functional for the reproduction of certain relations and class positions and contradictory for others…the formation of structures and relations is always the outcome of struggles between contending groups or classes and…this outcome is Janus-faced, being always simultaneously functional and contradictory. Which pole of the relationship will be dominant depends on the historically specific conditions of the social formation.[55]

One might say that there has been a shift in the relationship between capitalism and apartheid over the past forty years from the 'functional' to the 'contradictory' pole (although this statement will receive a very important qualification later in our analysis).

The National Party came to power in 1948 with a programme involving an intensification of the system of segregation and influx control which had evolved in the late nineteenth century primarily in response to the need of mining capital for ultra-cheap labour. Apartheid offered farmers and mine-owners a solution to the severe labour crisis which had developed during the Second World War.[56] The section of capital which these policies least favoured were the larger manufacturers, for whom the relaxation of influx control envisaged by the Smuts government in 1948 offered certain benefits, since their capital-intensive operations left them free to offer higher wages for more skilled African workers. However, they too were able to take advantage of the apparently quiescent and docile black labour force created by the repression of the early 1960s.

Nevertheless, the boom of the 1960s and early 1970s brought about structural changes in the South African economy—in particular the expansion of relatively advanced manufacturing industries increasingly dependent on semi-skilled and even skilled African labour. It is this underlying transformation which, more than any factor, is responsible for the upsurge in struggle since the early 1970s, and the consequent efforts to reform the apartheid system from above.

Thus, as John Saul puts it, 'the linkage between racial domination and capitalist exploitation is as potentially contradictory as it has been mutually reinforcing.'[17] Institutions and practices which were either of positive benefit to capital (such as influx control) or at least were worth tolerating because of the overall advantages of apartheid (such as job reservation) have become obstacles whose removal is a necessary condition for the long-term survival of South African capitalism.

It is important, however, to understand that the kind of reforms which big business advocates do not imply a transition to a welfare-state liberal democracy, contrary to the impression conveyed by some commentators.[18] Big business pressed for the abolition of the pass laws for a variety of reasons—for example, the bad press they gave South Africa abroad, and the fact that influx control was in any case breaking down. But it is also true that many of the *effects* of apartheid institutions would survive their abolition. Thus, very high levels of unemployment—reflecting the capital-intensive nature of investment, economic stagnation, and rapid population growth—guarantee all sections of capital a plentiful supply of cheap labour without the need for the centralised system of labour allocation erected by the National Party after 1948. Moreover, the abolition of various racist practices does not amount to the abandonment of labour repression at the point of production itself, as the willingness of supposedly 'liberal' employers such as Anglo-American to resort to mass sackings and the use of their own armed security forces to crush striking miners indicates.

More fundamentally, *big business, like the régime itself, is opposed to black majority rule.* Thus, interviewed before Botha's 'Rubicon I' speech in August 1985, Gavin Relly advocated the abolition of influx control and the establishment of 'a negotiating forum' with black leaders. However, he said, 'if the black attitude was that there could be no discussion unless it was about one-man one-vote in a unitary South Africa, the forum would not go far.' Relly went on to advocate, in the light of the 'different constituencies that make up South African society—whites, Coloureds, urban blacks, Zulus, homelands—that have achieved a degree of viability and places like Natal where racial integration is already relatively far advanced', 'a federal system in which everyone had the vote within these constituencies—some white, some black, and some already integrated—but not directly for the central authority.'[89]

There is, indeed, a convergence between the kind of political changes envisaged by Relly and other leading capitalists and the régime's own 'regional-federal' strategy. This is most clearly indicated in a document published by the Associated Chambers of Commerce (Assocom) in August 1985 and written by two leading National Party intellectuals, Jan Lombard and Johan de Pisanie. The authors warn that 'the kind of constitutional changes that allow unlimited, simple majoritarian government in South Africa' would threaten the 'foundations of the private enterprise economy'. They therefore advocate a Bill of Rights protecting private property, which would allow the courts to override legislation threatening these 'foundations', and a federal system which would involve autonomy for local, racially defined 'communities'.[90] While there are differences between big business and the National Party government, reflected, for example, in the latter's rejection of the Indaba proposals for a multiracial 'KwaNatal' administration, they are agreed in seeking for political devices which would permit the political incorporation of the black middle class while preserving effective white control over the state.

The degree of convergence was reflected during the white referendum in 1983 on the tricameral constitution, when Van Zyl Slabbert expressed his frustration with the big capitalists who were supposed to be the main backers of the PFP. He was unable to persuade more than a handful (which included Harry Oppenheimer, then still Anglo chief, but not his successor Gavin Relly) to oppose the constitution on the grounds of its exclusion of Africans: 'The business community had bought the Yes vote—if not the Constitution—hook, line and sinker.'[91]

Similarly the black leader with whom big business is clearly most comfortable is not Tambo or Mandela but Buthelezi. The Zulu leader's support for 'free enterprise' and his evident willingness to settle for less than majority rule plainly endeared him to South African capitalists. As Relly put it, 'you can't really expect us to run away from the single black leader who says exactly what we think.'[92]

The crisis of 1984-86, combining as it did township insurgency, industrial militancy, a flight of capital and economic recession, pushed big business into a more critical stance towards the régime. One of the outspoken critics was Tony Bloom, chairman of the Premier group of mills, bakeries and stores, who declared in 1984: 'Negotiations with ANC are a historical inevitability. The question is not whether, but rather when such negotiations will take place.'[93] But he later acknowledged:

> I don't think it's a coincidence that the business community became most vocal when the economy was in the worst recession for fifteen years, profits were declining, and South African businessmen were shunned in the captitals of the world.[94]

But even at the height of the political crisis—between July and September 1985, when the first emergency was imposed, 'Rubicon I' provoked the collapse of the rand, debt repayments were suspended, and Relly and Bloom met the ANC in Zambia—the South African bourgeoisie did not swing round to support the resistance's main demand: one person, one vote in a unitary South Africa. Anthony Sampson summed up their mood:

> The businessmen knew they were approaching an abyss, and that they must find some way round it: but they could not bring themselves to look down it for long. They knew that they would not run their factories and mines for long without the consent of the black workers, and that black political ambitions could not be suppressed indefinitely. Many even agreed that there could even be a black government in ten years time. *But they could not visualise any likely transition between now and then. They were prepared to offer blacks almost anything except the one thing they demanded: one man, one vote. Most found it impossible to contemplate majority rule, or to deal with the blacks who were likely to command it.*[95]

The central difficulty lies in the transition to black majority rule. The ANC could perfectly well provide capital with a bourgeois black government which would guarantee the conditions of continued capital accumulation: both the professions of Tambo, Mandela and company and the experience of countries such as Zimbabwe show this. But capital also needs to be able to rely on the existence, during the transition to majority rule, of a state apparatus capable of defending bourgeois property relations against the black working class. Such a state apparatus exists at present—

above all in the formidable might of the SADF and the SAP. But the cohesion of the existing state machine is inseparably interwoven with the white population and the material privileges they derive from the prevailing system of racial domination.

Any break from effective white control of the state would threaten to disintegrate the state machine. Some white soldiers and policemen might participate in a fascist putsch against the reformers; others might simply conclude that it wasn't worth fighting for a black government and emigrate. The existing state apparatus might disintegrate more rapidly than the ANC could construct a new one capable of defending capitalist relations of production. Given the strength and militancy of the black working class, the outcome would be an extremely threatening situation for the South African bourgeoisie.

The dilemma this poses them is well put by the Marxist Workers' Tendency:

> Because of the challenge of the black proletariat from below, the ruling class have to try to reform the state system; they have to try to change the state itself. But they cannot afford to weaken the repressive power of the state in the face of this black challenge.[96]

Ultimately, South African capital depends on the existing state apparatus to guarantee its existence. This means that it will, albeit with hesitations, criticisms, and many justified forebodings about the future, fall in behind the National Party régime. However unsatisfactory Botha may be, better the devil big business knows than the devil it doesn't know.

This fundamental strategic choice became evident after the September 1985 meeting in Zambia. Relly found himself isolated even within Anglo (Harry Oppenheimer was critical, for example), and began to distance himself from the ANC.[97] The second state of emergency, and its success in repressing the township risings, rallied big business behind the régime. Relly told Anglo shareholders in July 1987: 'In the circumstances the imposition of the state of emergency last year and its recent renewal, though regrettable, were necessary to contain the widening cycle of senseless violence.'[98]

Tony Bloom announced in January 1988 that he was giving up the Premier Group chairmanship to move to Britain. He gave two reasons for the retreat of big businessmen from overt political activity:

They've been cowed into silence by the state of emergency, worried that what they say could be construed as a subversive statement. There's no doubt they were very frightened by what happened to Chris Ball. If that was intended as a message to the business community, it worked.

Secondly, there's a lull because we're back into an economic upswing, and a lot of people have gone back to just running a business—which many think is all they should be doing anyway."

The shifts in big business's relationship with the Botha régime, from critical support in the early 1980s through open criticism in 1984-86, to rather grudging quiescence under the second emergency, should not in any case have come as a surprise. The South African state is a capitalist state, but it does not follow that it is a simple instrument of big business. The state and private capital may come into conflict for a number of reasons. In the first place, the state must try to develop an overall strategy for the capitalist class as a whole which may involve overriding the interests of specific capitals. Secondly, the state is faced, unlike individual firms, with the problem of maintaining political order, which involves attempting to develop ways of eliciting the consent of at least a section of the population. Thirdly, the state bureaucracy may develop interests which bring it into conflict with sections of private capital, especially if (as is generally true in twentieth-century conditions) it develops as a capitalist in its own right, directly involving itself in the accumulation process.

To these general sources of conflict is added, in the case of South Africa, the close association between the National Party and one particular fraction of capital, the Afrikaner bourgeoisie. Craig Charney argues:

Although the split [which led to the formation of the KP] has freed the NP to further the interests of capital, the Afrikaner capitalists remain much more reluctant to share political power than some of their English-speaking counterparts, despite their increasingly similar view on economic questions. The explanation of this apparent paradox lies in the fact that the political interests of these sections of the bourgeoisie remain opposed, even though their economic interests are convergent. Accumulation by Afrikaners remains largely dependent on the state and its organisations. Afrikaner managers in the parastatal industries and civil service obviously owe their position to Nationalist power... Even much of Afrikaans private business, often the weak sister of its English competitors, remains dependent upon state patronage and protection, while the agricultural bourgeoisie relies on farm pricing, input and credit policies.[100]

The implication of this arguement is that Afrikaner capital is likely to favour a slower pace of political reform than its English-speaking rivals. But these divisions within the bourgeoisie extend also to economic policy. One of the main planks of the Botha government's platform was deregulation designed to integrate the South African economy more deeply into the world market. Economic recession and the flight of capital in the mid-1980s, however, helped to create a powerful lobby in favour of import controls and even a siege economy closed off to the rest of the world.

A key figure in this lobby was Fred du Plessis, head of the Afrikaner business empire SANLAM and a close adviser of Botha's. SANLAM took advantage of disinvestment by Western multinationals to buy up the subsidiaries of many departing companies. Its growing stake in local manufacturing industry encouraged du Plessis to become increasingly critical of policies, for example over the exchange rate, which, he argued, made the South African economy vulnerable to the icy blasts of world competition. Similar pressures for more greater reliance on economic protectionism came from the military, the National Party right wing, and the KP. In a situation where Botha had political reasons for resisting demands by Western governments that he negotiate with the ANC, these demands for a siege economy may have found an audience at the highest levels of the régime.[101]

It would be a mistake, however, to exaggerate the extent of the divisions within the bourgeoisie. There were counter-pressures to the protectionists—for example, from Gerrit de Kock, governor of the Reserve Bank of South Africa, and from many leading capitalists, both English-speaking and Afrikaner. The highly monopolistic character of the South African economy means that it is difficult sharply to differentiate between distinct fractions of capital based in specific sectors. Thus Anglo has interests spanning mining, finance, manufacturing and agriculture, and was the major beneficiary from disinvestment, which allowed it to secure control over the First National Bank (formerly Barclays), the South African Motor Corporation, and Citibank.[102]

The South African economy is too dependent on world markets to retreat into a full-scale siege economy—only by exporting raw materials can it secure the foreign exchange required to finance imports of capital goods. In the economic as well as the political sphere the régime is likely to oscillate from expedient to expedient rather than follow a consistent path.

The distance between English-speaking capital and the state itself can, in any case, be exaggerated, Thus in 1980 Botha established the Defence Advisory Council to help co-ordinate the SADF and the armaments industry. Its members included not only such leading Afrikaner capitalists as Fred du Plessis and Willem De Villiers of General Mining, but also Gavin Relly and Mike Rosholt, chairman of Barlow Rand, a business empire closely associated with Anglo.[103]

The common interests of big capital and the white state ultimately outweigh their conflicts. They are caught in a shared dilemma—the reforms necessary to stave off revolution may help to provoke such a revolution both by stimulating black revolt and by so alienating poorer whites as to undermine the existing state machine. They are united in their fear that an end to white rule will threaten the very survival of capitalism itself—a fear well expressed by Jan Lombard when he wrote: 'If an unqualified one-man, one-vote election was held today in the Republic, a non-white leader with a communistic programme would probably attain an overall majority on a pledge to confiscate and redistribute the property of the privileged classes.'[104]

Faced with the pressure from both left and right, from black rebellion and white reaction, both state and capital will vacillate between reform and repression. Neither has any solution to the crisis facing South African capitalism.

The workers' movement under populist leadership

The relationship between apartheid and capitalism, while, as Wolpe puts it, in the abstract 'contingent', is therefore unlikely, in the concrete circumstances of contemporary South Africa, to be broken. Capital and the white state will hang together—in every meaning of the word. This analysis accordingly confirms the general argument of this book, that only a socialist revolution made by the black working class can achieve national liberation for the oppressed majority. How well, then, has the workers' movement weathered the second emergency?

Here, at least initially, there was a striking contrast between the collapse of township resistance and a *rising* curve of workers' struggles. In 1986 1.1 million strike-days were 'lost'—a conservative estimate which excludes another 3.5 million strike-days caused by political stay-aways, particularly on May Day and 16 June, the tenth anniversary of the Soweto uprising. This was only a foretaste, however, of what happened in 1987, the first year of the emergency. Strike figures rocketed—6.6 million working days 'lost', in addition to another 2.5 million on the May Day stay-away, and many more in protests against the white elections on 5-6 May and on 16 June.[105]

To a large extent 1987 saw the key line of confrontation between the régime and the resistance shift to the labour front. 'Protracted trials of strengh in key industries were a notable feature of the year's pattern of strike activity,' commented labour consultant Andrew Levy. '...labour mobilisation during the past year has advanced the aims of the broad anti-apartheid movement far more than those of the labour movement, despite the fact that it has focused on routine workplace issues'.[106]

The year began with a ten-week strike ending in February, by 11,000 workers employed by the OK Bazaars retail chain. Among the most important strikes to follow were a 46-day stoppage at Mercedes-Benz and four disputes involving postal workers—a highly significant development, since it represented the spread of independent unionism to the state sector. Public employees were also involved in the spectacular strike between 22 April and 5 June 1987 by 20,000 railway workers employed by South African Transport Services (SATS) during which COSATU House was twice invaded by the SAP and then wrecked by a bomb. But the most important struggle of all was the first national wages strike mounted by the National Union of Mineworkers (NUM), which took place between 9 and 30 August 1987, and involved at its height 340,000 workers.

The scale of workers' militancy was also reflected in the growth of trade-union organisation itself. **The Financial Mail** reported: 'Contrary to the declining trend in union membership elsewhere in the industrial world, South African unions overall increased their membership in 1987'. By the end of the year membership of registered unions was estimated at nearly 1.87 million, 18 per cent of the economically active population (members of unregistered unions were estimated at 240,000.)[107] These figures reflected more than quantitative growth. The established white-dominated unions were in crisis. The Trade Union Council of South Africa, squeezed from both left and right, disbanded at the end of 1986, having seen its membership shrink from nearly half a million in 1983 to a mere 150,000. Even the all-white South African Condederation of Labour found itself under pressure from the even more right-wing Mine Workers' Union.

The growth of the independent unions was in sharp contrast to this disarray. COSATU emerged as the largest union grouping, with a paid-up membership in early 1988 of 750,000 and a signed-up membership of one million. Its closest rival was the National Council of Trade Unions (NACTU), formed in October 1986 through the fusion of the two main black consciousness groupings, CUSA and AZACTU. It claimed 450,000 signed-up members, although observers placed its paid-up membership much lower, at 150,000.[108]

The disintegration of TUCSA helped to spawn a large number of unions outside any federation—known as the independents, some of which were drawn towards COSATU. The South African Boilermakers Society, for example, co-operates with the National Union of Metalworkers of South Africa (NUMSA—formerly MAWU). In some cases the process went further: thus in November 1987 two former TUCSA affiliates, the National Union of Garment Workers and the Textile Workers Industrial Union merged with the National Union of Textile Workers, a COSATU-affiliate, to form the Amalgamated Clothing and Textile Workers Union of South Africa, bringing an additional 40,000 members into the federation.

The response of the ruling class to these developments was double-edged. On the one hand, their tactics became significantly tougher. This was reflected in the growth in large protracted strikes—the average length of strikes grew from 3.1 days in 1986 to 9.9 days in 1987—and in the fact that in the first nine months of 1987 issues such as redundancies and union recognition triggered 38.6 per cent of all disputes, dismissals 20.5 per cent and wages only 33.7 per cent.[109] A number of big lockouts also indicated the harder line taken by the bosses. But the clearest indication of this line came during the miners' strike, when the Chamber of Mines, under the leadership of Anglo-American, forced NUM to accept an only marginally improved pay offer after 60,000 workers had been sacked.

The Botha regime more than matched this approach. Thus it dramatically upped the stakes in the rail strike, which was denounced by SATS director-general Bart Grove as 'part of a revolutionary strategy' and which led to a government-directed campaign of intimidation and harassment aimed at COSATU itself. Further attacks followed. The Minister of Manpower published in September 1987 the Labour Relations Amendment Bill, which was widely seen as a significant retreat from the concessions made to black trade unions after the Wiehahn report in 1979. Perhaps the most important restriction proposed was a ban on sympathy strikes. Then, as part of the package of measures imposed on resistance organisations in February 1988, COSATU was prohibited from engaging in political activity.

The attacks on the independent unions by both employers and the state did not, however, represent a systematic attempt to smash the black workers' movement. Thus the rail strike revealed considerable divisions on the bosses' side. SATS management had held an inquiry into labour relations which had come out in favour of encouraging collective bargaining on the railways. Ten days before the strike began, the official SATS journal carried an article by Professor Nic Wiehahn, who had headed the inquiry, arguing for the extension of collective bargaining and even a limited right to strike to the public sector.

Moreover, the strike ended in a retreat by management, who made significant concessions to the demands of the South African Railways and Harbours Workers Union (SARHWU). The 18,000 workers whose dismissal had precipitated the confrontation were re-instated, the workers' right democratically to elect their representatives was recognised, and black workers were included under the provision granting SATS employees' permanent status after two years' service—previously a condition reserved for whites.[110]

The rail strike was by no means the only dispute which the employers failed to win. The OK Bazaars strike for example ended with management making major concessions to the workers' wage demands. Sometimes the outcome was more evenly balanced. The Postal and Telecommunications Workers Association (POTWA), having won major concessions, including recognition, in two local strikes in East London and the Witwatersrand in April 1987, saw many of these gains clawed back when management adopted a much harder line, provoking a national strike in August and September which ended after 3,000 workers had been dismissed.[111]

But even when the employers did take a hard line, this did not reflect a break with the historic decision to incorporate rather than to crush black trade unionism. Thus even before the miners' strike had ended on terms set by the Chamber of Mines, Bobby Godsell of Anglo-American's Industrial Relations Department said:

> I think there's a very positive aspect to the strike, which is that it's a sign of a growing maturity in the South African nation. I think both sides are, broadly speaking, playing the game according to the collective bargaining rules. I've been encouraged by the initial response of the South African government, which has been to say that it will not interfere. In an important way a strike is a test of the vibrancy of an industrial relations system.[112]

From the point of view of big capital, then, the miners' strike was an important test of whether such a powerful group of workers could come out on strike without this leading to a generalised political confrontation with the state. In those terms, the strike was a success for them. Paradoxically, the strikes under the second emergency marked a certain stabilisation of South African industrial relations. Andrew Levy commented: 'As a result, industrial disputes, at least in the private sector, have become far more institutionalised. It [*sic*] now centres far more on the content of bargaining than on whether there will be bargaining at all.'[113]

A similar objective—of containing rather than crushing the unions—can be detected even in the Labour Relations Amendment Bill. A key provision reduces unions' indemnity from civil claims for damages caused by unlawful strikes and creates the presumption that union members and officials responsible for such damages are acting in the name of the union: 'The intention of this provision is to force unions to stop wildcat strikes because of the consequences of not doing so.'[114]

The aim, in other words, would be to get union officials to police their members for fear of otherwise becoming liable to massive damages. This kind of measure closely resembles the main thrust of the Thatcher government's Employment Acts in Britain, which were intended not to dismantle trade unionism but rather to strengthen the power of the full-time bureaucracy over the rank and file. Although in South Africa the régime and private captial are by no means fully in agreement—both the Labour Relations Amendment Bill and the restrictions imposed on COSATU have been criticised by some employers, they both seem to have the same kind of trade-union movement in mind—one that engages in genuine collective bargaining and even sometimes leads strikes, but which keeps out of politics.

On the face of it, COSATU represented a style of trade unionism far removed from economism of this sort. On the contrary, its commitment to engagement in broader political action became if anything firmer during the second emergency. This commitment increasingly took the form of support for a broad democratic alliance under ANC leadership. Thus on 5-6 March 1986 Jay Naidoo, COSATU general secretary, Sydney Mafumadi, his deputy, and NUM general secretary Cyril Ramaphosa met Tambo and other leaders of the ANC and SACTU in Lusaka. The communiqué issued after these talks declared that 'lasting solutions can only emerge from the national liberation movement, headed by the ANC, and the entire democratic forces of our country, of which COSATU is an important and integral part'.[115]

The COSATU leadership's espousal of popular-front politics was reflected in the emergence of a permanent alliance between the federation and the UDF such that joint UDF/COSATU statements became a routine matter until the February 1988 bannings. The relationship was formallised in July 1987, when COSATU's second congress adopted the Freedom Charter, the ANC's main programmatic document. This resolution followed similar decisions by a number of key unions, notably NUM, NUMSA and the Food and Allied Workers' Union (FAWU).

This shift represented a decisive victory for the 'populist' supporters of the ANC inside the unions in their struggle with 'workerist' opponents of union involvement in political alliances. Within COSATU the main workerist unions, most of which had originated in the old Federation of South African Trade Unions (FOSATU)—notably, the Metal and Allied Workers Union (MAWU) and National Automobile and Allied Workers Union, both which were merged into NUMSA in May 1987, NUTW, and the Commercial, Catering and Allied Workers Union of South Africa (CCAWUSA)—were forced onto the defensive politically.

Other unions which had previously taken a more ambiguous stance swung decisively into the populist camp. The NUM played a crucial role in this respect. Although it had broken from the black-consciousness grouping CUSA only in 1985, the miners' union rapidly become a stronghold of ANC politics. After the NUM congress had adopted the Freedom Charter in February 1987, union leader Cyril Ramaphosa explicitly endorsed the two-stage strategy:

> People in general want apartheid dismantled. Socialism is something you start building and learning and working through and discussing and so forth, and you move towards it—and between the two there is no gap. There is immediately a movement from one towards the other, but of necessity the end of national oppression has to be achieved first.[116]

How had this remarkable shift within the independent unions occurred? To some degree, it simply reflected the higher political profile enjoyed by the ANC thanks to the 1984-86 risings and the activity of its supporters and those of the South African Communist Party (SACP). The second emergency did not see any relaxation of the efforts of Congress supporters to win control of COSATU and other resistance organisations—indeed this was intensified. The demoralisation induced by the collapse of popular insurgency in the townships and by the defeats suffered by some workers may indeed have provided a more fertile soil for these activities, since the ANC and MK seemed to offer the hope of a liberating army moving south from Lusaka to rescue the oppressed from their plight. It would not be the first time that workers, lacking confidence in themselves, looked to some outside force to substitute for their own self-activity. ANC sympathisers, in their efforts to establish what sometimes seemed like remote control from Lusaka, enjoyed both far greater resources than their opponents, and the support of white liberals and international opinion.

The ANC's efforts to win control of all resistance forces sprang from its fundamental strategy of forcing the régime to the negotiating table. As Howard Barrell put it:

> the ANC's vision of negotiations with the government—if they come—is of the ANC heading a broad front of political, trade-union and other anti-apartheid forces.
>
> This front—the ANC would hope—would sit across a 'two-sided table' from the government and its allies. The ANC would resist attempts to introduce into the talks a multiparty or round-tabled design which would introduce a plethora of small and supposedly autonomous parties which it would regard as irrelevant to the central

conflict.[117]

To make plausible its claim to be sole negotiator for the popular resistance with the régime, the ANC would have to control all the different anti-apartheid organisations. Inclusion of the independent unions in this 'broad front' would be especially important if the ANC leadership were to convince the ruling class that it could deliver an acquiescent working class in exchange for political power. In pursuit of this strategy, a wide range of anti-apartheid opinion, including both white liberals and black-consciousness supporters, was cultivated by the ANC.

The struggle for control over the independent unions assumed an especially bitter form. Battles raged, for example, over the regional structures established by COSATU, with the key Witwatersrand region captured first by the workerists and then by the populists. In December 1986 fifteen trade unionists regarded as prominent workerists received a letter from 'the internal command of the national liberation alliance' which began:

> Despite several serious warnings to some of your reformist and Trotskyite collaborators, you still persist in spreading reactionary sindicalist workerist ideologies to confuse and divert the spontaneous mass worker resistance into accepting fraudulant 'reforms' instead of a revolutionary transformation of South Africa. The fact that you talk endlessly about the leading role of the working class to overthrow capitalism proves that you are only armchair revolutionaries who in practice reject all forms of disciplined revolutionary organisation.

The letter concluded by warning its recipients in particular not to 'prevent COSATU from affiliating to the national liberation movement,' and by declaring: 'If you do not comply with these demands be sure that you will be dealt with by our military command.'

Perhaps this document was the work of an *agent provocateur*. That an atmosphere had been created, however, where such vulgar threats could credibly be attributed to ANC supporters is suggested by a resolution adopted at much the same time by the MAWU Johannesburg shop stewards' local. Addressed to the corresponding COSATU body, the resolution complained that nearly a year after COSATU's formation:

> nothing constructive has been discussed in our local.
>
> We are being mocked whenever we put our views, COSATU structures are being ignored or overlooked. Some comrades would

like to force undemocratic decisions down our throats.

We bring mandates from our workforce, and decisions from our local but these are not discussed. Instead we would be snubbed. We believe it's time to work together with progressive organisations but structures, procedures and constitutions of different progressive organisations be respected.

The resolution went on to argue that 'workers have socialist ideas' and that they prefer 'worker controlled shop steward councils. Independent from community-based organisations and working with such organisations on disciplined alliances.'

The most coherent opposition to such ideas was provided by the Communist Party. Thus Joe Slovo, who became SACP general secretary in 1987, declared: 'It can only be an indigenous representative of the disastrous Pol Pot philosophy who can project a pole-vault into socialism and communism the day after overthrow of white rule.'[118] There were some signs of growing support for the SACP within the country. Two workerists, for example, were denounced for 'pass[ing]... over in complete silence the actual existence' of the SACP, 'a vanguard, workers' party with a socialist programme'.[119]

One feature of SACP propaganda was its attempt to lump together the workerists—and indeed socialist activists—with revolutionary organisations outside South Africa, for example the Socialist Workers Party in Britain. The following sample is fairly typical:

The 'workerist' clique has always sought, at best, to turn the democratic trade union movement into a political party. Such a party would become the central opposition to the political vanguard of the working class—the SACP—and the mass democratic movement. At worst, they would create an opposition parallel to, and within, the trade union movement. The so-called Socialist Workers Party is a case in point.[120]

The lead-up to COSATU's second congress in July 1987 was accompanied by a rising crescendo of denunciation of the left. Jay Naidoo declared in May 1987 that COSATU, through its alliances with UDF affiliates, was 'breaking away from the theoretical clutches of intellectuals and organisations that excel in resolution-writing, but who reduce all theory and practice to ideas that exist outside of mass organisation and struggle.'[121] Rapu Molekane, general secretary of the South African Youth Congress, made an explicit attack on the intellectuals—many of them white—who had been instrumental in building the former FOSATU unions when he warned the newly established National Education, Health and Allied Workers Union in June 1987 against 'academics' with 'half-baked theories of a working-class struggle in their attempt to cause divisions within the workers' movement... These so-called socialists should be isolated... The criterion for having people working for trade unions should not be a university degree.' [122] At the COSATU congress itself both the Marxist Workers Tendency, which is sympathetic to the British Militant Group, and the Socialist Workers Party were attacked by name.

The creation of a witch-hunt atmosphere is not, however, sufficient to explain the comparatively easy ride which the populists enjoyed. The political weaknesses of the workerists themselves cannot be ignored. One current among the workerists simply sought to continue their traditional 'survivalist' strategy. While refusing to capitulate to the populists, they at the same time avoided any major confrontation with them.

The best example of this was provided by the leadership of the metalworkers' union, NUMSA. Although the product of a merger in May 1987, the union to a large degree continued the traditions of the previous FOSATU-affliate, MAWU. The workerist leaders were careful to prevent a populist takeover: the UDF-aligned South African Allied Workers Union (SAAWU) was excluded from the merger after failing to submit proof of its paid-up membership. But the NUMSA founding congress, while reaffirming MAWU's commitment to socialist goals, also endorsed the Freedom Charter as 'a good foundation stone [on] which to start building our working-class programme'—a formula calculated to concede the populists' demand that all unions back the Charter while preserving some space for a working-class politics independent of the Congress and its supporters. [123]

Some workerists, however, went much further, actually capitulating to the populists. This tendency was most visible among some of the socialist intellectuals who had been often closely associated with the development of the independent unions in the 1970s and early 1980s.

One spectacular example of such a shift was provided by Rob Lambert. In 1980 he had published an article, cited in chapter four, which argued that the South African Congress of Trade Unions' subordination to the Congress alliance had led to the collapse of its efforts to build strong workers' organisations in the late 1950s and early 1960s; the conclusion he and many others drew was that it was therefore necessary for the independent unions to avoid similar alliances. By 1986, however, Lambert had changed his account of SACTU history, now arguing that there was 'a real *continuity* between practices of the 1950s and the "discoveries" of the 1970s and 1980s.' The strategic conclusions derived from this analysis were also new. The 'essential goal of the working class', which Lambert called 'radical democracy', could 'only be realised within a commitment to the national struggle, for it is the national struggle that has the greatest potential to unite different classes, and segments of classes, in a common liberation struggle. In taking the lead, COSATU has accepted the responsibility of imprinting working-class, socialist demands on the nationalist cause.' [124]

As Lambert's formulations suggest, the typical form taken by such capitulations to populism is not a simple collapse into a Stalinist stages strategy. The recommendation by Eddie Webster—another example of this trend—that the unions should 'consolidate the embryonic alliance, take up the concerns of working people as a whole and engage directly with the national liberation movement' is characteristic of the kind of blurring of the boundaries between workerism and populism that is involved. [152]

Rather than argue explicitly that national liberation is a distinct, prior stage to socialism—as the SACP continue to insist—the ex-workerist intellectuals tend to take the kind of line pursued by Karl von Holdt, editor of the **South African Labour Bulletin**, who, while defending what he calls a 'national liberation position', qualifies this by saying: 'This is not of course to say that nationalism guarantees full social transformation. It is a question of the balance of class forces within nationalism'. [126]

This position, which espouses participation in a modern version of the Congress alliance of the 1950s alliance while leaving open the question of whether or not the overthrow of apartheid will involve socialist revolution, corresponds to a current within COSATU itself. Perhaps most frequently identified with Jay Naidoo, this involved the claim that both, workerism and populism represent partial and inadequate perspectives and that COSATU has achieved a synthesis of the best in both approaches. Thus he declared:

The democratic structures of COSATU will not allow so-called 'workerist' and 'populist' fringe groupings to impose their own undemocratic control over militant, politicised, organised workers in South Africa. Underlying both the 'workerist' and 'populist' minority positions is a lack of confidence in the organisation, strength and vision of millions of workers in the country.

Workers are facing forward—in the direction of national liberation and socialism... The struggle for socialism is already unfolding within the struggle for national liberation.[127]

It is open to question to what extent this 'left', or perhaps better 'centrist' populism represented a genuinely independent or coherent position. Naidoo for instance claimed: 'There might be tactical differences but the goals of all sections of the community are the same. What we say is that we reject the present economic system because it has denied people fundamental human rights. We believe that the wealth should be democratically controlled.'[128]

This statement could mean that black capitalists want socialism—an absurdity— or it could simply be a reaffirmation of the traditional Congress demand for some diffusion of economic power which would leave capitalism intact.

Such vague formulae, while of no use in any serious analysis of the struggle, may nevertheless, by blurring key issues, enable Naidoo to perform the no doubt difficult balancing act between two powerful forces within COSATU—the assertive and increasingly Stalinist populist faction, and the workerists, on the defensive but still with formidable bases of strength in unions such as NUMSA. Workers might be facing forward, but facing both ways suited Naidoo better.

The general triumph of various forms of populism was not, however, unqualified. The toughest resistance to 'Charterism' came from the main retail union, CCAWUSA. On 27-28 June 1987 it was due to merge with two smaller unions to form a single union for the sector, also to be known as CCAWUSA, a fact which reflected the former's dominance—with 73,000 members compared to 17,000 in the two other unions. The merger congress instead led to a split when the leaders of the Johannesburg and Cape Town CCAWUSA branches refused to recognise the populist officials elected after the meeting had been closed, claiming that UDF supporters had tried to hijack the new union.

The tensions underlying the split had been present two weeks earlier at the last congress of the old CCAWUSA. There a polarisation had developed between the Johannesburg and Cape Town branches, who had a majority of the delegates, and the Orange-Vaal, Natal, Pretoria and Eastern Cape branches. In particular, the congress had passed, against the minority branches' opposition, a Johannesburg resolution refusing to endorse either the Freedom Charter or the black-consciousness Azanian Manifesto on the grounds that to do so would risk 'serious divisions' and instead proposing to 'discuss at all levels of the union and our Federation the importance of a Socialist programme of action which will bind together all workers regardless of political affiliation.'[129]

By contrast, the minority branches at the abortive merger meeting endorsed the Freedom Charter.

The Johannesburg and Cape Town branches could credibly claim to represent a majority of CCAWUSA's membership. The Johannesburg branch alone had 40,000 members. The branch had been at the centre of the wave of militancy which had shaken the retail sector in 1986-87. Specific conditions in the industry—its domination by a handful of huge supermarket chains, the poor wages and conditions, a young, urbanised and literate workforce—had favoured the growth of militant, rank-and-file trade unionism. CCAWUSA was the main, though not the only expression of this development—another, albeit much smaller socialist-led union, the remarkably dynamic and independent Federation of Commercial, Retail and Allied Workers (FEDCRAW), flourishing on the Rand despite its mistaken refusal to join COSATU.

Shopworkers were able to use a wide range of tactics—including the occupation of supermarkets—in order to take advantage of the retailers' need, in a highly competitive sector, to keep their stores open. The regime paid its own tribute to this militancy by detaining more leading members of CCAWUSA under the second emergency than of any other union.[130]

But the retail strike-wave and state repression contributed to the development of socialist political consciousness among shopworkers, reflected, for example, in an intensive education programme for shop stewards.

Now this dynamic, socialist trade unionism came into conflict with the drive to bind COSATU to the ANC. Jay Naidoo was quick to recognise the populist minority, headed by Papi Ngare, as the official leadership of CCAWUSA. The COSATU Central Executive Committee endorsed this decision, with no effective opposition, to their shame, from workerists representing unions such as NUMSA. The CCAWUSA majority however, did not simply stand firm, but raised the stakes politically, in particular by organising a rally attended by 5,000 workers at Jabulani Stadium in Soweto on 12 November 1987 around the themes 'Defend CCAWUSA! Defend Socialism!' For the first time a section of the leadership of the new working-class movement were willing openly to confront the populist bandwagon on the basis not simply of a workerist defence of independent trade-union organisation but of the political assertion of socialism as the main goal of the strike.

Something of the flavour of the CCAWUSA majority's politics is provided by a paper written by one of their officials:

> The opportunists, the renegades, the so-called 'pro-COSATU wing' have adopted the programme of an alien class—the petty bourgeoisie—programme which calls merely for the reforming of a present-day racial capitalism to a more 'Democratic Capitalism'...the most democratic capitalism will not mean the emancipation of the working people, it will only open the road for the oppressed petty bourgeoisie, the small businessmen, the petty proprietor to have a larger share of the South African Cake, one which we the working people have built up and developed. To adopt and fight for the programme of reforming capitalism is to betray the historical interests of the working class, it is to betray the daily struggle of the working people to free themselves from the bondage of wage-slavery...
>
> ...We believe that the working class must have its own class programme, its own policy, its own class platform and its own organisation, in a word it must develop its own *class leadership* distinct from and opposed to all nationalist leadership...
>
> All talk of alliances in South Africa has always been the basis of the subordination of the working class to nationalism... We in CCAWUSA comrades have never rejected the absolute necessity for alliances, but we insist that in order to enter into alliances the working class must have its ideas, its programme, its policies and its independent leadership.[131]

The politics of the CCAWUSA majority is by no means unproblematic. After the president of Mozambique, Samora Machel, died in a plane crash in October 1986, CCAWUSA issued a leaflet which did not simply declare its solidarity with the Frelimo regime against the barbarous policy of destabilisation mounted against it by Pretoria but described 'Comrade Machel' as 'a great thinker' who 'contributed immensely to socialist thought'—a strange tribute from anti-Stalinist trade unionists to a ruler who would certainly not have allowed them to organise in Mozambique. More immediately, the CCAWUSA majority's linking of their union's defence to the cause of socialism could, in the absence of the commitment to build an independent political party, degenerate into a form of 'red' trade unionism, with CCAWUSA becoming a substitute for the political organisation required to win the majority of workers to revolutionary socialism.

Moreover, despite the CCAWUSA majority's constantly affirmed commitment to COSATU, it did seem as if some at least among them were drawn towards NACTU and the National Forum, whose Azanian Manifesto after all explicitly avowed socialist objectives. Any move towards building a rival federation would, however, have been a disastrous mistake, since it would isolate some of the best militants in the South African workers' movement from the class's main organised strength in COSATU. The real battle was to fight for leadership inside COSATU. But that would require political as well as trade union organisation. The CCAWUSA majority's explicit defence of socialism was nevertheless an important step in this direction.

What kind of practical leadership did the dominant populist faction within COSATU offer in the meanwhile? The federation's main national initiative was the National Living Wage Campaign, launched in April 1987 and intended to provide the focus for a generalised wage offensive. COSATU, however, found itself rapidly forced onto the defensive after its confrontation with the state during the April-June rail strike. After the SAP invasion and subsequent bombing of COSATU House the national officials launched a 'Hands Off COSATU' campaign. Any real hopes for offensive action by workers came to focus on the disputes provoked in July and August and the wage claims of COSATU's two most important affiliates, NUM and NUMSA. Both proved to be severe disappointments.

Inevitably the confrontation between NUM and the Chamber of Mines attracted the most attention, involving as it did the first national strike in South Africa's most important industry. As we have seen, the strike represented a severe defeat for the union, which accepted the Chamber's terms after 60,000 miners had been sacked.[132] This defeat was by no means inevitable. Trends within the industry favoured the miners—in particular, the tendency towards a much more stable workforce of long-term migrants recruited primarily from within South Africa, probably as a step towards largely replacing migrant labourers with miners resident with their families in the cities.[133]

Nevertheless, a confrontation with the most powerful group of capitalists in Africa would require careful preparation and, above all, the full mobilisation of rank-and-file miners. Instead the NUM leadership called on their members to leave the mines and to sit the strike out in their mainly rural homes. Fortunately this foolish tactic—'Operation Exodus'—was largely ignored by the strikers, but it was indicative not merely of the NUM leadership's lack of seriousness, but also of their attitude towards the union rank and file.

The NUM congress in February 1987 had seen clear evidence of a marked tendency towards the union's bureaucratisation: congresses were henceforth to be held every two years, mine shaft stewards' councils were abolished, and full-time shaft stewards introduced. These measures were clearly attractive to a union leadership who so distrusted their members that they actually sent them off the field of battle during NUM's first national strike.

Ramaphosa finally called the strike off without consulting the rank and file. It was hardly surprising that following the defeat there was considerable bitterness towards the union leadership among rank-and-file miners, especially those victimised, who naturally included many militant stewards. In February 1988 a delegation of sacked workers from one mine visited NUM headquarters asking to see Cyril Ramaphosa on three successive days. Each time he was unavailable, so eventually in anger and desperation they wrecked the offices. Union membership fell in the wake of the strike from 270,000 to 210,000.

The miners' strike showed that the union movement was experiencing not simply a conflict between different political tendencies, but also one between rank-and-file workers and an embryonic but distinct bureaucracy of full-time officials. According to a survey published in late 1987 the independent unions had at least 24,701 shop stewards, compared to some 6,000 in 1984. But unions also had 715 paid officials (excluding administrative staff), nearly two and a half times the number reported at the end of 1985.[134]

The relative weight of this officialdom and its preoccupation with conserving the union apparatus rather than prosecuting class struggle were factors behind the NUMSA leadership's feeble conduct of the union's 1987 wage claim. They called off a one-day strike by 60,000 metalworkers on 14 July after the Minister of Manpower had made it illegal by extending the relevant national agreement. Rather than organise co-ordinated defiance of the law, the NUMSA leadership left it to the union members to pursue local disputes— as, for example, 6,000 metalworkers at ISCOR's Vanderbijlpark and Pretoria plants indeed did. This and other instances of militancy give some indication of the opportunity thrown away by the NUMSA leadership. A national metalworkers' strike in July/August 1987 would have had an enormous impact, coinciding as it would have done with a substantial strike-wave, not only in the mines, but also among workers in the Post Office, SASOL, the milling industry, and Mercedes-Benz. Bureaucratic conservatism cut across the divisions between populism and workerism within the union leadership.

The miners' defeat set the scene for a period of reflux for the union movement. COSATU nationally suffered a series of setbacks. It became drawn along with the UDF into a savage factional warfare in the Pietermaritzburg townships with Inkatha and its labour front, the United Workers Union of South Africa (UWUSA). COSATU's close indentification with the ANC tradition, reflected in its adoption of the Freedom Charter and alliance with the UDF, made it difficult for it to appeal, as FOSATU had to some degree been able, to Zulu-speaking workers whose political loyalties were bound up with Inkatha but who could be won to common struggles on economic issues. Then came the February 1988 bannings, which made illegal what had become the main activity of COSATU's National Office, joint initiatives with the UDF. And in the future there loomed the Labour Relations Amendment Bill. Jay Naidoo claimed that these measures would 'effectively ban' COSATU.[135]

Faced with what the **Weekly Mail** called 'the bleakest period in recent union history',[136] COSATU held a special congress on 14-15 May 1988. Its central executive committee, meeting in mid-April, made a grim appraisal of the federation's situation, identifying the following problems:

—The structures of merged unions have not always been properly integrated.

—Almost all union structures are weak.

—There is poor union participation in COSATU structures.

—There has been a failure to implement and build COSATU campaigns and this has meant that workers have often been left in isolation from the strength of the federation.

—There is a lack of financial self-sufficiency and of resources in terms of skills and organisational experience.

—Division and factionalism within and between unions affects COSATU's ability to act effectively.

—There are problems of financial maladministration in some unions.

—There is a problem with responding and adapting to repression.

—Bosses' strategies like mass dismissals, lock-outs and interdicts are not dealt with adequately.

—Certain sectors in COSATU—like farm, domestic, unemployed, construction and public sectors—are still weak.

—Weak education programmes in most unions mean that COSATU education cannot operate efficiently.

—Distribution of information to our membership is still poor.[137]

The special congress did not move far towards resolving any of these problems. Instead debate was dominated by a proposal to convene 'a conference of a broad range of anti-apartheid organisations to focus on apartheid repression'. Among the main issues was precisely how broad the range should be. Should it include white liberal groups such as the Five Freedoms Forum? And what about the NACTU, which rejected the Freedom Charter, according to COSATU president Elijah Barayi the resistance's 'guiding light'?

A compromise resolution left it to the central executive committee and COSATU's 'traditional allies' (presumably the UDF) to draw up a programme of action for the conference. Clearly the dominant forces inside COSATU were still committed to populist alliance politics.

One positive aspect of the congress, however, was the decision to mount protest action against the Labour Relations Amendment Bill. Despite the sectarianism of Barayi and others, COSATU and NACTU united to call a three-day strike on 6-8 June 1988. It took place in a highly-charged atmosphere, with big business lining up behind the government. The South African Employers Consultative

Committee on Labour Affairs (SACCOLA), headed by Bobby Godsell of Anglo, placed newspaper advertisements endorsing the Bill as in line with the practice of 'many Western democracies'. A number of employers threatened reprisals against unions taking part in the strike. One labour consultant returned from an industrial relations conference saying that 'war had been declared' on the unions.

The outcome confounded all expectations. Black workers responded massively to the strike call, producing the greatest proletarian mass action in South African history. Perhaps three million workers took part. The PWV area—core of the South African economy—was paralysed, with 81 per cent of African manufacturing and 67 per cent of African retail workers on strike on the first day; not only the ANC strongholds of the Eastern Cape but also Natal, despite Inkatha opposition, were similarly affected. Unlike previous stay-aways, pressure from township youth played a minor role: the protest was closer to a genuine, workplace-based general strike.

Big business' hard line crumbled. Godsell rushed off to Cape Town to see Manpower Minister Pietie du Plessis, who announced that he was willing to discuss amendments to the Bill with COSATU representatives. SACCOLA also opened discussions with COSATU which aimed at meeting union objections to the Bill.[138]

The strike—which was rapidly followed by another big stay-away on 16 June to commemorate the twelfth anniversary of the Soweto rising—was a dramatic demonstration of the formidable power of the organised black working class. But it did not mean that the problems facing the unions under populist leadership had been overcome.

This was underlined by the fate of the NUM's 1988 wage claim. Ramaphosa had justified his capitulation in August 1987 on the grounds that the strike was merely a 'dress rehearsal' for 1988. In the event he quickly accepted a pay offer from the Chamber of Mines, lower than that imposed at the end of the 1987 strike. This collapse reflected the weakness of union organisation (significantly, the mines were largely unaffected by the general strike of 6-8 June), responsibility for which lay with the NUM's pro-UDF officials. The black working class showed its enormous potential strength during the second emergency, but it lacked the leadership required to make the best use of this strength.[139]

Results and prospects

South Africa at the end of the 1980s faces four possible scenarios for future change. The first is least likely, namely a gradual negotiated transition to black majority rule. The obstacles to such a solution are, as we have seen, gigantic. Faced with the prospect of the disintegration of the existing white-dominated state apparatus, even the most liberal sections of big capital are likely to prefer a somewhat reformed version of the *status quo* to an ANC government. The possibility of a Lancaster House-type settlement in South Africa is remote.

Almost as unlikely is the second scenario, an ANC victory based on the use of traditional methods of guerrilla warfare. South Africa is a massively urbanised and proletarianised country. According to official statistics only 6.8 million Africans, 32.2 per cent of the African population, lived in urban areas in 1980. These figures are, however, misleading since they leave out of account the very large proportion of the Bantustan population effectively integrated into the urban economy.

Thus on the borders between the Bantustans and the main metropolitan areas 'peri-urban' settlements have mushroomed, whose residents depend on wages earned in the urban areas. Deeper into the Bantustans are the great resettlement camps, places such as Onverwacht-Botshabelo in Bophuthatswana, created by the apartheid regime's policy of forced removals, which affected 3.5 million people between 1960 and 1983. Although classified as rural, these are better understood as 'quasi-urban' settlements, since their inhabitants also rely mainly on the income of urban wage-labour, and they must therefore be regarded as 'functionally urban'.

According to one estimate, once such disguised forms of urbanisation are included, no less than 66 per cent of the African population in 1980 was urban.[140] When we take into account that the 20 per cent of the African population resident in the 'white' rural areas depend on the income of farm labour, we are faced with the fact that perhaps more than 80 per cent of all Africans are effectively proletarian—an enormous proportion by Third World standards.[141]

The social conditions therefore do not exist for a classic guerrilla strategy based upon the slow growth of rural 'liberated zones'. As I argued in the last chapter, urban areas do not provide a favourable terrain for the kind of military campaign waged by Umkhonto weSizwe. During the township risings of 1984-86 MK failed to achieved its objective of moving from the stage of 'armed propaganda', conducted by elite groups of trained guerrillas infiltrated from abroad, to the creation of 'mass combat units' recruited from township youth and trained and armed on the spot under the direction of the guerrillas.

The putative urban 'liberated zones', such as Alexandra, which were supposed to provide the basis for 'people's power', were pacified by the SADF and often made the object of 'upgrading' programmes directed by the State Security Council, on which R3.2 billion were spent in 1987-88 alone.[142] MK was able to sustain a low-level armed campaign, but the only realistic way open to it to escalate the military struggle was to overcome the inhibitions of the ANC leadership, despite the decision of the 1985 conference, against attacking 'soft' civilian targets.

An American analyst, if anything inclined to overestimate MK's effectiveness, argued that:

> ...the most the ANC could count on achieving would be a sort of 'rebellion of attrition', in which the intensity of both peaceful and violent resistance would grow dramatically, together with militant competition among black groups, but fail to reach a breakthrough to successful revolution. A stalemate characterised by deadly and continuous turmoil would result.[143]

Armed struggle was therefore likely to remain ancillary to the ANC leadership's search for the chimera of a negotiated solution.

Far more likely, unfortunately, is a third scenario, what one might call 'Lebanisation', the effective fragmentation of the South African polity into a conglomeration of warring baronies like the Lebanon. Two main features of the regime's strategy favour such an outcome.

One is the pursuit of 'power-sharing' on the basis of ethnic representation. This of course builds on the Bantustan regimes. These have typically had relatively narrow bases, reflecting networks of kinship and patronage, but the case of Inkatha demonstrates that ethnic politics can reach further, into even the urban working class of Durban and Pietermaritzburg. And the rise of the vigilantes elsewhere in the country indicates the potential for alliances between the regime and local conservative African leaders, which can mobilise often quite significant numbers of people on the most reactionary basis. The fears and strains created by the experience of rapid urbanisation and proletarianisation need not take the form of involvement in the independent unions and in anti-apartheid organisations. Instead they sometimes lead to identification with movements such as Inkatha which offer a degree of meaning and security by stressing continuities with an idealised, pre-colonial past—a past, what is more, that is exclusive to the putative descendants of a specific chiefdom or paramountcy rather than embracing all South Africans.

Secondly, the regime is increasingly relying on armed personnel recruited from the black population. In part this reflects a long-term shortage of SADF manpower, especially in the professional Permanent Force. This has led to the steady expansion since the early 1970s in the number of black units—the Cape Corps, the Indian Corps, African battalions usually though not exclusively recruited on an ethnic basis, and the armies of the four 'independent' Bantustans (Transkei, Ciskei, Bophuthatswana, and Venda). By the early 1980s some 40 per cent of the SADF and the South West African Territorial Force (SWATF) were black, many of them serving in front-line counter-insurgency units in Namibia.[14] The township risings of the mid-1980s led the regime further to expand the number of blacks under arms, especially through the establishment of the *kitskonstabels*, recruited to police the townships after three weeks' basic training.

Philip Frankel argues that, for blacks, deciding to join the SADF

> is not entirely irrational in terms of the material rewards made available to those willing to make such a commitment. A rural black of reasonable age, with a primary school education and without rights to live in 'white' urban South Africa, has precious few life-chances in apartheid society, least of all when economic recession and intensified application of influx controls combine to keep him poor and outside the cities. As a member of the Defence Force, on the other hand, he is able to acquire a substantial salary relative to his counterparts in the open labour market and, unlike the common black worker, he is able to enjoy a number of ancillary benefits and 'perks' in the form of on-the-job training, housing, free medical and dental care, uniforms, thirty days of annual vacation and a guaranteed pension at the age of sixty. The SADF is also an important means for rural blacks to ingratiate themselves with tribal headmen and local

chiefs (many of whom act as informal agents of the military in the Homeland areas) and the Defence Force, being a relatively encapsulated institution, is also able partially to shield its members from the unrequited racism of wider South African society.[145]

These reasons are, as Frankel notes, 'instrumental'—they are conditional on the black soldier or policeman believing that the balance of advantage lies in serving the white state. Should that judgement change, his loyalty to his masters would vanish.

Two incidents in late 1987 indicated just how conditional Pretoria's black mercenaries' loyalties were. In November the **Weekly Mail** reported that more than 400 members of the SWATF 101 Battalion had mutinied and refused to serve in Angola. Unrest was also reported in three other SWATF units.[146] Then on 10 December sixty African municipal policemen exchanged fire with a SAF unrest unit after they had been prevented from marching to the home of the mayor of Lekoa township in the Vaal Triangle to complain about poor pay. These and other similar incidents are all the more remarkable in occurring when the regime had succeeded in crushing large scale popular resistance.

The South African ruling class is caught in a contradiction. To rely primarily upon white soldiers and policemen would be both to suffer endemic manpower shortages and, if conscription were tightened even further, to increase the already serious rate of white emigration, especially of professional and managerial employees. But to look instead towards armed forces composed largely of black mercenaries would be to place their future on troops who might easily switch sides—like the black troops crucial to the Rhodesian settler regime's counter-insurgency war against Zimbabwean guerrillas, who rapidly changed allegiances after the ZANU-PF election victory in March 1980. Pretoria is likely, here as so often, to vacillate, relying on a core of white troops but recruiting more blacks.

The prospect of growing numbers of blacks under arms presents a possible solution to the problem of how to arm the black masses. But the experience of every revolutionary situation since 1789 shows that there are two conditions essential to winning sections of the armed forces to the side of the masses—first, that the existing state is already weakened, and, secondly, that a political force exists capable of offering a coherent alternative. What if the first condition exists without the second?

In that case we might well see instead political fragmentation. The regime might be strong enough to hang onto the core industrial region round the Rand. Elsewhere other forces, each with their private armies, would take control—Inkatha in Natal, and perhaps some of the other Bantustan regimes. The ANC might be able to carve out its own patch of territory, using MK's small conventional army currently based in Angola. So might other, far less atractive forces—the AWB might in these circumstances be able to mobilise its paramilitary wing and SAP/SADF sympathisers and create a fascist *Boerestaat*. South Africa would disintegrate into a larger version of the Lebanon, with rival warlords fighting over its mutilated corpse amidst economic collapse and mass emigration by capital and the middle classes.

Such a scenario is by no means a fantasy. Elements of such a situation are already present. The bloodshed in 1987-88 in the Pietermaritzburg area indicated the potential divisions among the oppressed. Several of the Bantustan regimes are dangerously near to escaping the control of even Pretoria: 1986-88 saw a near-war between the Ciskei and Transkei, two successful military coups in the Transkei, and an abortive coup in Bophuthatswana which was put down by the SADF. Pretoria itself has been instrumental in 'balkanising' neighbouring African states, especially Angola and Mozambique. Mozambique by early 1988 seemed in danger of becoming an African version of Kampuchea, with 100,000 dead at the hands of South African-backed rebels, more than two million refugees, a government in control only of the cities, and a famine of Ethiopian proportions. A ruling class capable of inflicting such horrors on others may in its own death agony unleash an even greater disaster in South Africa itself.

In the absence of any revolutionary transformation, probably the most likely outcome of the South African crisis is a slow drift into barbarism, as a progressively enfeebled regime is forced to concede effective control over parts of the country to local mafias. This analysis, if correct, underlines the urgency of realising the fourth scenario, socialist revolution.

The collective strength of the black working class is underlined by its ability to weather the second emergency far better than the township movements. That strength gives it the capacity to offer a positive, revolutionary solution to the crisis of South African society. Only the working class, by developing a hegemonic political project for the socialist transformation of South Africa, offers any real prospect of overcoming the ethnic divisions among the oppressed themselves. Only the working class, by unleashing a wave of mass strikes which go beyond purely economic demands and begin to raise the question of political power, can split the existing state apparatus, winning over black soldiers and policemen to the side of the masses and demoralising whites within the SADF and SAP.

While the black working class is the only social force with the capacity to achieve national liberation, and this only by carrying through a socialist revolution, it is still far from exercising that capacity. This is in part a consequence of objective factors—the relative youth and inexperience of the independent unions, their limited reach over the black proletariat, and the absence as yet of any strike wave on the scale of Russia in 1905, France in 1968 or Poland in 1980. But the dominant political tendencies within the working-class movement also have their part in explaining its limitations—the polarisation between two inadequate strategies, the narrow and defensive syndicalism of the workerists, and the vacuous popular-frontism of the populists. The populists, now in the saddle within COSATU, must take the lion's share of the blame for the setbacks suffered by the independent unions under the second emergency, but the workerists cannot escape responsibility, having left a political vacuum which the nationalism of the ANC tradition could then fill.

From an international perspective, what one might call the dialectic of workerism and populism was by no means unique to South Africa. Indeed, it seems to be a relatively common feature of the new workers' movements which developed in various semi-industrialised countries in the 1970s and 1980s. Rapid capital accumulation under authoritarian regimes provoked the explosive development of often very militant movements of industrial workers—South Africa after 1973, Iran 1978-79, Brazil in the late 1970s and early 1980s, Poland 1980-81, South Korea 1987. These movements tended to display a strong sense of workers' strength within the industry. Nevertheless, the conditions under which they developed meant that distinctively socialist, working-class political traditions were weak. Consequently workers would look for political solutions towards forces typically addressing workers as members of some *national*, cross-class community and invoking continuities between past and present—for example Islamic fundamentalism in Iran, the Catholic Church in Poland, the fervently nationalist 'Nicaraguan' tendency that came to dominate the Brazilian Workers' Party—and, in South Africa, the ANC.[147]

So rapid and apparently decisive was the ANC's rise to dominance in the mid-1980s that many left-wing intellectuals are attracted to the idea of some kind of 'dialectical' synthesis of workerism and populism under the ANC banner. One variant of this approach might be called the 'It'll be alright on the night' argument.[148] This consists in denying that support for the ANC implies accepting any sharp distinction between 'national-democratic' and 'socialist' stages of the revolution. Thus even Joe Slovo of the SACP argued in August 1986 that 'revolution is a continuing process' and that 'there is no Chinese Wall' between the stages. He claimed that

> In practice, the question as to which road South Africa will begin to take on the morning after the liberation flag is raised over Union Buildings, will be decided by the actual correlation of class forces which have come to power.'[149]

In fact, as I have argued, such formulations hark back to Stalin's original dogma of 'uninterrupted revolution'. But they appear attractive to some to the left of the ANC. John Saul, for example, put his faith in the 'actual dynamic of the South African revolution—a radicalisation that cuts right across South African society, across presumed historical stages and across proposed organisational divisions of labour, as "popular-democratic" and "proletarian" demands reinforce and push each other forward'.[150]

Passages of this kind conjure up a picture of revolution as an objective process realising its goals independently of the actual configuration of class and political forces, implying a Second-International version of Marxism—proved bankrupt since 1914.

Saul might instead be tempted to argue that 'a positive simultaneity of popular-democratic demands and proletarian-cum-socialist assertions' under 'ANC hegemony'[151] could be achieved by making nationalist ideology a vehicle for working-class interests. Such, indeed, was the position taken by Karl von Holdt, who accused workerists of 'class reductionism' in treating 'national oppression and struggles against it' as 'a veil concealing the real relations of capitalist exploitation.' He insisted: 'Nationalism is not simply a negative force. It is a very potent and deep political force that has been generated in resistance to colonisation and national oppression... Any serious struggle has to situate itself within this deep popular current.'[152]

Lurking behind this kind of argument seems to be the 'post-Marxist' theorising of Ernesto Laclau and Chantal Mouffe, who claim that ideological discourses such as nationalism are socially and politically indeterminate, capable of articulating the most diverse and even contradictory programmes. Such a position indeed avoids 'reductionism', but at the price of detaching ideologies from any anchorage in the forces and relations of production.[153]

To argue that nationalism can become a vehicle of 'proletarian-cum-socialist assertions' is to claim that the interests of the different classes making up the oppressed population can be reconciled in a post-apartheid South Africa. But is this remotely plausible?

Assume that by some peculiar and quite unanticipated combination of circumstances the ANC came to power. How could the interests of the African petty bourgeoisie be furthered? Either it could come to some accommodation with Anglo-American and the other big corporations, perhaps leaving the private sector to them and colonising the state apparatus in the way the National Party did after 1948—this would be a variant of the situation in Zimbabwe since independence. Or—much less likely but possible—the bulk of private capital would be expropriated and some kind of state capitalist regime installed. In either case, the African petty bourgeoisie would have a strong interest in ensuring that South African capitalism were as competitive as possible in the international arena, and in maintaining the flow of foreign exchange generated by gold exports. That would require appealing for 'discipline' and 'sacrifice' on the part of the working class, and if that were not forthcoming, attacking the workers' movement, as the Mugabe regime did in Zimbabwe in the early 1980s.

Now von Holdt and his like could reply in two ways. One would be to argue that such policies would be in the interests of all classes, including the working class. In this case, it would become plain that, despite all their protestations, their model of 'socialism' is none other than the bureaucratic monstrosities of the Eastern bloc. Any commitment to an independent workers' movement would have been abandoned in an abject collapse into Stalinism.

Alternatively, they might argue that such an outcome would indeed be undesirable, but that it could be prevented by the assertion of working-class interests *within* the national liberation movement prior to an ANC victory. But this is to suppose that the conflict between aspirant bourgeoisie and existing proletariat could be reconciled within the framework of one movement. Far more likely, given the scale of the class antagonisms that would be unleashed after national liberation, would be attempts to suppress the assertion of socialist aspirations within the Congress alliance. Is this not precisely what has happened in COSATU since its formation?

The hope that somehow socialism and nationalism can be reconciled under the ANC banner amounts to nothing less than an attempt to wish away the class struggle and the structural contradictions underpinning it. The nature of a post-apartheid South Africa will indeed, as Slovo says, depend on the 'actual correlation of class forces' at the time. More than that: the very possibility of such a South Africa will depend on the black working class assuming the leadership of the struggle in pursuit of socialism as well as national liberation. But such a favourable 'correlation' itself presupposes the political independence of the working class, which requires organisational expression in the shape of a revolutionary socialist party.

The experience since the beginning of 1986, when chapter four of this book was written, provides overwhelming confirmation of this conclusion. On the one hand, the populists have come to dominate COSATU, with the largely negative results described above. On the other hand, the workerists have been on the defensive, and in some cases have actually capitulated. But there exists a layer of working class militants in unions such as CCAWUSA and NUMSA who have gone beyond a purely trade union consciousness towards the adoption of an explicitly socialist programme. These workers represent the potential nucleus of a revolutionary party which could, in the testing years of struggle ahead, win a majority of the proletariat to the objective of socialist revolution. For this possibility to take concrete shape, however, the basis of socialist organisation must be laid now.

Unfortunately, the South African left has yet to take up this task. Thus the Marxist Workers' Tendency remains committed to the utopian strategy of transforming the ANC into a revolutionary workers' party. This led its supporters, for example, to side with the populists against the CCAWUSA majority. As an anonymous document entitled 'In Defence of Socialism' and produced after the COSATU congress in July 1987 put it, this placed the MWT 'in danger of becoming the *fingermen* of the Stalinists'. The authors of this document, however, while calling for 'a bloc of socialists' in the face of the populist offensive against the left, themselves argued for entry into the UDF, apparently with illusions similar to those of the MWT 'of winning some space within COSATU and UDF (and therefore in the ANC itself) for socialist propaganda (and ultimately for transforming the ANC and the SACP)'. The document displayed no awareness that the MWT's adaption to the politics of the ANC flowed from the very logic of a perspective aimed at converting a bourgeois-nationalist organisation into a Marxist party.

On the independent left, the Cape Action League has made some attempt under the second emergency to respond to the problems which were outlined in chapter four. CAL was reorganised along unitary rather than federal lines, and its activists became more involved in the unions, in particular participating in defence of the left-wing CCAWUSA against populist attacks.

An article in the CAL journal on the question of the party nevertheless showed the limits of this evolution. A confused and rather pretentious piece, it set out two main models—'the self-proclaimed party nucleus' (meaning a Leninist vanguard party) and 'the organic party' (meaning a broad labour party analogous to the Brazilian PT). The first was dismissed without argument as 'sectarian' and Stalinist, while the absence in South Africa of the conditions favouring the 'stabilisation' of the PT—above all, 'the transition towards the disappearance of the dictatorship'—was stressed. Although favouring 'the mass workers' party', the author left the resolution of the problem to 'the evolution of the social formation':

> The choice of a middle way between sectarian self-proclamation and the 'workers' party' model would mean cutting across the fields…only those who know the ground can decide which path is best to follow.'[154]

This kind of fatalist reliance on objective historical processes is nothing but an evasion. What is required in South Africa above all is indeed a mass workers' party, but one which seeks to overcome though political leadership the divisions and unevenness of consciousness within the working class, and not, as a broad labour party would, simply to reflect them.

But how to achieve such a party? The layer of politicised militants in the unions would, as I have already suggested, be essential to its ability to relate to the majority of the working class. But it is not in the unions where the basis of the party will be laid. Here the history of Russian Marxism offers an instructive example. The Bolsheviks in 1917 were a mass revolutionary workers' party profoundly rooted in the *soviets* and factory committees. Their origins, however, were in the Emancipation of Labour Group, founded in 1883 by Georgi Plekhanov and four other exiled intellectuals, which spent over a decade building tiny Marxist discussion circles. It was only after a core of revolutionary socialists had been created by these means that the Russian Marxists could go on to engage in factory agitation and to build the disciplined organisation of the Bolshevik party.[155]

Historical analogies are always imperfect, and the timescale of revolutionary struggle in South Africa is likely to be far more concentrated than in Russia. Nevertheless, the starting point for a mass workers' party is the creation of a nucleus of revolutionary militants trained in the Marxist tradition. Of course, once formed, they would not, as the CAL article suggests, simply 'proclaim' themselves the vanguard of the working class (South African Marxists too often confuse the Leninist party with its Stalinist or orthodox Trotskyist distortions), but would seek to win workers' confidence through their active participation in the class struggle. The point of the revolutionary party is not to substitute itself for workers' struggles, but to make these fully conscious and directed to the objective of socialist revolution. But without it there can be no successful revolution.

There is no tide of history which will carry the South African masses inexorably to national liberation and socialism. Unless the working class is won to the goal of overthrowing both apartheid and capitalism and of conquering power for itself, the most likely outcome is a slow, agonising drift into economic decline, social decay and endemic civil war. Rarely has the primitive accumulation of cadres indispensable for the construction of a revolutionary party been more urgent.

Notes

Abbreviations used in the notes

AC   **African Communist** (London)

CSAS Centre for Southern African Studies, University of York, Conference on the South African Economy and Apartheid, 29 September-2 October 1986

FM   **Financial Mail** (Johannesburg)

FT   **Financial Times** (London)

ICS   University of London Institute of Commonwealth Studies, Collected Seminar Papers

IS   **International Socialism** (London)

JSAS **Journal of Southern African Studies** (Oxford)

ROAPE **Review of African Political Economy** (London)

SALB **South African Labour Bulletin** (first Durban, now Johannesburg)

SAR   South African Research Service, **South African Review** (Johannesburg), volume 1: 1983, volume 2: 1984, volume 3: 1986, volume 4: 1987

WM   **Weekly Mail** (Johannesburg)

INTRODUCTION

1. S Friedman, **Building Tomorrow Today: African Workers in Trade Unions** (Johannesburg 1987) page 38.
2. Commonwealth Group of Eminent Persons, **Mission to South Africa** (Harmondsworth 1986) pages 43-44.
3. See for example D Innes, 'Monopoly Capitalism in South Africa', in **SAR** volume 1.
4. See L Trotsky, **Permanent Revolution and Results and Prospects**

(New York 1970), and **On China** (New York 1976).

5. E Webster, 'The goals of management and labour—Industrial relations in a post-apartheid South Africa', in **CSAS**. It is regrettable that Webster has not learned from the experience of workers' movements elsewhere in the newly industrialising countries and has instead capitulated to populism (see Chapter 5).

6. For general analysis of the economic and political implications of the rise of the newly-industrialising countries, see N Harris, **The End of the Third World** (Harmondsworth 1987), and my review of this, 'Imperialism, capitalism and the state today', in **IS** 2:35 (summer 1987).

Chapter 1: THE ROOTS OF THE CRISIS

1. V I Lenin, **Collected Works**, volume 13 (Moscow 1972) page 239. See also Barrington Moore Jr, **Social Origins of Dictatorship and Democracy** (Harmondsworth 1969). The analysis is this and the following chapters is heavily indebted to the so- called 'neo-Marxist' school of South African historiography, and in particular the work of Martin Legassick and his collaborators. It would not be appropriate to discuss here the methodological issues that have divided the school between those, such as Legassick, who give primacy to the contradiction between capital and labour and the group influenced by Nicos Poulantzas who accord greater weight to conflicts between different 'fractions' of capital. On these questions, see S Clarke, 'Capital, fractions of capital and the state', in **Capital and Class** (London) number 5 (summer 1978), and, for a discussion which does not refer specifically to South Africa but covers some of the same ground, A Callinicos, **Is there a future for Marxism?** (London 1982). Some of the main texts delaing with the background to this section of the book are: F A Johnstone, 'White prosperity and white supremacy in South Africa today', in **African Affairs** 69:275 (April 1970), and **Race, Class and Gold** (London 1976); S Trapido, 'South Africa in a comparative study of industrialisation', in **Journal of Development Studies** 7:3 (April 1971); H Wolpe, 'Capitalism and cheap labour-power in South Africa', in **Economy and Society** 1:4 (November 1972); M Legassick, 'South Africa: Capital accumulation and violence', in **Economy and Society** 3:3 (August 1974), and 'Legislation, ideology and economy in post-1948 South Africa', in **JSAS** 1:1 (October 1974); M Williams, 'An analysis of South African capitalism', in **Bulletin of the Conference of Socialist Economists** 4:1 (February 1975); D O'Meara, 'The 1946 mineworkers' strike and the political economy of South Africa', in **Journal of Comparative and**

Commonwealth Studies 12 (1975); M Morris, 'Capitalism in South African agriculture', in **Economy and Society** 5:3 (August 1976); **ROAPE** number 7, special issue on South Africa; M Legassick and D Innes, 'Capital restructuring and apartheid', in **African Affairs** 76:305 (October 1977); D Innes, 'The mining industry in the context of South Africa's development', in **ICS**, volume 21 (1977-78); R Christie, ' "Slim Jannie" and the forces of production', in **ICS**, volume 22 (1978-79); D Innes and M Plaut, 'Class struggle and the state', in **ROAPE** number 11; C Bundy, **The rise and fall of the South African peasantry** (London 1980); S Greenberg, **Race and state in capitalism development** (New Haven and London 1980).

2. The most comprehensive survey of the apartheid laws is the **Report of the Commission of Inquiry into Legislation affecting the Utilisation of Manpower**, RP32/1979 (Pretoria: the Government Printer 1979)—hereafter referred to as the Riekert report.

3. Quoted in the Riekert report, page 36.

4. Quoted in J Kane Berman, **The Method in the Madness** (London 1979) page 239.

5. G Lanning with M Mueller, **Africa Undermined** (Harmondsworth 1979) pages 148-9.

6. D H Houghton, **The South African Economy** (Cape Town 1973).

7. J Suckling, R Weiss and D Innes, **The Economic Factor** (Uppsala 1975) table 11, page 181.

8. Quoted in Legassick, 'Legislation, ideology and economy in post-1948 South Africa', in **JSAS** 1:1, pages 10-11.

9. Nedbank Group Economic Unit, **South Africa: An economic appraisal** (Johannesburg 1977) page 5.

10. See for example F H Cardoso, 'Dependence and development in Latin America', in **New Left Review**, number 74 (July-August 1972).

11. **FM**, 11 March 1977.

12. Nedbank, page 16.

13. **FM**, 25 April 1980.

14. G Airovich, 'The comparative advantage of South Africa as measured by export shares', in **South African Journal of Economics** 47:2 (June 1979).

15. **Sunday Times** (Johannesburg) 26 February 1979.

16. Nedbank, page 5.

18. Nedbank, page 206.

17. M Bienfield and D Innes, 'Capital accumulation and South Africa', in **ROAPE**, number 7, page 31.

19. **FM**, 23 March 1979.

20. C J Swanepoel and J van Dyk, 'The fixed capital stock and sectoral

capital-output ratios of South Africa', in **South Africa Reserve Bank Quarterly Bulletin** (September 1978) pages 36 and 38.

21. Swanepoel and van Dyk, page 37.
22. **South African Statistics 1978** (Pretoria: Government Printers 1978) section 9.4.
23. **FN**, 11 February 1977.
24. South African Institute of Race Relations, **Survey of Race Relations in South Africa 1978** (Johannesburg 1979) page 210.
25. N Harris, 'The Asian boom economies and the "impossibility" of national economic development', in **IS** 2:3 (Winter 1978-79) page 2.
26. **FM**, 27 April 1979.
27. D Innes and D O'Meara, 'Class formation and ideology: the Transkei region', in **ROAPE**, number 7.
28. **The Times** (London) 11 August 1980.
29. M Legassick and H Wolpe, 'The Bantustans and capital accumulation in South Africa', in **ROAPE**, number 7.
30. Kane Berman, page 244.
31. Swanepoel and van Dyk, pages 31-2.
32. **FM**, 26 August 1977.
33. **FM**, 19 January 1979.
34. A D Wassenaar, **Assault on Private Enterprise** (Cape Town 1977) page 86.
35. Nedbank, page 249.
36. **South Africa 1979** (Johannesburg 1980) page 371.
37. **Report of the Commission of Inquiry into Labour Legislation: Part 1—Key Issues**, RP47/1979 (Pretoria: Government Printer 1979)—hereafter referred to as the Wiehahn report—pages 2 and 1.
38. **South African Statistics 1978**, section 7.5.
39. The *locus classicus* of discussion of deskilling is H Braverman, **Labour and Monopoly Capital** (New York and London 1974).
40. See H Wolpe, 'The "white working class" in South Africa', in **Economy and Society**, volume 5, number 2 (May 1976).
41. Wiehahn report, page 1.
42. R Davies, 'Capital restructuring and the modification of the racial division of labour in South Africa', in **JSAS** 5:2 (April 1979) pages 183-6.
43. D Hemson, 'Trade unionism and the struggle for liberation in South Africa', in **Capital and Class**, number 6 (autumn 1978).
44. Institute for Industrial Education, **The Durban Strikes** (Durban and Johannesburg 1976) pages 144-5.
45. Wiehahn report, page 15.
46. J Natrass, 'The narrowing of wage differentials in South Africa', in **South African Journal of Economics** 45:4 (December 1977).

47. Hemson, page 30.
48. **FM,** 11 February 1977.
49. **FM,** 1 October 1976.
50. See Counter-Information Services, **Black South Africa explodes** (London 1977); **A Survey of Race Relations in South Africa 1976**; D Herbstein, **Whie Man we want to talk to you** (Harmondsworth 1977); Kane Berman; B Hirson, **Year of Fire, Year of Ash** (London 1979); A Brooks and J Brickhill, **Whirlwind before the Storm** (London 1980).
51. A Callinicos and J Rogers, **Southern Africa after Soweto** (London 1977) page 164.
52. Hemson, page 31.
53. Kane Berman, page 52.
54. **FM,** 6 May 1977.
55. See Callinicos and Rogers, pages 168-173, and Hirson.

Chapter 2: RATIONALISING APARTHEID

1. A Gramsci, **Selections from Prison Notebooks** (London 1971) page 178.
2. Kaplan, in **ROAPE** 15/16, page 142.
3. See R Davies, **Capital, State and White Labour in South Africa 1900-1960** (Hassocks 1979).
4. The best study of contemporary Afrikanerdom is H Adam and H Gilliomee, **Ethnic Power Mobilised** (New Haven and London 1979).
5. Adam and Gilliomee, pages 163-173.
6. **FT,** 29 February 1980.
7. Callinicos and Rogers, pages 165-6.
8. See D O'Meara, 'The Afrikaner Broederbond', in **JSAS** 3:2, and 'Analysing Afrikaner nationalism', in **African Affairs** 77:306 (January 1978).
9. J H P Serfontein, **Brotherhood of Power** (London 1979) page 107.
10. Serfontein, pages 176-7.
11. E Potter, **The Press as Opposition** (London 1975) pages 151, 183, 189-190 and 199.
12. Adam and Gilliomee, page 87.
13. See **Report of the Commission of Inquiry into Alleged Ireegularities in the former Department of Information,** RP113/1978 (Pretoria: Government Printer 1979).
14. Wassenaar, page 119.
15. **FM,** 25 June 1979.
16. International Defence and Aid Fund, **The Apartheid War Machine** (London 1980).

17. G-A Fiechter, **Brazil since 1964** (London 1975) page 29.
18. J A Lombard, 'The economic aspects of national security', in M Louw (editor) **National Security: A Modern Approach** (Pretoria 1978) page 85.
19. **The Economist** (London) 21 October 1978.
20. See **Newsweek** (New York) 29 September 1980.
21. J R Dutton, 'The military aspects of national security', in Louw, pages 107 and 114.
22. **The Apartheid War Machine**, pages 6-7.
23. Wassenaar, pages 148-150.
24. **South African Reserve Bank Quarterly** (March 1980).
25. **FM**, 4 April 1980. The **Financial Mail**, hitherto one of the regime's most intelligent capitalist critics, underwent a sad degeneration after the installation in 1979 of a new editor, a committed monetarist and author of a book titled **Milton Friedman in South Africa!**
26. **FM**, 3 August 1979.
27. Lombard, in Louw, page 86.
28. Riekert report, page 167.
 29 **FM**, 22 June 1980.
30. Kane Berman, page 234.
31. Riekert report, page 168.
32. Wiehahn report, page 18.
33. See R Davies and D Lewis, 'Industrial relations legislation: one of capital's defences', in **ROAPE**, number 7.
34. Wiehahn report, pages 18-19.
35. **FM**, 11 May 1979.
36. H Cheadle, 'A Guide to the Industrial Conciliation Act No 94 of 1979', in **SALB** 5:2 (August 1979).
37. **FM**, 11 May 1979.
38. **FM**, 18 May 1979.
39. **FM**, 25 January 1980.
40. **FM**, 15 June 1979.
41. Interview in A Starke, **Survival** (Cape Town, 1978) pages 155-6.
42. See Davies, in **JSAS** 5:2.
43. See A Sitas, 'Rebels without a pause: the MWU and the defence of the colour bar', in **SALB** 5:3 (October 1979).
44. See C Cooper, 'The mineworkers' strike', in **SALB** 5:3.
45. Interview in Starke, page 128.
46. **FM**, 3 December 1976.
47. **FM**, 15 June 1979.
48. **FM**, 13 July 1979.
49. **FM**, 14 September 1979.
50. **FM**, 13 June 1980.

51. **FM**, 21 September 1979.
52. **FM**, 14 September 1979.
53. **FM**, 20 July 1979.
54. Lombard, in Louw, pages 92-3.
55. Interview in Starke, pages 155-6.
56. Internview in Starke, page 177.
57. **FM**, 30 November 1979.
58. Adam and Gilliomee, page 204.
59. Compare the survey in **The Times**, 4 July 1980.
60. **FM**, 22 June 1979.
61. **The Times**, 2 and 3 September 1980.
62. Adam and Gilliomee, pages 221-232.
63. Adam and Gilliomee, pages 165-6.
64. **FM**, 9 November 1979.
65. See F Parkin, **Marxism and Class Theory** (London 1979).
66. **FM**, 16 November 1979.
67. Quoted in **The Apartheid War Machine**, page 7.
68. Wassenaar, page 153.
69. Dutton, page 113.
70. See N Poulantzas, **Fascisme et Dictature** (Paris 1970).

Chapter 4: WORKING-CLASS POLITICS IN SOUTH AFRICA

1. **Business Day** (Johannesburg) 10 January 1986.
2. See also N Lambert, 'South Africa: Reform of revolution?', in **Socialist Worker** (London) 5 October 1985, and C Green, 'South Africa: The struggle today', in **Socialist Worker** (London) 25 January 1986.
3. See especially Callinicos and Rogers, and A Callinicos, **South Africa: The Road to Revolution** (London 1985).
4. There are two outstanding histories of the South African struggle: J J and R E Simons, **Class and Colour in South Africa 1850-1950** (Harmondsworth 1969), and E Roux, **Time Longer than Rope** (Madison 1972). Simons and Simons is the richer work, and more focused on working-class politics, although the overall perspective is what one would expect from two former leaders of the Communist Party. M Benson, **The Struggle for a Birthright** (Harmondsworth 1966) is very much a court history of the ANC. T Lodge, **Black Politics in South Africa since 1945** (Johannesburg 1983) gives a more balanced account of the later period.
5. For an overview of this process, see J Grest and H Hughes, 'State strategy and popular response at the local level', in **SAR**, volume 2.
6. See D Hindson and M Lacey, 'Influx control and labour allocation', in **SAR**, volume 1.

7. There is a good summary of these changes in 'Reshaping the Constitution of Apartheid', International Defence and Aid Briefing Paper 16 (May 1985).

8. 'Cape Action League: Challenging the Cliches', an interview with A Abrahams, in **Work in Progress**, number 35 (February 1985) page 19.

9. Quoted in H Barrell, 'The United Democratic Front and National Forum', in **SAR**, volume 2, page 13.

10. Quoted in Barrell, in **SAR**, volume 2, page 13.

11. I Silver and A Sfarnas, 'The UDF: A "workerist" response', in **SALB** 8:8/9 (September-October 1983) pages 100-1 and 103.

12. See 'Building People's Power', supplement to **State of the Nation** (October/November 1985).

13. Interview in **SALB** 9:2 (November 1983) page 80.

14. D Innes, 'The Freedom Charter and workers' control', in **SALB** 11:2 (October/December 1985) page 37.

15. N Mandela, 'In Our Lifetime', in **Liberator** (June 1956), quoted in **South Africa's Impending Socialist Revolution** (London 1982) page 157.

16. 'Strategy and tactics in the South African revolution', in A La Guma (editor) **Apartheid** (London 1972) page 179.

17. 'A Lerumo', **Fifty Fighting Years** (London 1971) is very much an official history, by a veteran Communist Party leader, Michael Harmel. There is much useful material in Simons and Simons, and in **South African Communists Speak** (London 1981). In all likelihood our needs for a scholarly and critical history of the SACP will be met when Tom Lodge's study is published.

18. See Simons and Simons, chapters 13 and 14.

19. **South African Communists Speak**, pages 93-4. 'Native' was then the official term for 'African'.

20. See H Isaacs, **The Tragedy of the Chinese Revolution** (Stanford 1974), and L Trotsky, **On China, The Third International after Lenin** (New York 1970), and **Permanent Revolution and Results and Prospects**.

21. Tony Southall argues that Bunting, independently of Trotsky and the Left Opposition, developed his own critique of the notion of revolution by stages; see 'Marxist theory in South Africa until 1940' (MA thesis, University of York, 1978) pages 26-33.

22. 'Toussaint' (a leading Communist Party theoretician) provided a charming example in a review of **Southern Africa after Soweto**, 'Class and Nation in the South African revolution', in **AC**, number 78 (first quarter 1978). Among other things he insinuated that John Rogers and myself were agents of American imperialism. Our

request for right of reply was turned down.

23. 'Toussaint', 'A Mirror of our Times', in **AC**, number 100 (first quarter 1985) page 23.

24. **South African Communists Speak**, pages 313-4 and 307- 8.

25. **South African Communists Speak**, page 300.

26. 'Strategy and Tactics', in La Guma, page 195.

27. J Slovo, ' "Reforms" and Revolution in South Africa', in **Sechaba** (February 1985) page 8.

28. Slovo, in **Sechaba** (February 1985) page 6.

29. **South African Communists Speak**, pages 304-5.

30. SACP Central Committee, 'A United People will defeat the Enemy', in **AC**, number 96 (first quarter 1984) pages 48-9. See also 'Makelekelathini', 'We must win over the African middle class', in **AC**, number 100 (first quarter 1985).

31. **South African Communists Speak**, page 311. See also 'Strategy and Tactics' in La Guma, pages 202-3, on the 'special role' of the working class.

32. R Suttner, 'The Freedom Charter—the People's Charter in the 1980s', in **Free Azania** 2:1 (August 1985) page 41.

33. J Slovo, 'South Africa—No Middle Road', in B Davidson and others, **Southern Africa: The New Politics of Revolution** (Harmondsworth 1976).

34. See J Stalin, **On the Opposition** (Peking 1974).

35. **South African Communists Speak**, page 311.

36. 'Toussaint', 'A trade union is not a political party', in **AC** (second quarter 1983).

37. **Africa Confidential**, 3 July 1985.

38. T Lodge, 'The African National Congress 1983', in **SAR**, volume 2, page 25.

39. See for example Bundy, **The rise and fall of the South African Peasantry**.

40. M Lipton, **Capitalism and Apartheid** (Aldershot 1985) page 379, but for later figures see chapter 5 below.

41. R Bolus and N Muller, 'The drought and underdevelopment in the Transkei', in **SAR**, volume 2, page 291.

42. Lipton, page 379.

43. O Tambo, 'Render South Africa ungovernable', in **Sechaba** (March 1985) page 12.

44. Quoted in P Storey, 'South African Perspectives: Workers' revolution or racial civil war', supplement to **Inqaba ya Basebenzi**, number 16/17 (May 1985) pages 44-5.

45. 'Take the struggle into the white areas!', in **Sechaba** (December 1985) page 2.

46. See Hirson, chapters 11 and 12.

47. **Students of Young Azania Bulletin,** number 3.

48. See D Innes, 'Monopoly Capitalism in South Africa', in **SAR,** volume 1.

49. For a study of this tradition see G M Gerhart, **Black Power in South Africa** (Berkeley and Los Angeles 1978).

50. Quoted in Gerhart, page 60.

51. S Biko, **I write what I like** (London 1978) page 89.

52. Biko, page 97.

53. For critical assessments of Black Consciousness see Hirson, chapters 15 and 16, and A Callinicos, **Southern Africa after Zimbabwe** (London 1981) pages 146-9.

54. **Survey of Race Relations in South Africa 1978,** pages 32-3.

55. See Barrell, pages 11-12.

56. 'Azania' is the name used for South Africa by the Pan-Africanist Congress, Black Consciousness and the Cape Action League; the ANC and its allies do not use it.

57. Barrell, page 12.

58. See Simons and Simons, chapters 4 and 5.

59. See Southall, in various places.

60. On the early years of South African Trotskyism, see Southall, pages 20 and 34-7, and Roux, pages 311-3.

61. Southall, page 74.

62. Southall, pages 72-3.

63. L Trotsky, **Writings 1934-35** (New York 1974) pages 250 and 254.

64. Trotsky, **Writings 1934-35,** pages 249-250. Trotsky does, however, confuse the issue by interpreting black self-determination as involving 'a separate black state in South Africa' (page 251), in other words the partition of the country along racial lines. The South African Communist Party tended to interpret the 'Native Republic' demand similarly. Perhaps Trotsky, like them, was influenced by the Comintern policy of defending the right of blacks in the southern United States to their own state. See No Sizwe, **One Azania, One Nation** (London 1979) pages 49-53.

65. Wolpe, 'Capitalism and cheap labour-power', in **Economy and Society** 1:4, and Legassick, 'Capital accumulation and violence', in **Economy and Society** 3:3. Legassick also wrote an earlier path-breaking essay, 'The Frontier Tradition in South African Historiography', published in S Marks and A Atmore (editors) **Economy and Society in Pre-industrial South Africa** (London 1980).

66. N Alexander, **Sow the Wind** (Johannesburg 1985) page 130.

67. Legassick, in **Economy and Society** 3:3, page 269.

68. See J B Peires, editor's introduction to **Before and After Shaka** (Grahamstown 1981) page 17.

69. Wolpe, in **Economy and Society** 1:4, page 439.

70. Wolpe, in **Economy and Society** 1:4, page 450.

71. Wolpe, 'The theory of internal colonialism: the South African case', in I Oxaal and others (editors) **Beyond the Sociology of Development** (London 1975) page 249.

72. Wolpe, in Oxaal and others, page 250.

73. Wolpe, in Oxaal and others, page 241. Wolpe quotes here from Charles Bettelheim.

74. Wolpe, in Oxaal and others, page 248.

75. Williams, 'An Analysis of South African Capitalism' in **Bulletin of the Conference of Socialist Economists** 4:1, page 31. Jeff Guy dates the collapse of pre- capitalist society even earlier: 'It seems to me misleading to conceptualise the Zulu formation in the 1890s as a pre-capitalist mode of production coming into articulation with the capitalist mode. To do this is to confuse form and content . . . Capitalism dominated Zulu society in 1889, when the first hut-tax was successfully collected. From this time it was made to serve the interest of capital accumulation.' ('The Destruction and Reconstruction of Zulu Society', in S Marks and R Rathbone (editors) **Industrialisation and Social Change in South Africa** (London 1982) pages 189-190).

76. Williams, in **Bulletin of the Conference of Socialist Economists** 4:1, page 3.

77. R Davies and others, 'Class struggle and the periodisation of the state in South Africa', in **ROAPE**, number 7 (1976) page 5.

78. See S Clarke, in **Capital and Class**, number 5; Innes and Plaut, in **ROAPE**, number 11; D Kaplan, 'Relations of production, class struggle and the state in South Africa in the inter-war period', in **ROAPE**, number 15/16; and the editors' introduction to Marks and Rathbone.

79. See Callinicos, **Is there a future for Marxism?**, chapters 5 and 6.

80. O'Meara, in **Journal of Comparative and Commonwealth Studies**, number 12, and O'Meara, **Volkskapitalisme** (Johannesburg 1983).

81. **Merle Lipton's Capitalism and Apartheid** is an example of this sort of challenge, and very feeble it is too.

82. See especially the conclusion to N Poulantzas, **Classes in Contemporary Capitalism** (London 1975).

83. Legassick, in **Economy and Society** 3:3, page 286.

84. See E Webster, **Essays in South African Labour History** (Johannesburg 1978) section three.

85. See Wolpe, 'The white working class in South Africa', in **Economy**

and Society 5:6 (1976), and A Callinicos and C Harman, **The Changing Working Class** (London 1987) chapter 1.

86. The best analysis of this process is E Webster, **Cast in a Racial Mould** (Johannesburg 1985).

87. Lipton, pages 381-2.

88. See Webster, chapter 6.

89. Webster, page 279.

90. **SALB**, August/September 1984.

91. J Lewis and E Randall, 'The state of the unions', in **SALB**, number 11 (October 1985) pages 74-6.

92. See Webster, pages 202-212 and 213 note 28.

93. See R and L Lambert, 'State reform and working-class resistance', in **SAR**, volume 1.

94. See Labour Monitoring Group, 'The November stay-away', in **SALB** 10:6 (May 1985).

95. For much useful information on the independent unions, see D MacShane and others, **Power!** (Nottingham 1984), and S Friedman, **Building Tomorrow Today** (Johannesburg 1987).

96. D Hindson, 'Union Unity', in **SAR**, volume 2, page 93.

97. See Callinicos, **Southern Africa after Zimbabwe**, pages 124-6, and, for a defence of FOSATU's tactics, B Fine and others, 'Trade unions and the state in South Africa', in **Capital and Class**, number 15 (1981).

98. A Erwin, 'The question of unity in the struggle', in **SALB** 11:1 (September 1985) pages 54 and 60-1.

99. Erwin, pages 68 and 67.

100. MacShane and others, page 125.

101. R Lambert, 'Political unionism in South Africa', in **SALB** 6:2/3 (September 1980) page 104.

102. Lambert, in **SALB** 6:2/3, page 104.

103. J Foster, 'The workers' struggle—where does FOSATU stand?', appendix 1 to MacShane and others, pages 149-150.

104. Interview with Nigel Lambert, **Socialist Worker**, 14 September 1985.

105. Webster, page 193.

106. Labour Monitoring Group, in **SALB** 10:6.

107. See M Swilling, 'Workers divided', in **SALB** (August/September 1984).

108. Swilling, in **SALB** (August/September 1984) pages 115 and 119-120.

109. Labour Monitoring Group, in **SALB** 10:6.

110. See Labour Monitoring Group, in **SALB** 10:6, in various places, and Socialist League of Africa [B Hirson], 'South Africa: Ten years of the stay-at-home', in **IS** 1:5 (1961).

111. The account that follows is based mainly on D Pillay, 'Community organisations and unions in conflict', in **Work in Progress**, number 37 (June 1985), and Labour Monitoring Group, 'The March Stayaways in Port Elizabeth and Uitenhage', in **SALB** 11:1 (September 1985).

112. See **SALB** 6:2/3, special issue on 'Working for Ford', and Callinicos, **Southern Africa after Zimbabwe**, pages 126-9.

113. Labour Monitoring Group, in **SALB** 11:1.

114. Pillay, page 12.

115. See interview with SACTU representative in **SALB** 11:2 (October/December 1985).

116. Lewis and Randall, page 84.

117. NUM, November 1985.

118. See P van Niekerk, 'NUM's first legal mine strike', in **SALB** (October/November 1984), and 'Briefings', in **SALB** 11:1 (September 1985).

119. See M Golding, 'Mass struggles in the mines', in **SALB**10:6 (May 1985), and 'Mass dismissals in the mines', in **SALB** 10:7 (June 1985).

120. Webster, pages 60-1.

121. See **The Workers' Movement, SACTU and the ANC** (London 1979).

122. **Inqaba ya Basebenzi**, number 1 (January 1981).

123. See **Inqaba**, number 16 (May 1985) for the Marxist Workers Tendency's side of the story.

124. Storey, page 25.

125. **South Africa's Impending Socialist Revolution**, pages 152-3.

126. Webster, pages 226 and 230 note 51.

127. Storey, page 43.

128. Storey, page 30.

129. Storey, page 38.

130. **South Africa's Impending Socialist Revolution**, page 147.

131. **South Africa's Impending Socialist Revolution**, page 139.

132. Storey, page 38.

133. See for example 'Claris', 'Conference expels "left-wing" deviationists', in **Sechaba** (August 1985).

134. See D Lewis, 'Registered trade unions and Western Cape workers', in Webster (editor), Hirson, and Callinicos, **Southern Africa after Zimbabwe**, pages 130-5.

135. See I B Tabata, **The Awakening of a People** (Nottingham 1974) and Roux, pages 354-9.

136. See I B Tabata, **Imperialist Conspiracy in Africa** (Lusaka 1974) chapter 3.

137. Tabata, **Imperialist Conspiracy**, page 34.
138. O'Meara, in **Journal of Comparative and Commonwealth Studies**, number 12, page 153.
139. See Webster, pages 202-212.
140. R O Dudley, interview in **Free Azania** 2:1 (August 1985) page 31.
141. **Cape Herald**, 11 May 1985.
142. **Cape Herald**, 11 May 1985.
143. Dudley, in **Free Azania**, page 31.
144. New Unity Movement, **A Declaration to the People of South Africa** (Cape Town 1985) page 7.
145. New Unity Movement, page 13.
146. **Cape Herald**, 11 May 1985.
147. Abrahams, in **Work in Progress**, number 35, page 20. Information about the Cape Action League is drawn mainly from this interview and from two collections, **Cape Action League Documents** and **Cape Action League—A Product of Mass Struggle**.
148. S Gastrow, **Who's Who in South African Politics** (Johannesburg 1985) pages 27-9.
149. No Sizwe, in various places.
150. N Alexander, 'An approach to the national question in South Africa', in **Azania Worker** 2:2 (December 1985) page 5.
151. Alexander, **Sow the Wind**, page 49.
152. Alexander, in **Azania Worker** 2:2, page 12.
153. Alexander, in **Azania Worker** 2:2, page 13; see also **Sow the Wind**, pages 139-150.
154. No Sizwe, page 125.
155. Abrahams, in **Work in Progress**, number 35, page 21.
156. **Socialist Organiser**, 19 September 1985.
157. Alexander, **Sow the Wind**, pages 13-16.
158. Alexander, **Sow the Wind**, page 15.
159. See 'Points on the Role of Liberals', in **Cape Action League Documents**.
160. See Socialist League of Africa, in **IS** 1:5.
161. 'Breaking the Chains', in **Workers Liberty** (September 1985) page 4.
162. T Cliff and D Gluckstein, **Marxism and Trade Union Struggle** (London 1986) chapter 1.
163. T Cliff, 'The economic roots of reformism', in **Neither Washington nor Moscow** (London 1982).
164. Webster, page 250.
165. N Haysom, 'The Industrial Court', in **SAR**, volume 2.
166. 'Breaking the Chains', in **Workers Liberty**, page 10.
167. M Mayekiso, 'Towards a Workers' Party?', interview in **Socialist Worker Review** (London) number 80 (October 1985) page 19.

168. T Rigby, 'Why a Workers' Party?', in **Socialist Organiser**, 12 September 1985.
169. 'Breaking the Chains', in **Workers Liberty**, page 10.

Chapter 5: STATE OF SIEGE

1. 'South Africa's Socialist Revolution has begun', supplement to **Inqaba ya Basebenzi** 20/1 (November 1986) page 2.
2. D Webster, 'Repression and the State of Emergency', in **SAR**, volume 4, page 142.
3. **WM**, 12 June 1987.
4. **WM**, 24 December 1987.
5. For a detailed analytical narrative of the 1984-86 upsurge, see M Murray, **South Africa: Time of Agony, Time of Destiny** (London 1987).
6. See for example **Socialist Worker**, 1 March 1986.
7. 'South Africa's Socialist Revolution has begun', in **Inqaba ya Basebenzi** 20/1.
8. See for example D Gluckstein, **The Western Soviets** (London 1985).
9. See for example 'Two Trade Unionists', 'Errors of Workerism: a response', in **SALB** 12:3 (1987) pages 70-1.
10. See C Markham and J Matiko, 'State of the Unions', in **SALB** 13:1 (1987) page 109.
11. K O Grady, **The Militarisation of South African Politics** (Bloomington, Indiana, 1986) page 21.
12. T Lodge, 'The African National Congress after the Kabwe Conference', in **SAR**, volume 4, pages 7-10. For a detailed analysis of the ANC's military campaign in the 1970s and 1980s, see S M Davis, **Apartheid's Rebels** (New Haven 1987).
13. Lodge, in **SAR**, volume 4, page 6.
14. See 'Notes of a Meeting at Mfuwe Game Lodge, 13 September 1985' (copy in my possession); also A Sampson, **Black and Gold** (London 1987) chapter 13.
15. 'Minutes of Evidence taken before the Foreign Affairs Committee', **Hansard** 29 October 1985, page 4.
16. Commonwealth Group of Eminent Persons, pages 69-70.
17. Quoted in 'NUM Congress: Mineworkers ready to struggle', in **Inqaba**, number 23 (April 1987) page 11.
18. **WM**, 11 July 1986.
19. Sampson, page 302.
20. See Commonwealth Group of Eminent Persons, chapter 6.
21. Similar processes have been detected in other mass struggles: see L Trotsky, **History of the Russian Revolution** (three volumes,

London 1967) volume 3, and C Harman, **Class Struggles in Eastern Europe 1945-81** (London 1984) pages 243 and following.

22. See Commonwealth Group of Eminent Persons, chapter 6. The pattern present in the EPG affair was repeated on a minor scale when one of the leading accused at the Rivonia trial, Govan Mbeki, was released in November 1987. The release of Mbeki, a veteran leader of the ANC and SACP, was surrounded by widespread speculation that it was 'a test-run before the big one: freeing Mandela' (**WM,** 13 November 1987). The government was believed to be considering both freeing Mandela and the unbanning of the ANC as part of an attempt to accelerate negotiations with Buthelezi and perhaps even Nelson Mandela himself. Winnie Mandela, no doubt with this in mind, appealed to the 'oppressed and exploited' to react with 'restraint, caution and circumspection' (**WM,** 20 November 1987). Once again the hopes of an opening were dashed: Botha, finding the water still too hot, withdrew his toe, and imposed paralysing restrictions on Mbeki, virtually reducing him to house arrest.

23. My account of the struggle at Crossroads is based on J Cole, **Crossroads: The Politics of Reform and Repression 1976-86** (Johannesburg 1987).

24. Cole, page 87.

25. Cole, page 120.

26. Cole, page 131 and chapter 10.

27. **Socialist Worker,** 7 June 1986.

28. The following section draws heavily on Webster's account in **SAR,** volume 4.

29. Webster, in **SAR,** volume 4, pages 151-2.

30. See **WM,** 24 December 1987.

31. See Webster, in **SAR,** volume 4, pages 169-172.

32. See N Haysom, **Mabaugalala** (Johannesburg 1986).

33. I draw heavily in discussing Buthelezi and Inkatha on G Mare and G Hamilton, **An Appetite for Power** (Johannesburg 1987).

34. 'Minutes of Evidence', in **Hansard**, page 2.

35. 'NEC Political Report: Part 3', in **Sechaba** (December 1985) page 3.

36. **FM,** 9 November 1979.

37. 'NEC Political Report', in **Sechaba** (December 1985) page 4. See also Mare and Hamilton, pages 136-149.

38. See Mare and Hamilton, chapter 6.

39. See D Glaser, 'Behind the Indaba', in **Transformation**, number 2 (1986), and G Mare, 'Mixed, Capitalist and Free', in **SAR,** volume 4.

40. See Mare and Hamilton, pages 116-133.

41. **WM,** 26 February 1988.

42. For an important account of these events, see A Sitas, 'Inanda, August 1985', in **SALB** 11:4 (1986).

43. **WM**, 22 April 1988, which reports the findings of a Natal University conference on the Pietermaritzburg fighting.

44. Centro de Estudos Africanos, 'The Coming South African Election and the Far Right Factor', in **Transformation**, number 3 (1987) page 72.

45. One of the main themes of Harold Wolpe's recently published book, **Race, Class and the Apartheid State** (London 1988), is that this is a subject that has been badly neglected by radical scholarship in South Africa. Although marred by a post-Althusserian tendency to detach politics from any general material determination, this book makes many valuable points which correct the excessive functionalism of previous Marxist work on South Africa.

46. See for example B Bunting, **The Rise of the South African Reich** (Harmondsworth 1969). For critiques of the theory of South African fascism, see O'Meara, **Volkskapitalisme**, pages 9-11, and Wolpe, **Race, Class and the Apartheid State**, pages 40-47.

47. See the discussion of Kaplan's formula in Murray, pages 107-9.

48. See Wolpe, **Race, Class and the Apartheid State**, especially chapter 4.

49. See Haysom, 'The Industrial Court', in **SAR**, volume 2, and P Benjamin, 'Trade Unions and the Industrial Court', **SAR**, volume 4.

50. See O'Meara, **Volkskapitalisme**.

51. This is a point emphasised by the Marxist Workers Tendency: see 'South Africa's Socialist Revolution has begun', in **Inqaba** 20/1, especially pages 23 and following.

52. C Charney, 'Class Conflict and the National Party Split', in **JSAS** 10:2 (1984). I refer to the KP by its Afrikaans name partly because of the possible confusion caused by its English initials, which not long ago led a **Guardian** sub-editor to delight South Africa-watchers by calling Treurnicht the 'leader of the Communist Party'!

53. There are a number of studies of the political rise of the SADF, including P Frankel, **Pretoria's Praetorians** (Cambridge 1984), D Geldenhuys, **The Diplomacy of Isolation** (New York 1984) chapters 4 and 5, and Grundy, **Militarisation**.

54. The **Weekly Mail** has carried a succession of stories about the development of the National Security Management System.

55. F Van Zyl Slabbert, **The Last White Parliament** (London 1985) page 114.

56. L Platzky, 'Restructuring and Apartheid', in **SAR**, volume 4.

57. What follows is heavily indebted to W Cobbett and others, 'Regionalisation-Federalism', in **SALB** 10:5 (1985), and 'South

Africa's Regional Political Economy', in **SAR**, volume 3.

58. S Greenberg, **Legitimising the Illegitimate** (Berkeley 1987) pages 56-7, and see especially chapter 3.

59. Cobbett and others, in **SAR**, volume 3, page 141.

60. Cobbett and others, in **SAR**, volume 3, page 138.

61. See Glaser, in **Transformation**, number 2.

62. Glaser, in **Transformation**, number 2, page 20.

63. **FT**, 4 March 1988.

64. **WM**, 15 April 1988.

65. **WM**, 31 July 1987, and M Swilling, 'Whamming the Radicals', in **WM**, 20 May 1988.

66. Cobbett and others, in **SAR**, volume 3, page 154.

67. Cobbett and others, in **SAR**, volume 3, page 158.

68. **WM**, 29 April 1988. For recent analyses of the economic crisis, see S Gelb, 'Making Sense of the Crisis', in **Transformation**, number 5 (1987) and F Cassim, 'Economic crisis and stagnation in South Africa', in **SAR**, volume 4.

69. **FT**, 4 March 1988.

70. J Hyslop, 'The Impact of the Ultra-right in South African Politics', in **SAR**, volume 4, page 395.

71. **WM**, 12 February 1988.

72. Quoted in Sampson, **Black and Gold**, page 197.

73. **WM**, 4 March 1988.

74. **WM**, 31 March 1988.

75. The account given here draws on Charney, 'Class Conflict', in **JSAS** 10:2, Centro de Estudos Africanos, 'South African General Election', in **Transformation**, number 3, and Hyslop, 'Ultra Right', in **SAR**, volume 4.

76. **WM**, 11 March 1988.

77. Slabbert, page 157.

78. Slabbert, page 159.

79. Greenberg, page 154.

80. Greenberg, page 187.

81. Wolpe, **Race, Class and the Apartheid State**, page 80. The rise of General Magnus Malan, formerly chief of the SADF, minister of defence since 1980, and widely tipped as a possible successor to Botha, is sometimes seen as a symptom of the 'silent coup'. But he was never a simple soldier: 'Malan was a key figure in the Afrikaner establishment, son of a speaker of the House of Assembly, brother of a Springbok rugby captain, a member of the Broederbond, and a soldier who not only had direct observer experience in the Algerian civil war from the perspective of the French **colon**, but was a graduate of the American military academy

and a close student of Israeli and Taiwanese military methods' (T R H Davenport, **South Africa: A Modern History** (third edition, Houndmills 1987) page 438). Malan's elevation to the deputy leadership of the Transvaal National Party is an indication that the Nationalist parliamentary caucus and party machine are still crucial bases of political advancement.

82. For a useful, albeit journalistic survey of the relationship between big business and apartheid in recent years, see Sampson, **Black and Gold**.

83. Quoted in J McCarthy, 'Contours of Capital's Negotiating Agenda', in **Transformation**, number 1 (1986) page 130.

84. The most detailed statement of this case is M Lipton, **Capitalism and Apartheid** (London 1985); see Bill Freund's excellent review in **Transformation**, number 4 (1987).

85. Wolpe, **Race, Class and the Apartheid State**, page 8. Wolpe, however, in his eagerness to avoid any taint of functionalism and to offer a sophisticated rationale for ANC strategy comes close to detaching political struggle from any anchorage in the forces and relations of production.

86. See especially S Greenberg, **Race and State in Capitalist Development** (New Haven 1980), M Lacey, **Working for Boroko** (Johannesburg 1981), and O'Meara, **Volkskapitalisme**.

87. J Saul, 'South Africa: The Question of Strategy', in **New Left Review** 160 (1986) page 5.

88. See for example H Adam and K Moodley, **South Africa after Apartheid** (Berkeley 1986).

89. **FT**, 12 August 1985.

90. McCarthy, in **Transformation**, number 1.

91. Slabbert, page 112.

92. Quoted in Sampson, page 192.

93. Quoted in Sampson, page 30.

94. **WM**, 29 January 1988.

95. Sampson, page 32. Emphasis added.

96. P Storey, 'Workers' revolution or racial civil war', supplement to **Inqaba**, number 16/17 (May 1985) page 24. The MWT, however, combined this correct analysis of 'the essential barrier to the transformation of society—the racist capitalist state machine' (Story, in **Inqaba** 16/17) with a catastrophist economic analysis which leads them to deny that there is **any** scope for reforms more limited than the transfer of political power to the black majority. Thus, for example, they ruled out the possibility of the abolition of influx control—see Storey, in **Inqaba**, number 16/17, pages 22-4.

97. Sampson, pages 261-2.

98. 'Abridgement of the Annual Statement of the Chairman of the Anglo-American Corporation', in **WM**, 17 July 1987.

99. **WM**, 29 January 1988.

100. Charney, in **JSAS** 10:2, pages 280-1.

101. P Le Roux, 'The State as Economic Actor', in **CSAS**.

102. See D Innes, 'Disinvestment: The Big Boys do it with Mirrors', in **WM**, 24 December 1987.

103. Frankel, pages 80-1.

104. Quoted in Story, in **Inqaba**, number 16/17, page 14.

105. Figures from Markham and Matiko, in **SALB** 13:1, **FM**, 8 January 1988, and **WM**, 20 May 1988.

106. **FM**, 8 January 1988.

107. **FM**, 8 January 1988, and **WM**, 20 May 1988.

108. **WM**, 13 May 1988.

109. **WM**, 20 May 1988, and **FM**, 8 January 1988.

110. 'Victory for SATS workers', in **SALB** 12:5 (1987).

111. 'Postal strikes—need for unity', in **SALB** 13:1 (1987).

112. **WM**, 14 August 1987.

113. **FM**, 8 January 1988.

114. P Benjamin and H Cheadle, 'Proposed amendments to the Labour Relations Act: A Critical View', in **SALB** 13:1 (1987).

115. 'Document: ANC-SACTU-COSATU Talks', **SALB** 11:5 (1986) page 29.

116. 'Cyril Ramaphosa on the NUM Congress', in **SALB** 12:3 (1987) page 49.

117. **WM**, 13 November 1987.

118. J Slovo, 'Speech at the 65th Anniversary Meeting of the South African Communist Party, London, July 30th 1986', in **An Alliance Forged** (London, no date (1986)) page 12.

119. Isizwe Collective, 'Workerism and the Way Forward—a Rejoinder', in **SALB** 12:5 (1987) page 74.

120. ' "Workerism" and the Freedom Charter', in **Umsebenzi** 3:3 (1987). The SACP's paranoia about revolutionary socialists outside South Africa is well illustrated by a piece entitled 'How the Ultra-Left play into the hands of the Ultra-Right', in **African Communist**, number 109 (1987), in which the original version of chapter 4 of this book earns me the title 'a tireless anti-Communist Party crusader'. The author, Thando Zuma, whose invokes among others CPUSA leader 'Gus Hall (a master in polemics!)' (!), concludes by stressing the need for 'political education'—of which his own article is ample proof.

121. Quoted in R Lambert, 'Trade Unions, Nationalism and the Socialist Project in South Africa', in **SAR**, volume 4, page 246.

122. **WM**, 3 July 1987.
123. 'NUMSA Political Resolutions', in **SALB** 12:5 (1987) page 12.
124. Lambert, 'Trade unions', in **SAR**, volume 4, pages 235 and 251. Compare the same author's 'Political Unionism in South Africa', in **SALB** 6:2 and 3 (1980). Assessment of Lambert's claims about the 1950s must wait upon his publication of his history of SACTU. The evidence which he has presented so far—in 'Trade Unions and National Liberation in South Africa', in **CSAS**—shows that there were differences within the SACP in the 1950s over the extent to which to give priority to the national liberation struggle, and that SACTU practice varied across the country, which seems to add nuances to, rather than to require fundamental revision of, the left critique of SACTU.
125. E Webster, introduction to 'Section 3: Labour', in **SAR**, volume 4, page 218.
126. K von Holdt, 'The Political Significance of COSATU', in **Transformation**, number 5 (1987) page 103.
127. 'Jay Naidoo on COSATU', in **SALB** 12:5 (1987) pages 62-3.
128. Quoted in Murray, page 439.
129. 'CCAWUSA Congress', in **SALB** 12:5 (1987) page 20.
130. Markham and Matiko, in **SALB** 13:1, page 117. For useful analysis of the retail sector's strike wave, see **WM**, 27 February 1987.
131. Copies of this and other CCAWUSA material cited are in my possession.
132. See C Markham and M Mothibile, 'The 1987 Mineworkers' Strike', in **SALB** 13:1 (1987).
133. J Crush, 'Restructuring Migrant Labour on the Gold Mines', in **SAR**, volume 4.
134. Markham and Matiko, in **SALB** 13:1, page 102.
135. **WM**, 26 February 1988.
136. **WM**, 13 May 1988.
137. **COSATU News**, May 1988.
138. See **WM**, 3 and 10 June 1988, for detailed reports on the strike, its background and aftermath.
139. It is significant that the NACTU congress in August 1988 saw Africanists win control of the executive away from supporters of AZAPO. A number of observers have commented on signs of a revival in influence in the PAC under the second emergency—a sympton perhaps of disillusionment arising from the impasse to which the dominant ANC/UDF/COSATU bloc has led the resistance.
140. D Hindson, 'Alternative Urbanisation Strategies in South Africa', in **CSAS**.

141. It does not follow that all even of the urbanised majority have lost all connection with their rural origins. On the contrary, a crisis in which state power was seriously weakened would see some proletarianised layers involved in struggles over the land, leading perhaps to the division of white farms and the 'peasantisation' of some workers. But discussion of the land question in South Africa, apart from some important recent historical work—see T J Keegan, **Rural Transformations in Industrialising South Africa** (Johannesburg 1986), W Beinart and others, **Putting a Plough in the Ground** (Johannesburg 1986) and W Beinart and C Bundy, **Hidden Struggles in Rural South Africa** (Johannesburg 1987)—has been largely confined to fairly empty rhetoric on the part of the SACP and even the left. For a historical survey, see C Bundy, 'Land and Liberation: Popular Rural Protest and the National Liberation Movements in South Africa 1920-1960', in S Marks and S Trapido (editors) **The Politics of Race, Class and Nationalism in Twentieth Century South Africa** (London 1987), and, for an attempt at least to pose some pertinent questions, see J Krikler, 'Problems of a Transition to a Socialist Agriculture', in **SALB** 12:5 (1987).

142. **WM**, 20 May 1988.

143. Davis, pages 210-211.

144. Frankel, pages 107-123.

145. Frankel, page 117.

146. **WM**, 20 and 25 November 1987.

147. See for example P Marshall, **Revolution and Counter-Revolution in Iran** (London 1988), C Barker, **Festival of the Oppressed** (London 1987), and D Beecham and A Eidenham, 'Beyond the Mass Strike: Class, Party and Trade Union Struggle in Brazil', in **IS** 2:36 (1987).

148. See M Plaut, 'A Rejoinder to von Holdt', in **Transformation**, number 5 (1987) page 105.

149. Slovo, in **An Alliance Forged**, page 9.

150. Saul, in **New Left Review** 160, page 18. Despite Saul's willingness to give the populists the benefit of the doubt, some fairly mild criticisms of the SACP were sufficient to bring down the usual curses from the **African Communist**, which placed him in the special hell reserved for 'ultra-left sectarian "Marxists" ' such as myself: see Zuma, in **African Communist**, number 109.

151. Saul, in **New Left Review** 160, pages 19-20.

152. Von Holdt, in **Transformation**, number 5, pages 97-8 and 103.

153. E Laclau and C Mouffe, **Hegemony and Socialist Strategy** (London 1985). Among the many forceful criticisms of this book are E M

Wood, **The Retreat from Class** (London 1986) chapter 4, N Geras, 'Post-Marxism?', in **New Left Review** 163 (1987), and P Kellogg, 'Defending the Orthodoxy', in **IS** 2:38 (1987).

154. All quotations from 'The Class Struggle and the Question of the Workers' Party', in **Free Azania**, May 1988.

155. See T Cliff, **Lenin**, volume 1 (London 1975) chapters 1 and 2. The three volumes of Cliff's **Lenin**, together with J Molyneux, **Marxism and the Party** (London 1978), and C Harman, **Party and Class** (Chicago 1986), provide the theory of the revolutionary party still absent from the South African left.

Index

Other publications from Bookmarks

Racism, Resistance and Revolution
by Peter Alexander

Racism may be seen as an irrational prejudice, to be opposed with education and legislation. Alternatively, it is seen as 'natural' to white society, to be opposed only by separate black organisations. This book shows how both views have been tested and failed—and argues that racism can only be understood as the result of material causes. If that is so, it has a material solution: the defeat of the social system which depends on racism. £3.95 / $8.50

The Fire Last Time: 1968 and after
by Chris Harman

The year 1968 was a political watershed, when millions of workers struck in France, the black ghettoes of the US rose in protest at the murder of Martin Luther King, when Czech workers and students challenged the Stalinist monolith... The world may not have been turned upside down but the shock waves broke the fetters on the minds of millions of people, showing that society could be changed. This book shows how 1968 was the product of contradictions in the world system, contradictions that are with us still. £6.95 / $13.50

The Revolutionary Road to Socialism
by Alex Callinicos

Here is the case for revolutionary socialism, taking up the issues of why capitalism is in crisis worldwide, how the reformist parties have failed the workers, and what went wrong in Russia after the revolution of 1917. This is the case for the Socialist Workers Party. *£1.50 / $3.00*

Revolutionary Rehearsals
edited by Colin Barker

Five essays on the five times in the past 20 years when the working class has taken mass action: France 1968, Chile 1972-3, Portugal 1974, Iran 1979 and Poland 1980-1. This book examines the potential for working-class revolution in the world today. *£4.95 / $9.50*

Festival of the Oppressed
Solidarity, reform and revolution in Poland 1980-1
by Colin Barker

In the brief sixteen months of its existence, the Polish independent trade union Solidarity proved itself the most impressive working-class movement the world had seen for half a century. Yet it was suppressed—along with the hopes of millions of people—with appalling ease. This book looks at the reasons why. *£4.25 / $8.50*

These and many more publications are available from bookshops and local branches of the socialist organisations listed at the front of this book, or by mail order from:

Bookmarks

* 265 Seven Sisters Road, Finsbury Park, London N4 2DE, England.
* PO Box 16085, Chicago, Illinois 60616, USA.
* GPO Box 1473N, Melbourne 3001, Australia.